What I
Mission?

What Is Mission?

THEOLOGICAL EXPLORATIONS

J. Andrew Kirk

FORTRESS PRESS
MINNEAPOLIS

WHAT IS MISSION?
Theological Explorations

Phototypeset by Intype London Ltd

Library of Congress Cataloging-in-Publication Data

Kirk, J. Andrew
    What is mission? : theological explorations / J. Andrew Kirk.
    p.   cm.
    Originally published: London: Darton, Longman & Todd, 1999.
    Includes bibliographical references and index.
    ISBN 0-8066-3233-8 (alk. paper)
    1. Missions. I. Title
BV2061 .K57 2000
266'.001—dc21
                                                    99-088224
                                                    CIP

The paper used in this publication meets the minimum requirements for American National Standard for Information Sciences—Permanence of Paper for Printed Library Materials, ANSI Z329.48–1984.   ⊗™

Manufactured in the U.S.A.   AF 1-3233

04   2   3   4   5   6   7   8   9   10

Contents

Acknowledgements

I was most fortunate in being able to take a period of study leave in the summer of 1998. In spite of a family wedding in the middle of the time (a great occasion it has to be said), I was largely undisturbed and able to do some very concentrated writing. Some of the material was already written but unpublished, and I was able to adapt it for the purposes of this book. Most of the content, however, has come through the stimulus of engaging with the thinking of others and in the course of preparing courses in mission.

I would like first to thank all my colleagues in the School of Mission and World Christianity at the Selly Oak Colleges for their support, encouragement and stimulus to go on engaging with the crucial mission issues of the moment. In particular my gratitude goes to Philip Seddon who deputised for me in the overall running of the operation in my absence. I know how much it cost him to do it.

Michael Taylor, Allan Anderson, Peter Fulljames, Laurence Taylor, Dan Beeby, John Peters and John Corrie most generously read parts of the manuscript in draft form and gave me exceedingly helpful comments. If they were to read the finished book they might recognise my indebtedness to their insights. However, responsibility for the end product is entirely mine.

In a special way I am grateful to Beverley Stubbs, the School of Mission's administrator and my personal assistant, for the long hours she spent in getting the whole manuscript in a presentable form, and particularly for struggling to bring the notes into some kind of order. As an agreed date for finishing the work fast approached, she increased her commitment to digging me out of the embarrassment of a badly missed deadline.

Finally, I wish to thank Morag Reeve, the editorial director of Darton, Longman and Todd, not only for agreeing to publish the book, but for doing so with enthusiasm. I hope this will be matched by subsequent interest on the part of the public. I have found every step of our collaboration to be smooth and very professional. The same is true of Katie Worrall, the commissioning editor, Helen Porter, the managing editor, Allison Ward, the publicity officer, and Pauline Shelton, the copy editor. They have all been helpfulness itself.

I dedicate this book to all the students who have sat through my classes, seminars, tutorials and supervision sessions over many years. It may not always have been as obvious to them as it should have been that learning is a multi-way process: *mea culpa*. Understanding 'What is Mission' is a matter for the whole people of God, listening to what the Spirit of Jesus says to the churches, hearing the sorrows and joys of people's daily lives and listening to one another. In part, 'I am, because you are'. Thank you.

Andrew Kirk

Introduction

Every author justifies writing another book on a subject already well-served with the comment that there is nothing else quite like it. This author is no exception. In the course of being involved over a number of years in mission education, I have become aware of the lack of a book which offers a manageable overview of the main topics under the heading, 'Theology of Mission'.

I am aware of the standard books included in most lists of suggested reading for courses on the subject. At the top of the list is David Bosch's *magnum opus, Transforming Mission*. This will remain the standard textbook into the foreseeable future. It is doubtful whether, even once in a generation, such a book will be written. It represents a lifetime of involvement in mission and the study of it from almost every conceivable angle. There are few people who are able to master so expertly such a wide range of material with such care, balance and sensitivity.

David Bosch's book is a systematic theological presentation of the whole subject of Christian mission. It is like a journey of exploration in which the traveller takes sufficient time both to cover a wide territory and to do so with much attention to detail. My book is more of an introduction. It is an attempt to present the crucial material on theology of mission in a convenient form. It is intended *purpose* to be a handbook helping to guide the student through some of the relevant discussion on a fairly wide range of issues. The difference between the two might be likened to the scale of a map: David Bosch's is large scale, showing individual houses, clumps of trees, pathways and contours; mine is smaller scale, giving only the location of large villages, small towns and cities.

I believe both are required. *Transforming Mission* and other books which cover a large terrain are resource books to which one returns time and time again, checking out one's own knowledge and understanding of the subject. However, just because of the scope of these studies, some people find them somewhat intimidating, particularly if English is not the student's first language. There is also needed an exploration of the land which encompasses important matters relatively briefly, though without being superficial.

As indicated in the text, and much to my surprise, David Bosch's book is not quite as exhaustive as I had imagined. In his chapter, 'Elements of an Emerging Ecumenical Missionary Paradigm', the subjects that I touch on in chapters 8–10 are not covered. Given the important place that they have occupied within the ecumenical movement in recent decades, and given the previous situation of South Africa under apartheid (when the book was being written), this is strange. In mitigation, it can be said that rarely, if at all, do they feature in other books on mission. Perhaps they are only now beginning to become a part of the missiological agenda.

Enough of comparisons. It goes without saying that I am deeply indebted to David Bosch both as a scholar and a person (I had the privilege of knowing him personally). I have also benefited greatly from a number of other people's writings. I hope that their inclusion in the text, footnotes and bibliography will go some way to acknowledging their contribution to the issues under discussion. If I have omitted any significant studies, the reason will be ignorance rather than lack of appreciation.

Outline and scope

As already indicated, my main intention in writing this book is to provide all students of Christian mission with a handbook that will help them do their own exploration of a wide range of issues in this field. The focus will be on some of the theological questions that are current, and it will attempt to reflect existing debate from a variety of perspectives and different parts of the world. I have also tried to make the presentation user-friendly by breaking the text up into manageable sections with frequent headings and subtitles, and by setting out various opinions as clearly as possible.

frcst

As can be seen, the book divides into three parts. The opening three chapters deal with questions of foundations and methods. I recognise certain differences of opinion over the nature of the *missio Dei* and the Church's relationship to it. By and large these spring from the way we approach fundamental matters to do with God and his purposes, and the place that Jesus Christ and the Christian community has within them.

The second section is dedicated to seven main themes. The choice is the result of many years involvement in mission education on more than one continent. It would be perfectly legitimate to suggest other subjects, though not necessarily possible to include all of them within one volume. They all cover extensive areas and present complex matters. Quite enough to be getting on with! There is a danger, I realise, in presenting them as separate items, whereas in reality they interlock at a number of points. I have endeavoured to point out the connections.

The third part consists of one chapter only. This is dedicated to a review of what the Church might be and do if it were sufficiently conscious of its nature as a Church for the sake of mission. In some ways, this part also gives an opportunity to tie up some loose ends by including discussions not properly addressed elsewhere. The epilogue is a personal appraisal of the state of the debate and an intrepid peep into the future. It was written only after I had received the helpful comments on, and criticisms of, the main body of the text from friends and colleagues.

I would expect readers to look at chapters separately, according to their particular interests in a subject, rather than read the book through from cover to cover – though this latter will give an overview of the scope of the study. In each case I have attempted to lay out in broad outline the state of the debate. In some instances I have given my own observations. I trust that they will not be considered intrusive. For the sake of providing a useful educational tool, I have tried to rein in my own convictions. In a few cases, where I think that certain views are due to genuine misunderstandings or to a seriously inadequate line of reasoning, I have found this difficult. I would not want to give the impression that I have a settled view on all these questions – far from it.

Some of them – like the legitimisation of violence, the means of evangelism and the nature of the Church's involvement in politics – have been debated for most of two millennia. No easy answers here! Others, such as interfaith dialogue, inculturation and the preferential option for the poor, are of more recent concern. Each one represents a storm of controversy through which Christians may have to sail for some time to come before reaching calmer waters. Care of the environment, as a subject of mission concern, is even more contemporary. And yet, in spite of unsettled business, mission implies conviction and commitment, even if it has to be provisional and open to correction. Even those who appear to reject firm beliefs about the Church's mission have their (firm) reasons for doing so.

In concluding, I would like to say something about the use of gender-explicit language in the book. I have scrupulously tried to avoid the generic use of the masculine to refer to both halves of the human race. For me there should not be any doubt that this procedure is right. Personally, I prefer to use both pronouns, 'he' and 'she' ('his' and 'hers'), rather than some people's contrived use of the feminine to cover both sexes. The day may come, when it will be acceptable to use the plural 'they'/ 'their' to refer to the singular, bringing English into line with other languages which do not make a gender distinction. This has not yet happened and we are therefore left still with the awkwardness of repetition.

The one case, however, where I still have difficulty is with the designation of God. The problem is not with ascribing to God in equal measure both masculine and feminine attributes – I see no grounds for disputing this; the problem is, rather, aesthetic – the extreme ugliness of repeating God, in place of he/she, his/her, over and over again.

Other conventional ways of getting round this dilemma, such as using terms like 'creator', 'sustainer', 'redeemer', do not properly address it, for they isolate one part of God's work, whereas God is simultaneously all of these (and more) all of the time. Reluctantly, therefore, and acknowledging that the use of the feminine exclusively for God brings with it another unresolved and highly charged agenda, I continue for the moment to use the masculine pronoun for God. Some may reject my timidity, prevarication and unjustifiable excuses. I hope that no one will conclude that I hold a patriarchal view of God. Difficult though it is to rid ourselves of a human tragedy almost as old as humanity itself, the masculine must not be equated with domination, authoritarianism and control.

1

What is Theology? And Theology of Mission?

First impressions

Where to begin? Theology is an unusually broad subject. Given the worldwide spread of the Christian faith, an amazing variety of people are doing theology from many different angles and in distinct situations. Many people, however, instinctively have a somewhat negative view of theology. In their minds, it has the image of being a rather abstract and theoretical pursuit, undertaken largely by trained professionals who use language and concepts beyond the reach of most ordinary folk. However, theology is an enterprise which all kinds of Christians can enter into. Part of the purpose of this book is to show how important and useful it is in deciding how the Church should carry through its mission.

At the beginning of one of our courses in the School of Mission at the Selly Oak Colleges, we look at the ways in which various people understand theology and mission. At the same time, we emphasise that, in the course of studying together, each person must come to his or her own conclusions. As with so much in life, the meaning becomes clearer in the doing. Therefore, for those who use this book, the hope is that you will be wiser about the meaning and practice of mission as you yourself grapple with many of the questions that will be raised and discussed.

Towards a working definition

In beginning with a few attempts at defining theology the idea is to call upon the rich tradition of views, not to decide the meaning in advance. Inevitably short descriptions are incomplete; but to extend them beyond a sentence or two is to risk the danger of being long-winded and ponderous. The intention is to offer what are often called 'working definitions' – explanations that lay out the area of study, but without pretending to be comprehensive or unchangeable.

So what is theology all about? One writer calls it 'the reflective self-understanding of faith'.[1] Presumably this idea follows the ancient formula of 'faith seeking understanding', which implies the desire to think as deeply as possible about the reality of one's belief and its relationship to other sources of knowledge about life.[2] Some people stress the intellectual nature of theology as 'rational thought or talk about God' or 'reasoned discourse about God'.[3] According to this concept, theology is a discipline which helps the trained mind come to a more comprehensive and justified judgement about the claims of faith.

In the Western world, the eighteenth-century Enlightenment challenged Christians to defend their view that theology was a proper subject to be taught at university. This was the beginning of the attempt to demonstrate that theology could legitimately claim a scientific status. Thus, for example, Charles Hodge called it 'the science of the facts of divine revelation'; while E. H. Bancroft said that it is 'the science of God and of the relations between God and the universe'.[4]

This kind of language is, however, ambiguous, if not dubious: firstly because it restricts the scope of theology, and secondly because the perception of the nature of science has changed, freeing other disciplines to be studied according to their own criteria. If the use of the word 'science' is intended to convey a commitment to intellectual rigour in the pursuit of understanding the different aspects of faith, then it is appropriate. However, in the hands of some, the use of the word 'scientific' to specify certain theological disciplines has become pretentious and inappropriate.[5]

At least since the middle of the 1960s, there has been much emphasis on the practical nature of theology or, to put the matter the other way round, on the nature of theology as reflection on practice. The explosion of various liberation theologies on to the scene at the end of the 1960s certainly shifted the discussion of the theological task away from the rather narrow intellectual struc- ture it had come to assume in academic circles. The famous definition of Gustavo Gutiérrez, that theology is 'critical reflection on historical praxis in the light of the Word',[6] brought to the forefront the close relationship between thinking, being and doing, between faith, life and action. He showed how, in the case of theology, rational discussion cannot be divorced from a person's entire situation in the world nor from the reality of the communities with which he or she is identified. Thus:

> The classic meaning of theology is an intellectual under-standing of the faith – that is, the effort of human intelligence to comprehend revelation and the vision of faith. But faith means not only truths to be affirmed, but also an existential stance, an attitude, a commitment to God and human beings ... We affirm that theology is the intellectual under-standing of this commitment.[7]

David Ford, at the end of his comprehensive survey of contemporary theology, concludes that any adequate theology has to be 'self-involving', 'world-involving' and 'God-involving'. God ultimately is the author of theology, the whole of nature and culture forms the horizon, and the subject matter 'has a specific concern with the radical transformation of selves'.[8] For the time being, and tentatively, we might describe theology as a disciplined reflection on the reality of God and God's relation to the world, whose intention is to clarify God's purposes and actions and, in this light, to evaluate the faith and practice of those who claim to know God. Of course, we need to develop the implications of such a statement, and concentrating on the missionary nature of God and of faith is a crucial perspective from which to do this.

Theology's assumptions

This attempt at a definition raises many interesting questions. Before pursuing them, it is important to clarify some of the assumptions on which the doing of theology is based.

1. Open enquiry
Firstly, because critical reflection is involved in theology, it has to adopt a stance of open enquiry. What may be discovered in the

course of theological exploration cannot be arbitrarily restricted
either by ecclesiastical traditions, secular world-views, political
ideologies, moral fashions – or even by current academic consensus. Investigation must be open to a number of possibilities,
even though, as Schubert Ogden argues, the adequacy or validity
of theology is measured both by its appropriateness 'to Jesus as
Christians experience him' and by its credibility 'to human experience as any man or woman experiences it'.[9] Theology uses a critical
method: this involves an awareness of and engagement with alternative views, a refusal to employ *ad hominem* arguments or to
misrepresent others' opinions, a willingness to respond to criticisms of one's own position and a commitment to clarity, charity
and honesty in argument.

2. Unavoidable tensions

Theology is also involved in a number of unavoidable tensions. Its
subject matter is given both by the actuality of revelation (God
doing and speaking) and the reality of social and cultural situations. Discovery, however, is not closed either by church dogma
or by social or cultural analysis. Theology is a human construct in
the sense that it is done by fallible humans trying to make sense
of two givens – God's self-revelation and our human experience.
Nevertheless, it is not a matter of mere personal whim or invention.
If, as John Yoder suggests, 'we need in the body of Christ a few . . .
persons whose sensitivity to the fragility of language and its sus-
ceptibility to abuse enables them to watch defensively over the
usefulness of our words',[10] there have to be firm criteria for
judging 'usefulness'.

Although the global reach of Christian faith means that theology,
to have integrity, must be approached from many different standpoints, a pluralistic free-for-all is unacceptable because it would
mean that particular theological stances (e.g. patriarchal, nationalistic or free-market) could not be challenged. Whatever the claims
of postmodern culture, Christian faith is necessarily based on a
'grand narrative' whose message counters the possibility of
manipulation in the interests of sectarian concerns. Some attempts
at a radical reinterpretation of the language and symbols of
Christian belief, from whatever philosophical or ideological per-

spective they may come, should be seen as oppressive impositions of alien views on a discourse having its own integrity and acknowledged meanings.[11]

Not everything, then, is legitimate in theology. There are boundaries which from time to time have to be clarified – particularly when the Christian community is faced with unprecedented challenges (e.g. those arising from gnosticism, clericalism, colonialism, racism and secularism). Of course, the location of the frontiers is open to dispute, for the Church ideally is *reformata semper reformanda* (reformed and always reforming). Nevertheless, the community of faith would have no grounds for fulfilling its various callings unless it had settled views on its central beliefs. Its theology would be trivial and vacuous. Freedom to leave the Father's house is always available, but in the absence of adequate frameworks for deciding on appropriate action away from home it soon turns into riotous living!

3. No theology without mission

The final assumption, highly relevant to the subject of this book, is that there can be no theology without mission – or, to put it another way, no theology which is not missionary. This is partly a matter of observation in that theology is, by its nature, about fundamental concerns which affect life at all levels. People engaged in theological reflection invariably take up positions on a whole host of important matters, even if they do so from vastly different stances, with conflicting results and sometimes without being aware of what they are doing. Theology, even when it claims to be nonpartisan, is in reality thoroughly committed, as has so often been pointed out in recent years. In countless respects, it is in the business of persuading others to believe and act in specific ways. Its missionary nature is unavoidable.

Theology's tasks

1. Critical assessment

If we interpret theology broadly, there is no justification for discounting any of a wide range of goals. There is no such thing as 'pure' theology. As already described, perhaps its major function

is to provide a critical assessment of the beliefs and actions of
Christian individuals and communities. Schubert Ogden says that
theology, in its proper sense, is 'used to refer to either the process
or product of a certain kind of critical reflection – namely, the kind
that is required to *validate the claims to validity* that Christians
either make or imply in expressing their experience'.[12] According
to Robert Schreiter, this is only one part of what theology is about.
He says that 'theology is a pedagogical process' that 'liberates
consciousness', but then adds that it also 'incites to action'.[13]

2. Analysis of reality
In this latter mode, theology may contribute to any analysis of
reality. Certain social disciplines have the function of uncovering
ideological commitments that underlie political and economic
strategies. Psychoanalysis may be used to strip away levels of
unconsciousness in order to explain mechanisms of repression and
types of behaviour. Theology, at another level of discernment, may
engage in the exposure of the perennial idolatries that humans
create to avoid ultimate truth about human existence. Such
(theological) analysis implies a call to conversion, theology being
a tool which helps to identify the reasons for change and a new
beginning.

3. Empowering the poor
Under the influence of liberation theologies, it is now commonplace to identify one of theology's tasks as empowering the poor.
Although the phrase may be somewhat ambiguous, the assumption is that theology has a responsibility to help in the process of
affirming the worth and dignity of those people who are excluded
from normal society and to use its resources in aiding their full
inclusion.[14] In this context, it has been suggested that theology has
a subversive role, understood from its Latin derivation to mean
'turning something over from below'. In this sense, theology helps
to articulate in the language of faith the aspirations of those at the
base of society.

4. Apologetics

By extension, theology has a responsibility to promote in its own way all types of action to which the Church is called (as we will explore in subsequent chapters). Thus, for example, in supporting evangelism, one of its tasks will be engaging in apologetics – namely, responding to objections to belief in God (e.g. that God is no more than a code for strategies of domination or a projection of people's inability to cope with social alienation or psychological distress), showing how and why Christian faith is true and how other belief systems or moral values may distort reality. In this sense, theology is much more than a study of the phenomenon of religion in which an attempt is made to sideline faith.[15]

5. Relating to the world

Closely aligned to apologetics is theology's task to help Christians arrive at a 'Christian mind' on how to relate their faith to the contemporary world. Instead of Christians unthinkingly adopting current values and practices in any given situation, they should use theology to aid a reflection which is attuned to 'the mind of Christ' (Eph. 4:20–4; Col. 3:2; Rom. 12:1–2; 2 Cor. 10:5). This means a meticulous, disciplined process of thinking through, from Christian first principles, attitudes, behaviour and action which can be shown to spring consistently from the message of Jesus Christ.

6. Training leaders

Finally, theology is the major tool for training leaders for Christian communities. In accordance with the rediscovered vocation of the whole people of God, this does not mean just the traditional ordained ministry, but all kinds of ministry done on behalf of the community by Christians working in secular occupations as well as voluntary agencies. The shift (at least in theory – practice usually takes a long time to catch up) from a clerical model of theological education to a comprehensive one entails a major reconsideration of both the content and potential of theology.[16]

Theology's sources

It was Karl Barth who famously said that theology is to be done
with the Bible in one hand and the newspaper in the other. More
recently liberation theologians have spoken about the two books –
the book of God and the book of life. Others have spoken of a
double listening: to the voice of God (as recorded in Scripture) and
to the cry of people. This dual outlook on theological reflection
combines the universal nature and intention of the Christians'
foundation document with the particular reality of every situation
into which the message and life of Christ comes. Theology is a
constant process of understanding and relating the two.

The task is somewhat complex. To do it in the best way possible,
other sources, sometimes referred to as 'mediations', can be used.[17]
Classically, the two most prominent have been tradition and
reason.

Tradition

Tradition refers to the accumulated wisdom of the Christian community through time, inherited and passed on from one generation
to another. For some branches of the Christian Church, tradition
is a privileged tool for interpreting the meaning of the faith. They
affirm that, under the providential leading of God's Spirit, tradition
manifests for later generations what may have remained unseen
for previous ones.

Tradition thus enables the Church to possess an accumulated
understanding of the message entrusted to it. The experience of
Christians of other times and places gives today's Church a greater
range of options in its interpretation and application of its founding
text. Other branches of the Church, however, are suspicious of any
notion of the development of tradition which might be used for
promulgating dogmas which appear to them to be contradicted by
Scripture.[18] Their belief in providence is tempered by a realistic
appreciation of the way Churches have and can manipulate their
teaching for ideological ends.

Reason

Reason has come to prominence as part of the advent of the modern world since the seventeenth century. Confidence in the intrinsic rationality of the scientific method and its universal application gave cause for thinking that knowledge of the real world could be based on indisputable foundations transparent to the light of reason. Reason was pitted against ignorance and superstition, and was judged the sole necessary criterion for distinguishing truth from error. Applied to the Christian Scriptures and Christian doctrine it became the measure of what was deemed to be credible.

Much has changed since the most heady days of rationalism. Claims made for reason today are more modest. For example, it has been noted, after much debate, that the use of reason alone to judge what is reasonable (e.g. the possibility of miracles) is illegitimate, since another criterion beyond reason, which is neither defined nor defended, has to be (secretly) introduced into the discussion. Reason is legitimate and valuable as a tool for weighing up the force of arguments made on behalf of different beliefs and actions. It has a genuine though limited role in assessing the coherence, consistency and non-contradictory nature of the evidence adduced for particular interpretations of the Christian faith in relation to contemporary life.

Analysis and action

In recent discussion, less emphasis has been placed on reason and more on the mediations of historical investigation, socio-political analysis and transformative action. Adaptations of Marxist thought have contributed both to new ways of understanding the message of Christ and to new ways of doing theology. Historical method has shown the importance of structural forces in shaping and defending particular forms of economic and social management. Social analysis has uncovered defining concepts like the alienation of working conditions and the conflict between labour and capital. Transformative action has demonstrated the degree to which theory has to be modified as a result of lessons learnt in the struggle for change.

Each of these disciplines in its own way helps to enlarge Christianity's self-understanding as a message of universal salvation.[19]

Theology as a tool for a comprehensive liberation has been called a 'political hermeneutic of the gospel', a way of weaving together the biblical text, history, an understanding of social systems and action to bring about God's liberating plan for human beings.

Theology's methods

Contemporary theology has been self-conscious about its methodology. Much has been written about this from diverse backgrounds.[20] In the light of the conviction already expressed, that theology can best be assessed by seeing it in action (what this book is about), this section will only offer one or two brief guidelines.

We begin where most theological courses begin, with an appreciation of the nature, content and role of the Bible. The Bible can only be understood when looked at from a number of different angles. It is a document from the rather remote past which presents a story of how the God of the people of Israel acted and interacted on the world stage. It contains an amazing diversity of literary material including history, stories, laws, aphorisms, liturgical material, poetry, exhortations, promises, threats, teachings and visions. It claims to be the result of God's communication with certain chosen people and to possess a message about the solution to humanity's deepest needs which is valid for all times and places.

The task of theology is to understand this document (in the first place on its own terms) by allowing it to speak for itself, and to discern how its story and teachings are applicable and significant to subsequent generations. This delicate and complex task can best be seen as one of translation:[21] discovering how the word of God which was written down and lived out 2000 and more years ago can be recognised as God's word today in such a way that it commands allegiance and obedience. This is part of what is meant by hermeneutics (the discipline of interpreting and applying the message).

The hermeneutical enterprise will accompany us throughout this book. Along with translation, I understand this to be about both the translation and communication of texts and their message. It entails moving from the text's original *sense* to its contemporary *meaning*. The first, often called the *sensus literalis*, is the message which the original author intended to convey when writing.[22] The second, often called the *sensus plenior*, is the message which the Holy Spirit (the divine author of Scripture), who will guide the followers of Jesus into all truth (John 16:13), intends to convey to each new generation (Luke 24:27; Acts 8:31ff.). One assumes that the original author was writing with some immediate audience in mind, not for generations to come. Yet the word is written about God and his unchanging purposes fulfilled in Jesus Christ, and it is addressed to basic human conditions which do not change.

Another way of trying to understand the hermeneutical undertaking is through the distinction often made in linguistics between the word used as a *sign* and as a *symbol*. As a sign, the sense of the language is more or less controlled by the etymological origin and semantic development of words and by the grammatical situation in which they are placed. To be able to communicate at all, it is necessary to abide by a commonly accepted set of definitions; for this reason each written language has its dictionaries. If on the first occasion we do not communicate properly, we can try again until the other person is able to say, 'Now I understand what you mean'. This exercise is especially important when people are communicating in a language which is not their mother-tongue.

To use words in wholly novel or eccentric ways or to employ one's own private vocabulary is to invite incomprehension. Invention, in this case, is the mother of confusion. However, when used as a symbol, a word may take on new meanings according to the context in which it is found. Thus the text as a whole may have different levels of meaning, making it applicable beyond the original reader. The sense is not frozen in past history.

The Bible, then, speaks about a history of salvation. However, this history did not stop at the closing of the New Testament; it continues with us today. The Christian community, having responded to God's offer of forgiveness and new life in Jesus Christ, is part of the same history of salvation as the early Church, and proof of its reality. The hermeneutical task is carried out today as we in our generation bear witness to the reality in our lives and world of God's salvation. Just as there is a continuity in history between the generations, so there is a continuity between sense and meaning.

Contrary to what certain literary theories may suggest, the text is not open to any interpretation which may take our fancy. To subject the text to arbitrary readings is to violate it, to deny its integrity. Moreover, the outcome of such reconstruction is merely that we hear the echo of our own voice or that of our surrounding culture. It is solipsism (the belief that we can only be certain about our own existence and ideas) at its worst. Hermeneutics is, then, a delicate art of finding both faithful and imaginative connections between sense and meaning.

Hermeneutics is obviously not possible without understanding the contemporary context into which the text is to be brought. Theology can only fulfil its task by availing itself of the tools of other disciplines. This is clearly not a straightforward matter as we live in the midst of an enormous conflict of interpretations. The person doing theology has to be aware of the range of explanations given for events in the contemporary world. He or she has to weigh up the reasons for the differences and has to make judgements about which of them appear to be the most plausible.

Perhaps one could summarise the methods of theology in terms of five aspirations:

1. There is open *inquiry.* In the theological task there is always more to learn: more information, facts and analysis to absorb; more insights to be gleaned and judgements made. Inquiry has two major goals: to discern what is important and what peripheral, and to make connections between different branches of learning.

2. There is *immersion* in the subject matter being studied. In so far as it is possible for any one person, the theological task requires the use of a variety of tools – historical studies, cultural studies, the analysis provided by the social sciences and, ideally, a working knowledge of philosophy as well.

3. There is *integrity* – a respect for the given-ness and value of the source materials and a refusal to make too hasty judgements on them. Integrity also demands that we acknowledge to our-

selves and keep under constant review our own assumptions and predispositions to ensure that they do not unknowingly distort the area we are working with.

4. There is *integration* – the ability to work across disciplines, bringing pieces of a jigsaw together into persuasive patterns, in order to show how knowledge gained in one area may help to illuminate others.

5. There is *imagination*. Although theology has to respect the integrity of the past, resisting the temptation to be carried away with fanciful reinterpretations, and has to try to achieve a sober assessment of the present, it is also orientated to the future. It is a creative task, requiring the vision to see different possibilities which can then be tested. The theologian is someone who is open to surprises, combining a cool head with a touch of inventiveness and originality.

And theology of mission?

The Christian world is in the midst of a crucial debate about the relationship between theology and mission. Traditionally, the study of mission has been treated as one discipline among many within the wider confines of the whole theological curriculum. David Bosch summarises the different ways in which missiology became related to the academic pursuit of theology.[23] Under the influence of Schleiermacher, missiology was appended to practical theology as a study of the self-realisation of the Church in missionary situations. It might equally well have become a branch of church history, being the study of the Church's expansion in different ages.

However, missiology has also been treated as a theological discipline in its own right, and chairs of mission were established in various universities, firstly on the Continent and later in the USA. However, missiology became isolated from other parts of the theological task. It became what David Bosch calls 'the theological institution's "department of foreign affairs", dealing with the exotic but at the same time peripheral'.[24] Other theologians did not see any need to reflect on the missionary nature and implications of all branches of theology. Moreover, missiologists tended to divide their specialised discipline into the same fourfold pattern as followed by theology 'proper' – biblical foundations, mission theory, mission history and missionary practice – and thus became self-contained.

Finally, in a bold move to try to break the stereotype of traditional theology, some have proposed that all theological disciplines should incorporate the mission dimension into their respective subjects. In theory this is correct; however, in practice it breaks down unless specialists working in other disciplines are fully aware of the mission dimension of their work. There are two formidable obstacles to overcome before theology, in whole and in part, is transformed into a missionary theology. First, there is confusion over the nature of mission. For far too long in the Western world it has been perceived as something which is done overseas, in places where the Church is not yet established or perceived to be still in its youth. People still betray their thinking by talking about 'going to the mission field', meaning somewhere else where the Gospel is needed. At best, mission is thought of as a vital *activity* of the Church, one among others; mission as the essential *being* of the Church has not yet been properly recognised.

Secondly, with too few exceptions, specialists in the various theological disciplines have not been challenged to view their subject matter as intrinsically missionary – this in spite of a greater willingness to perceive God as, by nature, missionary. For example, what a difference it would make to biblical studies if full justice were done to the Bible as a book about mission from beginning to end, written by missionaries for missionaries! Given its content and intent, how could one study it in any other way?

As mission is an expression of a deep commitment to the truth of a particular message, interpreted as good news for all people, some believe that it cannot constitute the proper field of study for an academic institution. Such thinking is confused, since all theological study is implicitly committed, and commitment and critical scrutiny are not mutually exclusive. Far better that all theological disciplines come clean and admit their implicit missionary agendas!

In concluding this first chapter, I will offer a provisional and tentative definition of how I understand theology of mission. This is by way of providing a bare map of the terrain, whose details will be filled in gradually as we proceed with our study:[25]

> The theology of mission is a disciplined study which deals with questions that arise when people of faith seek to understand and fulfil God's purposes in the world, as these are demonstrated in the ministry of Jesus Christ. It is a critical reflection on attitudes and actions adopted by Christians in pursuit of the missionary mandate. Its task is to validate, correct and establish on better foundations the entire practice of mission.

'Questions arise' because the world is complex and varied. Each new generation of Christians may have to tackle issues not faced or adequately addressed by previous ones. Questions also arise because Christians differ among themselves about God's purposes: for example, whether it is legitimate to evangelise people of other faiths; whether resistance to government is ever justified, and if so whether violence can be used in certain circumstances. Because there are questions, there need to be enquiring minds which wish to discover answers.

'God's purposes' are those things which God is about in the world. People committed to the reality of God seek understanding of his involvement in order to be immersed in his concerns. These purposes are not an enigma. God does not play cat-and-mouse with those he has created and loves. God is not hidden or remote. He has come among us as a person and spoken to us – 'Anyone who has seen me has seen the Father' (John 14:9). Jesus Christ is the normative understanding of God's historical project to establish his governance over the entire created order in justice, reconciliation, peace and compassion.

Theology of mission acts, then, as a means of 'validating, correcting and establishing on better foundations' the motives and actions of those wanting to be part of the answer to the prayer, 'Your kingdom come, your will be done on earth as in heaven'. In brief, it has the task of keeping under review and validating best practice in all areas of missionary obedience.[26] It tests theory and practice against the apostolic Gospel and history read eschatologically (i.e. from the perspective of the full realisation of God's rule on earth). The testing is carried out in the midst of the attempt to implement the new order of relationships, structures and attitudes which spell out life in the kingdom in detail. It is also measured against all known alternatives, be they religious, secular or ideological. Needless to say, theology of mission is a continuous task, as it seeks to point the Christian community in the right direction in its response to the mission to which it has been called.

Exercises

1. Give an account of theology which would be exciting to a group of young Christians.

2. Discuss how you would try to resolve a theological dispute between two groups of Christians over
   (a) the priority of experience over belief;
   (b) the notion that there is no salvation outside the Church.

3. Show how you would set about discovering best practice in the Church's attempt to overcome racism.

2

God's Mission and the Church's Response

The rights and wrongs of mission

In many places 'mission' and 'missionary' have a negative image. Much of the history of the modern missionary movement, beginning with the Spanish and Portuguese *conquistadores* in the sixteenth century, has been construed as an alliance between throne and altar, between states grabbing lands and Churches snatching converts. Even where such a direct link between colonial rule and the preaching of the Gospel cannot be established, missionary work is often seen as involving the destruction of indigenous cultures and the implantation of foreign ones.

The Western missionary enterprise – often planned meticulously as if a kind of business operation – has been interpreted as the forceful sale of European civilisation, considered by those who took it elsewhere to be the best product of human creativity yet witnessed. There is a good deal of truth in this image of mission. There is also much exaggeration. For those who wish to perpetuate a wholly negative reading of mission history there are plenty of stories and anecdotes in the archives of church and mission organisations to keep them going for a long time to come. There is also another history of heroic, selfless service which is still remembered with affection and admiration (as I have heard personally) among Christians in different parts of the world.

Linguistically, the outcome of this controversy has been to drop the term 'missionary' but retain 'mission'. Thus today the former are often called 'mission partners' (or 'exchange partners'), perhaps because 'partner' and 'partnership' are currently considered agreeable and appropriate terms in other contexts. Mission is a word that currently possesses a particular resonance in the secular world.

Every business and institution has been busy in the last few years
designing its own mission statement – the first sentence at the
beginning of the glossy brochure, setting out the reason for
the particular establishment's existence, its ambition and goals;
what it is about. We might even say that an organisation's mission
statement explains what it believes it is sent into the world to do.

Mission is here to stay, in Christian circles as well. In the English
language at least there is no real substitute. In the Orthodox and
Roman Catholic traditions, 'apostolate' is also used. It has the
benefit of linking back to the apostolic age of the early Church and
the marginal advantage, perhaps, of being derived from Greek
rather than Latin. However, it has not caught on widely – to speak
of apostolic societies or congregations doesn't seem quite right.
Slowly, and somewhat painfully, mission is becoming uncoupled
from its association with the previous Western movement of evangelism and church planting and being redefined to cover the calling
of the Church, at every level and in every place, to be part of God's
mission in the world.

Mission is no longer thought of as the Church's activity overseas
or in another culture. The mission frontier is not primarily a geographical one, but one of belief, conviction and commitment. Thus,
the Mexico City Conference of the WCC's Commission on World
Mission and Evangelism (1963) described it as follows: 'The
missionary frontier runs around the world. It is the line which
separates belief from unbelief, the unseen frontier which cuts across
all other frontiers and presents the universal Church with its
primary missionary challenge.'[1]

Mission is quite simply, though profoundly, what the Christian
community is sent to do,[2] beginning right where it is located ('you
will be my witnesses in Jerusalem . . . and to the ends of the earth',
Acts 1:8). Although fulfilled in different ways according to particular local circumstances, the obligations of mission are the same
wherever the community is established. The detailed nature of
these obligations will be explored throughout this book and, in
this sense, an understanding of mission will grow, as the current
scene is surveyed.

Missio Dei

God's *missio* (to use the word's Latin root) has become a popular place to begin an enquiry into the nature of mission. In the recent past, it was first used at the Willingen conference of the International Missionary Council (1952). Its primary reference is to the purposes and activities of God in and for the whole universe. The wideness of its scope means that it has become a tag on which an enormous range of meaning has been hung. Legitimately and illegitimately the *missio Dei* has been used to advance all kinds of missiological agendas. Nevertheless, as we shall see, there is a converging broad agreement about the theological interpretation of God's purposes, even though there is still considerable disagreement among Christians about how they should respond in detail.

Perhaps the *missio Dei* is rather too easily taken for granted. In this sense, it has become more of a slogan than a defining phrase. A careful investigation of its meaning should begin, in my opinion, by looking at the assumptions that have to be in place if it is going to act as more than a topical catch-phrase or rallying cry.

Implications

To assert that God has a *missio* presupposes that we are speaking about a personal God with particular characteristics. If one takes the line (as some theologians do) that it is impossible to speak accurately about God, because God must always escape our defining categories, or if one prefers to use abstract and impersonal categories of the divine like 'ground of Being' or 'the ultimately Real',[3] then mission would appear to be an inappropriate concept.

Mission is an activity which presupposes a personal subject. This is not the place to enter the philosophical discussion about the knowability of God or the use of propositions to understand who he is and what he is about. Along with all Churches in all places and at all times, it is necessary to presume that sufficient can be known and said truly about God to make sense of stating that he is actively fulfilling his will in the universe.

If this assumption is shaky, it would be illogical to affirm that God is concerned about every aspect of life, or that he is compassionate, a lover of justice, full of mercy and forgiving. It would, further, be improper to speak about God's kingdom or rule or to use any analogical language about God from human experience (such as the prophet's expression of God's love: 'I took them up in my arms . . . I was to them like those who lift infants to their cheeks', Hos. 11:3–4). Those who use analogical language are well aware of the potential dangers; they are also aware of the much greater peril of refusing any kind of personal ascription to God.

Attempts to make sense of God by using impersonal terms have ended up, inevitably, either in extreme vagueness (because every statement is instantly and progressively qualified) or atheism by any other name. This can, perhaps, be well illustrated by two phrases that the British theologian Don Cupitt has used of his spiritual pilgrimage: *Taking Leave of God* and *The Sea of Faith*. Here, the voyage of exploration into the reality of human life is likened to emigration: God is left behind in the old country to which one never intends to return; now one launches out on a journey across the sea, which may take one anywhere (or nowhere – perhaps it doesn't matter), except back again to the old life.[4]

So, to speak intelligibly of the mission of *God*, one has to be situated within the monotheistic tradition of the designated Abrahamic faiths (Judaism, Christianity, Islam). If one believes that all language about God is nothing more than a human construction, groping for some kind of grand theory by which to make sense of the otherwise disjointed, fragmentary experiences of life, it would be better to speak of *missio hominis*. Of course, to maintain that it is quite legitimate and meaningful to speak of God in personal terms, and to speak truly about him, does not mean that all such talk is right (that would be historically absurd); it does mean, however, that there is a sufficient basis on which one may distinguish between true and false speaking.

God's purposes

This short discussion is a necessary prelude to an enquiry into the meaning of God's mission, for it shows why it is justified to employ otherwise extravagant concepts about God. There have been many ways of interpreting the reasons for God's action in creation and human history. Johannes Verkuyl describes it as God 'actively engaged in the reestablishment of His liberating dominion over the cosmos and all of humankind'.[5] Emilio Castro says that it is 'the purpose of God . . . to gather the whole of creation under the Lordship of Christ Jesus in whom, by the power of the Holy Spirit, all are brought into communion with God'.[6] Wilbert Shenk affirms that 'the redemptive power of God is now being guided by a particular strategy in order to bring the divine purpose to completion by delivering the creation from the powers of decay and death'.[7]

Which God?

Following the so-called Copernican revolution announced by John Hick, in which God, rather than Christian revelation, is the sun around which the different faith traditions of humanity circle,[8] some have thought of God's mission in broader terms than those given in the Christian faith. There is, as it were, a mission of God that breaks the bounds of the Christian texts with their centre fixed exclusively on Jesus Christ. This broader emphasis tends to subsume the mission of God around grand themes like 'justice' or 'liberation', and then see ways in which all traditions (religious and non-religious) contribute to defining their meaning.[9]

There are several reasons why most Christians have not followed this lead. As already discussed, to remove God, moral realities (like justice) or terms signifying new life (like liberation) from concrete and specific traditions is to create abstract and nebulous concepts. They need grounding in the particular usages of real communities. When Christian communities speak about God, by definition they have to speak about Father, Son and Holy Spirit. There simply is no other God. Therefore to speak about the *missio Dei* is to indicate, without any qualification, the *missio Trinitatis*.[10] If other faith traditions use alternative expressions to depict God (or an equivalent), that is a matter for them. To mix dissimilar languages, or to try to reinterpret them in unrecognisable ways, brings only confusion.

The driving force

The trinitarian nature of God's mission is indispensable if one is to understand why God acts in the world. Over and over again in all the most significant literature on the subject,[11] the *missio Dei* is

said to spring from God's boundless and matchless love for the
universe he has created, and particularly for the beings within it
that bear his image. If creation is itself an act of love, then love
has to be a reality within God before matter and being came to
exist in time. Love is a highly personal reality, only possible in
reciprocal relations (such as 'being in love'). This argues for a
relational perception of God – a God in whom interpersonal love
is active.

It is not surprising, therefore, that in recent mission thinking the
idea of the Trinity as community has come to the fore: 'God in
Trinity is a community of divine persons . . . The unity/community
which is God, established and maintained by love (agape), constitutes the plan for humanity.'[12] In other words, the mission of God
flows directly from the nature of who God is. It is impossible to
be more basic than that. God's intention for the world is that in
every respect it should show forth the way he is – love, community,
equality, diversity, mercy, compassion and justice. Although love
is usually singled out as the supreme quality, love can only be
understood in terms of the function of all God's other attributes –
his justice is merciful, his forgiveness is according to justice, equality allows for distinctiveness and his love is both tender and stern.

The logic of love

Divine love is the very opposite of narcissism (a self-absorbing
concern with oneself).[13] It is the passion which wishes the very
highest and best for the other and is willing to sacrifice all that
this might be achieved.[14] This is why Jesus spoke about loving
one's enemies (Matt. 5:44), interpreted as doing good to those who
hate us, blessing those who curse us, praying for those who abuse
us (Luke 6:28), feeding them and never taking vengeance on them
(Rom. 12:19–20).

Love is not a concept that can be understood theoretically. To be
appreciated it has to be seen in action. That is why the New
Testament insists that the most profound understanding of love
springs from God's action in the life of Jesus: 'In this is love, not
that we loved God but that he loved us and sent his Son to be the
atoning sacrifice for our sins' (1 John 4:10). Here is manifested
God's supreme response to the hostility of those he has made to

enjoy his presence and yet who refuse to live as he wishes: 'While we were enemies, we were reconciled to God through the death of his Son' (Rom. 5:10).

In other words, God is in himself mission through and through. Sending and being sent are integral to his nature, for love is uncalculating in the pursuit of its object. No one falls outside its compass. It perseveres even when opposed, rejected and misinterpreted. Love is centrifugal – it always tends outwards from its centre.

The kingdom of God

In contemporary mission thinking no one would contemplate trying to grasp the *missio Dei* without a thorough reference to the rule or reign of God. Although the reality behind the concept is reasonably simple, the language that is used sounds strange, if not alienating to modern ears. Speech about kingship sounds masculine, hierarchical, dominating and constraining. Therefore its significance within the purposes of God has to be explained, not necessarily to make it acceptable to modern thought-forms, but to make sure that it is not misunderstood. Given that this language is so common in the foundation document of the Christian faith, it still has to be used.

In one of the most visionary passages of the entire Bible, Paul speaks of Jesus Christ 'handing over the kingdom to the Father, after he has destroyed every ruler and authority and power' (1 Cor. 15:24). In this text the kingdom is understood as life free from the reign of all those forces which enslave humanity. These 'powers' are understood as enemies which act against human life here and now – the final enemy being death (1 Cor. 15:26). Elsewhere, Paul defines the powers as all those aspects of life which enslave: sin (Rom. 7:14), the law (Rom. 7:10), vanity and corruption (Rom. 8:19–21), this present evil age (Gal. 1:4), weak and miserable principles (Gal. 4:9), spiritual forces of evil (Eph. 6:12). By contrast, the kingdom is life where human beings are no longer subjected to destructive forces.

In another sense, the kingdom is the sphere of life where God's Spirit is in control, where justice, peace and joy are experienced completely and permanently (Rom. 14:17). It is the messianic

banquet, where everyone will enjoy equally and to the full God's
noble gifts, experiencing how another's enjoyment of being human
enhances one's own. It is the place where God will be 'all in all'
(1 Cor. 15:28): that is, recognised universally as the source of all life,
justice, love, wisdom and truth, the only redeemer, the Lord of
history and the righteous and merciful judge.

As we shall see when we have to relate the biblical statements
about the kingdom to both world history and the Church, it is
important to understand the kingdom in terms of a double liberation *from* slavery *into* the 'glorious freedom of the children of
God' (Rom. 8:21).

At the centre of the vision of the kingdom is a 'Lamb standing
as if it had been slaughtered' (Rev. 5:6). This picture is crucial in
enabling us to grasp the meaning of the kingdom, for it is by the
power of the self-sacrifice of the triune God that the hostile powers
are overcome and God's world is enabled to live again in the
power of true creativity and service:

> According to the witness of the New Testament, the cross is
> the place where to eyes of faith the reign of God is manifested
> in what seems to be its defeat ... This is the place where the
> meaning of the original gospel announcement is disclosed:
> the kingdom of God has drawn near. The church can hold and
> live by this faith because this Jesus, crucified in weakness, was
> 'designated Son of God in power according to the Spirit of
> holiness by his resurrection from the dead' (Rom. 1:4).[15]

Missio ecclesiae

Missionary by definition

Mission is so much at the heart of the Church's life that, rather
than think of it as one aspect of its existence, it is better to think
of it as defining its essence. The Church is by nature missionary
to the extent that, if it ceases to be missionary, it has not just failed
in one of its tasks, it has ceased being Church. Thus, the Church's
self-understanding and sense of identity (its ecclesiology) is
inherently bound up with its call to share and live out the Gospel
of Jesus Christ to the ends of the earth and the end of time. Without

a strong sense of vocation to its missionary work, the Church cannot consider itself either catholic or apostolic.

Failure to appreciate this self-defining reality has allowed some people to talk of the Church simply maintaining its own life and traditions, as if this were an alternative option. However, this cannot be so. If and when the Church exists for its own sake, it denies itself; it has become something other than the community called into being by Jesus Christ, crucified and risen:

> Mission is the fundamental reality of our Christian life. We are Christians because we have been called by God to work with him in the fulfillment of his purposes for humanity as a whole. Our life in this world is life in mission. Life has a purpose only to the extent that it has a missionary dimension.[16]

To clarify the nature of mission is to answer the question, what is the Church for? It is entirely for the purposes for which God called it into being. It has no liberty, therefore, to invent its own agenda. It is a community in response to the *missio Dei*, bearing witness to God's activity in the world by its communication of the good news of Jesus Christ in word and deed.

Election: getting it straight

God's way of relating to his troubled world has been to seek out a community of people who will dedicate themselves to fulfilling his compassionate and liberating will for all, on behalf of all. The Bible uses the two words – 'covenant' and 'election' – to describe this action. God enters into a specific relationship with those he calls, entrusting them with the special responsibility of transmitting his word of salvation in Jesus Christ to all who will hear. Unfortunately, in the course of history, this relationship has been interpreted far too often as a special privilege or as a superior power, seducing the Church into imagining it has explicit rights and prerogatives within society.

Election means appointment. As in the political process, it means accountability in the first instance to the one who has made the choice. In an age which emphasises so strongly equality and pluralism, it is extremely difficult to make sense of a particular divine call to one group of people out of all humanity; it is therefore necessary to make a few critical points:

1. The people of God are not called because they merit it. They are not of better quality than others or a cut above them. They are those who recognise the failure and poverty of their lives. Paradoxically, it is those who refuse to admit their need of God's forgiveness and a new beginning who have an exalted view of themselves. An arrogant Christian is a contradiction in terms.

2. The people of God are not called in order to gain benefits for themselves. Among certain 'new' churches, often working among the most destitute of the earth, there has arisen an illusory teaching that God will shower with gifts any who ask with enough faith. Sometimes called 'prosperity doctrine' or 'health and wealth' teaching, it deceives people into believing that they can enter into some kind of contract with God, who will bless them in return for some special performance on their part. This is the modern equivalent of the old 'cargo cult'.[17] Of course, there are incalculable gains to be enjoyed for those who know and love God; but, strangely, they only come when everything has been given up to follow Jesus Christ for the sake of God's rule on earth (Mark 10:28–31; 8:34–7).

3. God's calling to mission is a calling to service. Again, service is not so much a function as a definition of the Church. The community Jesus founded is *diakonia* (Mark 10:43–5). God's people are judged not by their formal piety but by the spontaneous compassion they show – or fail to show – to those in need with whom Jesus Christ identifies himself (Matt. 25:44; Acts 11:29; 12:25).

Covenant and *election* in biblical understanding are profitable to those who belong to God's people only in the strict sense that it is a privilege to be part of what God is about in the world, even when this means sacrifice and suffering. Christians in many parts of the world understand this all too well. They have renounced their own security or secular advancement for the sake of testifying faithfully to the truth of Jesus Christ. We Christians who live in the West find all kinds of plausible reasons why we should share the same comfortable lifestyle enjoyed by our friends and neighbours. We make seemingly convincing excuses for not responding to people in need or sharing the Gospel with them. Many of the assumptions of our societies are hostile to the Christian view of life, and rather than be exposed as a small minority in a sea of indifference or antagonism, we keep our heads down.

Granted, then, that the Church can guard against the various perversions to which its status may make it prone,[18] it has every right to rejoice in the glorious honour of knowing and communicating that Jesus Christ is good news both for individuals and whole nations – indeed, for the all-pervasive world order of today.

The kingdom of God and the Church

Mission through the Church?
During the last half century, a vigorous debate has been joined within the Church on the relationship between the *missio Dei*, the Church and the world. There have been times in the past when Christians assumed that all God's purposes would be fulfilled exclusively through the Church. There have been theologies which have either identified the kingdom completely with the Church or which have regarded the kingdom as a purely future event.[19] A Church-centred missiology undergirded the extraordinary missionary thrust of the last two centuries, with its emphasis on the planting of self-supporting, self-governing and self-propagating churches,[20] although perhaps the 'civilising' aspect of this mission reflected some kind of (distorted) reference to the kingdom.[21]

Mission through the world?
On the other side, there are theologies which almost bypass the Church altogether. These see God's direct activity in the world as the clue to his mission. They deny the distinction sometimes drawn between 'salvation history', which is focused on the community which God is saving, and 'world history', which is focused on the rest of humanity alienated from the ways of God and heading for judgement. In their thinking, the place of salvation is the world, and God works out his purposes through a process of humanis-

ation through which the conditions are created, step by step, to make human flourishing possible:

> Previous patterns of mission viewed the church as the bearer of God's mission to the world; now the world became the focal point with the church responding to people's search for humanization, evident in situations of injustice, racial hatred, loneliness, and other personal crises. In this study mission became identified with participation in programs for urban renewal, the civil rights movement, and in community development projects.[22]

The Church is somewhat peripheral to this view of God's mission, except in having the role of interpreting to the world what is going on.

The figures most often associated with this way of thinking about mission are the Dutch pair A.T. Van Leeuwen and J.C. Hoekendijk.[23] Van Leeuwen builds a thesis that God has brought about, in the course of historical progress, an abandonment of the distinction between secular and religious spheres, between holy vocations and mundane pursuits. The genius of Christianity, according to this view, is that as the Gospel itself begins to transform the whole of life, it makes itself unnecessary as a religion. God's principle work is being carried forward through the various revolutions (technological and economic) which are creating that kind of society in which an enhanced welfare for everyone becomes possible.[24]

Hoekendijk began from a profound study of the perversion of the Church's mission under the influence of Nazi ideology.[25] The *volkskirche* (the Church of the whole people) is either manipulated by the state to support its ideology or it becomes a passive and gullible institution whose role is played out in terms of conserving a people's self-identity. The problem with putting the Church at the centre of mission is that it becomes the judge and jury in defence of its own destiny and priority. There is no external, radical norm for self-criticism. The Latin American missiologist Ismael Amaya sees the modern missionary enterprise as an example of the Church accepting uncritically a calling with pretentious cultural dimensions.[26] He accuses the Church (in America in particular) of confusing the Gospel with the American dream of individual liberties and a free-market economy.

The solution, therefore, to the dangers inherent in the Church-orientated view of mission is to minimise the Church as an entity in itself and, excluding its pretentious, self-aggrandising claims, see it only operating against the horizon of the kingdom of God. Hoekendijk puts it starkly: 'The nature of the Church can be sufficiently defined by its *function*, i.e. its participation in Christ's apostolic ministry'.

Mission and community

However, concentrating on the Church as the centre and agent of God's mission is not as mistaken as it is often portrayed.[27] For example, in the Pauline captivity letters (Ephesians and Colossians), the Church is placed at the very heart of God's purpose to 'gather up all things in Christ' (Eph. 1:10). It is said not only to be an instrument of the Gospel, but part of the Gospel (Eph. 3:6). The reason for this is clear, if often forgotten: God's reconciling activity in Jesus Christ (2 Cor. 5:19) has as its goal not only individuals (Rom. 5:10–11) and the cosmos (Col. 1:20), but human beings with one another.

The overcoming of alienation is to be manifested in the end of hostility between antagonistic groups (Eph. 2:14–22). Reconciliation does not take place when groups of people merely decide to be friendly with one another, but when they form part of the same community, learning to submit their identity (Col. 3:11) and forgo their ambitions for the sake of a common goal. That is why the Church in mission is both a threat and antidote to nationalisms of all kinds – imagine the radical consequences if the Church took seriously, across all cultural and ethnic boundaries, the command, 'be subject to one another out of reverence for Christ' (Eph. 5:21).

Kingdom, Church, world

Though acknowledging the complexity of the relationship between kingdom, Church and world in the mission of God, some kind of theological integration needs to be attempted. The way that most missiologists have approached this task is by seeing the Church as the only *self-conscious* agent of the kingdom. If the kingdom is

aware

about the restoration of the fullness of life to a sick and fractured
world, then many people, without knowing it, may be agents of
the kingdom. However, without recognising and submitting to the
control of the king, they cannot be members of the kingdom. World
history is significant as the coming kingdom will be the completion
of all that is good, just, beautiful and true in the whole of human
life. However, it cannot be identified with God's salvation, for this
supposes the removal from the world of all that is corrupt, unjust,
ugly and false (Rev. 21:26–7).

The Church then intentionally bears witness to the meaning and
relevance of the kingdom, while not itself being identical with
that kingdom. It is called to the risky task of being the living
interpretation of that kingdom; otherwise, the kingdom can be
little more than a slogan, ideology or human programme of betterment.[28] In its preaching and teaching, the Church is an advocate
of the kingdom; in its worshipping life[29] it is an emissary of the
kingdom; in its work for reconciliation, peace and justice it is an
instrument of the kingdom. In Emilio Castro's words:

> The church is called . . . to be an anticipation of the kingdom;
> to show in its internal life the values of justice and supportive
> love; to develop a priestly servant vocation in interceding
> in Abrahamic tradition for the whole human community; to
> celebrate liturgically, in anticipation, the coming of the
> kingdom; to watch like the virgins of the parable for the
> coming of the Lord; and then to be the missionary people of
> God, called and sent all over the world to proclaim and serve,
> announcing and manifesting the kingdom of God.[30]

Wilbert Shenk has outlined the different relationships in a helpful
way: in the first place, 'the rule of God is prior to mission'; in the
second place, 'mission is prior to the church'; thirdly, 'at Pentecost
the Holy Spirit equipped the disciple community to continue the
mission of Jesus Christ in the world'.[31] It is to the third aspect
of mission that we will turn next, to see more concretely how the
Church is to carry through its calling to follow in the way of Jesus.

In whatever way one links kingdom, world and Church within
the one mission of God, it is important to safeguard certain fundamental facts:

1. The history and culture of human beings, even if they are not touched in a consciously direct way by the knowledge of salvation in Jesus Christ, are not rubbish. As human beings created in the image of God they will, shorn of inevitable corruption, constitute a part of God's new creation.

2. The gains made by human beings in the overcoming of injustice, diseases, oppression and violence of all kinds are not to be equated with the salvation which is offered in the Gospel of Jesus Christ (which removes the more fundamental problem of idolatry). Nor, however, are they something of a completely different order, for the transformation promised in the coming kingdom relates to the whole of life, internal and external, personal and social.

3. This means that God's mission is carried out in both the world and the Church; to a lesser degree in human history untouched by the Gospel, to a greater degree where the Gospel is believed and obeyed. To these different kinds of connection we will need to return many times in the course of our theological exploration. Getting them right is crucial for a wholesome view of mission.

Exercises

1. Discuss how the following aspects of God's nature shape God's mission: love, justice, holiness, anger and mercy.

2. Draw a diagram of how you think God's kingdom relates to the Church and the world.

3. Describe the symptoms of a Church which has lost its missionary vision and the steps it can take to recover it.

3

Mission in the Way of Jesus Christ

The significance of the theme

The title of this chapter has been inspired in part by the theme of
the conference on world mission and evangelism held by the World
Council of Churches at San Antonio, Texas, in 1989: 'Your Will be
Done: Mission in Christ's Way'. The choice was meant to indicate
an inseparable link between doing the will of God and following
Jesus;[1] between the *missio Dei* and the *missio Christi*. Unless God's
mission is rooted in what liberation theologians would call 'concrete practice', it becomes either empty or open to ideological,
political or religious manipulation (or all three).

Another point of reference has been Jürgen Moltmann's notable
christological study, *The Way of Jesus Christ: Christology in Messianic
Dimensions*.[2] He explains the reason for choosing this particular
title:

> What I wanted was . . . a christology for men and women who
> are on the way in the conflicts of history, and are looking for
> bearings on that way . . . Men and women who are living in
> the exile of history, and who are searching for life, need a
> christology for pilgrims . . . That means a christology of the
> way, which points beyond itself and draws people towards
> the future of Christ, so that they remain on Christ's path, and
> move forward along that path.[3]

The way of Jesus Christ has two obvious focal points: the first in
his own life's work and the second in the conduct of his disciples.
In the first case, we ask how Jesus carried out his vocation; in the
second case, we ask how those who follow Jesus should shape
their lives. This exploration is crucial if we wish to take seriously

the most all-encompassing of the New Testament's texts on mission, 'As the Father has sent me, so I send you' (John 20:21). We need to grapple particularly with the words 'as' and 'so': how exactly has Jesus Christ been sent into the world ? How does he send his disciples into the world?

Similar questions emerge if we take to heart an instruction like, 'Go and do likewise' (Luke 10:37), which refers to mercy shown to the victim of unprovoked violence who belonged to a despised ethnic group; or 'Be perfect, therefore, as your heavenly Father is perfect' (Matt. 5:48), which speaks of loving one's enemies. What sense does it make to go and do as Jesus did? What possibility is there of fulfilling our mission in the way of Jesus Christ when our circumstances are so vastly different?

And yet, in spite of the difficulties (which we will survey below), there has been a deep-rooted conviction throughout the history of the Christian community that following in the way of Jesus Christ (discipleship) is *the* test of missionary faithfulness. The Church has gone astray precisely when it has either ignored or reinvented the mission of Christ. How, for example, could the Spanish conquerors of Central and South America in the sixteenth century possibly have thought they were doing mission 'in the way of Jesus Christ'? Or how could ancient and modern defenders of the alliance between Church and state ever think that it was a faithful reflection of what Jesus was about? Though the problems of discovering and reapplying mission in the way of Christ may be complicated, the Christian community needs a standard by which to measure its own performance – a standard which is able to call in question its own policies, programmes and practices. Without this, mission simply becomes an arbitrary response to whatever a particular culture or moment of history throws up.

Conducting the investigation

Many questions concerning the relationship of the four gospels to the beginning of the Christian movement and to the Church's existence today have been controversial and disputed. A full discussion of the issue is not possible here; all I can offer is a short description of some of the problems and a summary of my own assumptions in trying to clarify mission in the way of Jesus Christ.

Some scholars believe that the chances are remote of discovering events in Jesus' life just as they happened. Recognising that the only access to the history of Jesus is through the writings set down by his followers some time afterwards, they assume that the gospel narratives are so full of the early Church's interpretation that recovery of the original Jesus is well-nigh impossible. The implication is that the gospel writers were not interested in reporting incidents in Jesus' life as 'bare facts', but only as they revealed theological insights into the meaning of Christ. Furthermore, according to this view, the picture of Jesus in the gospels has been shaped in order to give guidance on issues the Church faced at least 30 to 40 years after his death.

This position, at its most sceptical, takes for granted that historical detail did not interest the early Christian communities or those who opposed them. Rather, they were concerned to write an account of Jesus 'from faith to faith', that would provide an inspiration for struggling congregations under threat from powerful forces determined to stamp them out. The result of these widespread assumptions has been a minute investigation of the gospel texts with the aim of finding echoes of the early Church's life and witness contained in the stories about Jesus. The method of achieving this is called 'form criticism' (or 'tradition history') – the study of individual parts of the gospels with a view to ascertaining how they came to be written and rewritten within the Christian communities before assuming their final form.

And yet, despite the lack of interest in some quarters about the historical Jesus, the search for who he might have been has never lost its hold. New Testament scholarship is into its third so-called 'quest for the Jesus of history'. There is an almost irresistible pull to find Jesus as he was, behind the Jesus as preached by the early Church. There are a number of good reasons for this:

1. The fundamental presuppositions which undergirded the lack of interest in Jesus of Nazareth have all been questioned: for example, the view that a faith-perspective inevitably distorts history, or that faith does not need history to rest on, or that

the early Church was not interested in telling it the way it was because the Gentile world was mainly interested in universal ideals.

2. It was noted that form criticism or tradition history as a method of historical research is based on a circular argument: if the stories about Jesus are *assumed* to convey mostly information about the early Church, they will be found to do so; each one will be seen in the light of alleged communities reconstructed on the basis of the gospel stories. However, since there is no independent verification of these reconstructed histories, there is no way of testing the thesis that the gospel accounts speak more about the life of the early Church than the life of Jesus. The conclusions are already present in the premises and serious historical work has been bypassed.

3. The birth and growth of the 'Jesus movement' is an enigma, unless it is possible to recover the historical causes that set it going. There are serious historical facts that can be explained only by the original story of Jesus. There is the persecution of the early Church, indiscriminately carried out by Jews, Greeks and.Romans. What made this pathetically small and powerless community so loathed and feared? There is the opposition to Jesus recorded in the gospels. In some of the more imaginative reconstructions of Jesus his death by crucifixion would be inexplicable.[4] There is the belief of the early Church that, in some sense, the end of history had already arrived in its lifetime – and yet it did not happen as anyone had imagined. There is the existence of a community of followers of Jesus which did not disintegrate after his death. How on earth did they manage to base their existence on a story about a Messiah who had died at the hands of the pagan enemies of Israel and to convince Jews to believe that in this act God was already fulfilling his promises to overcome evil and re-establish the mission of his people in the world?

For these reasons, and others, the serious work of historical enquiry is being undertaken again; not this time into the circumstances of the early Church which produced the gospels, but into the circumstances of Jesus which produced the early Church. Nevertheless, some scholars are still working with the *a priori* assumption that the Jesus of the gospel narratives cannot be taken at face value as a figure who clearly fits into his own historical situation. In other words, the assumption that Jesus must have been other than the way the evangelists present him does not die easily. However, if one were to reconstruct the life of the Jewish people from the stories of Jesus, rather than that of the early Church, a pattern emerges which is consistent with what we know from other sources. Moreover, it is precisely these stories that are able to explain the riddle of the early Church.

The importance of history to mission

What Jesus said and did about God's plan of salvation is the starting-point for all discussion of the Church's mission, whatever the context.[5] This means that it is imperative to discover who Jesus was and what he was aiming at. In turn, this makes historical enquiry a necessary and legitimate task. There is no self-evident reason for trying to shield faith in Jesus Christ from searching historical investigation. Indeed, what happened and why is crucial for a faith based on a real figure of the past (even when this faith also confesses him to be alive and present).

The alternative is that Jesus becomes a figure of the imagination, a symbol of ideals or programmes which bear little or no relationship to what he himself stood for. When this happens, there is no possibility of objecting, on the grounds of historical integrity, to any kind of reconstruction of Jesus. Consistency would demand an absolute plurality of Jesuses. Experience suggests that, in contrast to the Jesus of the gospels, these recreated Jesuses are usually innocuous.

The most satisfactory explanation of the data is also the simplest. In other words, the more complex the theories needed to account for the evidence the further from reality they are likely to be. In general it is not unreasonable to assume that the stories and sayings of Jesus have been transmitted reliably, unless all plausible explanations for what seem to be discrepancies have been exhausted. Likewise it is justifiable to reject speculation about the way things might have been when there is no concrete and convincing evidence to substantiate the conjectures. This is sound historical common sense; before arriving at what seems to be the most credible version of the facts, the historian must be able to point to well-tested evidence.

Historical criticism involves examining hypotheses and weighing up the merits of alternative explanations. But the evidence produced has to be sufficiently solid to be verifiable in principle. Too often in gospel criticism theories have been built on tenuous connections between superficially related ideas, allusions, language and historical circumstances. Much of the speculation is interesting, even ingenious – but the evidence is far too meagre. Historical analysis cannot achieve absolute certainty; but to say anything significant it must be able to move from what is only possible to what is probable.

There are good reasons for treating the gospels as serious records of real events. This, at least, is what they claim implicitly and explicitly (e.g. Luke 1:1–4; 23:48; Mark 1:16–20; 6:1–3; 11:15–16; 14:43–6). The gospel writers knew and respected the difference between stories without a reference to events in the real world (e.g. the parables) and stories which happened largely as reported. Writing out of a Jewish milieu, they would have related their beliefs to historical occurrences through which they believed God was working. They could not have understood either the exodus, the settlement in Palestine, the end of the northern kingdom, the exile in Babylon, the restoration or the triumph of the Maccabees (to name some crucial moments in their history) as fables invented to drive home some moral lesson. Finally, the threat or reality of social ostracism, imprisonment, torture and martyrdom could not have been born merely on the basis of a good theory about how God brings about his righteous rule in the world, but on the conviction that, through certain events which happened in a particular locality at a concrete moment in time, God's salvation was accomplished.[6]

All in all, the best possible explanation for the existence of the early Christian communities is the story of Jesus as told in the gospels. The Jesus who best fits the available knowledge we have of the Jewish people of the first century under Roman occupation is also the Jesus of the gospels. These narratives throw up a credible portrait of an exceptional figure who became the founder of a missionary movement which spread with amazing speed, and survived both sporadic and sustained attempts at its elimination.

Turning from issues of historical method to issues of integrity in mission means exploring the questions about who Jesus was, what he intended to do, and whether he was successful.

Jesus' public life

In outline
A reasonably clear pattern emerges from the gospels about Jesus' activities in public. He first became prominent when a figure called John was baptising people in the river Jordan. He started an itinerant ministry of preaching, with the arrival of God's kingdom as the main theme. He also healed many people and called a small group of people to accompany him. He was involved in conflict with some political and religious leaders because he ate with people they considered unclean and made claims that they considered outrageous. Partly as the result of a dramatic incident in the temple, he was arrested, handed over to the Romans and executed in the manner habitually used for rebels. A few days later his followers claimed that he was alive again and had been with them.

Baptism
By undergoing baptism at the hands of John alongside many of his compatriots, Jesus identified himself with John's message to Israel of judgement, repentance and forgiveness of sins. This was given in the context of the announcement that God was about to act in a special way ('The kingdom of heaven has come near' – Matt. 3:2). Jesus interpreted his own action as the beginning of a special mission ('It is proper for us in this way to fulfil all righteousness' – Matt. 3:15).

Temptations
The story of the temptations confirms this sense of a special vocation, for in it the direction of his life is challenged and clarified.

Under dispute is the meaning of the phrase, 'Son of God', as a key to understanding his mission ('If you are the Son of God' – Matt. 4:3,6). Jesus was tempted not so much to doubt that this title applied to him as to interpret it to mean that he should perform some spectacular public miracles to convince the people of his credentials. His refusal to agree to Satan's suggestions indicates that he had already ruled out certain options.

It is generally assumed that the most powerful temptation for Jesus was to allow himself to become the focus of a rising against the Roman occupation of the land. A natural interpretation of the arrival of God's rule would have been that God was about to restore his people's fortunes by ridding them of the unclean presence of the foreign invader and by ensuring a renewed commitment to God's moral demands (Acts 1:6). The two were closely linked. Jesus' actual mission has to be seen as a radical reinterpretation of both these aspirations.

Controversies

Nevertheless, the choice he made did not rule out a number of contentious actions that were open to misinterpretation.[7] He continued John's preaching of the kingdom. He called a select group of people to share his work, among whom were some fairly suspect figures.[8] He publicly claimed to fulfil the Scriptures (Luke 4:21). He engaged in a round of healings and exorcisms all over Galilee (Mark 1:39). He provoked serious controversy by:

(a)   forgiving the sins of a paralysed man (Mark 2:1–12);
(b)   calling a tax collector to follow him (Mark 2:14); eating with the tax collector's friends (Mark 2:15–16);
(c)   not insisting that his disciples follow strict regulations regarding fasting (Mark 2:18–20),
(d)   apparently breaking the sabbath (Mark 2:23–7; 3:1–5).

Conflict

There has been great debate about whether Jesus consciously believed himself to be the Messiah (the expected agent of God's rule on earth). At one time, a theory called the 'messianic secret' was much in vogue. According to this, Jesus quite self-consciously refused the title of Messiah (preferring the less emotive title, 'Son of Man' – for example, Mark 14:61–2), forbidding various people from spreading abroad such a rumour (Mark 1:44) and withdrawing on various occasions from public view for fear of stirring up false hopes (Luke 5:15–16). The theory, however, ignores two vital facts: firstly, that there was no one settled opinion in the first century about the nature of the Messiah; secondly, that Jesus' actions spoke louder than his words. Perhaps the most convincing reason why we must assume that Jesus thought of himself as the Messiah (as he interpreted this) is the conflict which his teaching and actions stirred up.[9] This conflict is the direct result of the way in which he interpreted his relationship to the kingdom of God. The following are some of the main causes of the conflict between Jesus and those who opposed him – an unlikely coalition of political and religious leaders (Mark 3:6):

(a) Tradition and the Law
Although it is true that Jesus did not teach or practise a wholescale abandonment of the traditions of his people (Matt. 5:17–19), he did not absolutise them either. He taught that the purpose of the traditions was to guide and warn, never to dominate or enslave (Matt. 23:3–4). They had to be set in the context of the new order that God was in the process of creating: 'One puts new wine into fresh wineskins' (Mark 2:22). In this order, what counts are relationships of love and justice, which spring from a new heart (Jer. 31:33), not a conformity to codes of practice which may hide hatred, exploitation, deceit and violent intentions (Mark 7:14–15, 20–3).

The Sermon on the Mount is a description of the righteousness required by the kingdom (Matt. 6:33), which exceeds the current righteousness being practised (Matt. 5:20). Indeed, it might be interpreted as a heroic ethic, one not normally associated with ordinary mortals of flesh and blood; and yet clearly it is a way of life from which no disciple is excused. The teaching defines discipleship and its practice membership in the kingdom (Matt. 5:20; 7:21–3; 25:34ff.).

(b) Nationalism and kinship

The conflict between Jesus and certain Jewish leaders was not just about rules and regulations, but about the underlying identity that these signified.[10] The food laws, the sabbath, marriage customs, circumcision and the sanctity of the temple were symbols that pointed to the divine origin of Israel's peoplehood, now under serious threat. By relativising the importance of these symbols or declaring them to be redundant ('The sabbath was made for humankind, and not humankind for the sabbath' – Mark 2:27; 'Thus he declared all foods clean' – Mark 7:19), Jesus was making a major statement about the nature of belonging to a particular ethnic group.

Jesus' response to the disciple who (legitimately) sought permission to perform his family duty to his father – 'Let the dead bury their own dead' (Luke 9:60) – would have been considered scandalous by most people. It can only indicate that Jesus understood his mission, in response to the coming reign of God, as forming an alternative community with remarkably different values. This is emphasised by two further statements: 'Whoever does the will of God is my brother and sister and mother' (Mark 3:35), and 'There is no one who has left house or brothers or sisters or mother or father or children or fields, for my sake and the sake of the good news, who will not receive a hundredfold now in this age – houses, brothers and sisters, mothers and children, and fields' (Mark 10:29–30). This is a call to declare a new loyalty to Jesus' understanding of what God was doing through him. In this new community allegiance to kinship and ethnic groups was not the main source of a person's identity. This was radical preaching indeed![11]

In other words, Jesus' vision of the kingdom had nothing to do with safeguarding national sovereignty or the maintenance of ethnic purity. In the kingdom of God, race and national identity are not major matters; they do not offer grounds for discrimination. Thus attempts to keep people loyal to a particular state, cultural group or family by prohibiting them from responding to Jesus' invitation to the kingdom are condemned by the message that Jesus proclaimed and lived.

(c) The excluded

In recent times, one of the most noted of all the aspects of Jesus' mission is his willingness to associate with outsiders. Recent historical studies of the social conditions of first-century Palestine have provided a growing body of evidence that many of Jesus' contemporaries were excluded from the normal benefits of community existence.[12] They were lepers and other diseased people,[13] 'sinners' who were not sufficiently strict about the law, prostitutes, debtors, collaborators with Rome, bonded labourers. The gospels refer to these collectively as 'the poor': first, because they had no financial or family resources to fall back on; secondly, because 'normal' society considered them to be deviants in some way.

Jesus meets these people, eats with them, touches them, heals them, forgives them and proclaims that they will enter the kingdom of God before the 'insiders':

> The kingdom of God which Jesus proclaims and which he demonstrates through his dealings with the poor, the sick, sinners and tax collectors does not merely bring the lordship of God over his whole creation; it also brings the great and joyful banquet of the nations . . . (Isa. 25:6–8; Luke 13:29) . . . It is in this context that we have to see Jesus' eating and drinking with sinners and tax collectors: together with these 'unrighteous persons' he is . . . demonstrating in his own person what acceptance by the merciful God and the forgiveness of sins means . . . Jesus celebrates the feast of the messianic time with those who are discriminated against in his own time . . . In this celebration he is reflecting God's own way of doing things.[14]

The poor were a wider category than those who were bereft of the basic necessities of life, although these latter formed a large group in Palestine at the time of Jesus. They were also those whom the ruling system disadvantaged: 'the multitude', defined by those in power as useless to society, social misfits, subversives. They had no opportunity to become a full part of civil society, because of discrimination, prejudice and the defence of privilege. The preaching of the kingdom came to them as good news because it spoke of another kind of system (Luke 6:20):

No one came close to matching Jesus' perception of the nature of the Domination System and what was needed to replace it. That new alternative he called the 'kingdom of God'. In order to specify its actual content I paraphrase that expression as 'God's domination-free-order.[15]

(d) Money, prestige and power

Jesus' idea of the kingdom was in almost every conceivable aspect different from that of the leaders of his time:

> Because money is an idol that seeks to be an absolute, it is not possible to serve God and money (Matt. 6:24) . . . Jesus stands on the wrong side, with those no one wants to be with . . . He declares that God is on the side of the little people, those who have no value for society (cf. Matt. 8:10) . . . He is glad that the Father's self-revelation has been to the simple, not the wise (Matt. 11:25ff.) . . . He unmasks political power when he says 'those who claim to govern nations behave despotically and the powerful oppress the people' (Mark 10:42).[16]

Tom Wright links Jesus' call to sit loose to possessions with an idolatrous attitude to the land. Many of Jesus' sayings about the deceitful nature of money (e.g. Matt. 6:19–21; Luke 12:13–15; 33–4; Luke 14:33; Mark 10:21–2) make best sense in the context of a defence of the right to the 'promised' land at any cost. The land was one of the centrepieces in the world-view of the Jewish people, but it was luring them into 'a war in defence of her land, that she [i.e. Israel] could not win'.[17] In the same vein, one might say that the defence of the right to land, understood as private property in any form, even at the cost of excluding the vast majority of people from an adequate livelihood, was (and is) a denial of God's will that all should be blessed with enough.[18]

The gospel narratives do not give us sufficient information to construct a detailed picture of Jesus' attitude to political power. However, there are a number of hints that suggest his version of the kingdom conflicted with the practice of power by the Romans, Herod and the Sadducean party. In response to the famous question about paying taxes to sustain the Roman empire, Jesus clearly distinguishes between God's authority and that of the earthly power (Mark 12:17). His reference to Herod as 'that fox' (Luke 13:32) conveys both an indifference to Herod's pretensions and a view of him as a calculating and dishonest pragmatist. His contempt for the proceedings of the Sanhedrin (John 18:19–23; Matt. 26:57–68) shows his refusal to accept the distortion of justice, even when practised by the highest religious authority in the land. There can be little doubt that Jesus refused for himself and his disciples the option of violence (a subject we will return to) as a way of achieving his goals (Mark 14:48–9; Luke 22:38, 49–51; Matt. 26:52; John 18:36–7). His words imply a criticism of all who believe that violence is a legitimate means of bringing about God's kind of righteousness.

(e) The temple

The events surrounding the beginning of the last week of Jesus' life – the entry into Jerusalem, the withering of the fig tree and the cleansing of the temple – give us the most important clues for understanding his mission. The crowds in Jerusalem for the Passover feast, swarming over the Mount of Olives, urged Jesus to deliver them from the hated occupation of Rome. They cried out for political liberation, for national independence:

> 'Save us. Blessed is the one who comes bearing the Lord's name, and in his protection. Blessed is the coming kingdom like the one that our father David ruled over. Save us' (Mark 11:9–10).

In the corner of the temple mount, overlooking the whole area, was the dreaded Tower of Antonio which housed the Roman garrison, present in force to control the crowds at this volatile festival. Jesus was carried by the surge of people to the temple. In that place there was a dramatic parting of the ways. Instead of leading an assault on the military power of the Republican Guard, Jesus attacked the economic power of the temple traders. His choice of which of the two to set upon (both considered defiling presences in a sacred space) was significant. The episode of the fig tree (Mark 11:12–14, 20–1) gives us a clue to Jesus' action: representing Israel, God's chosen people, outwardly the fig tree promised much, but it was devoid of fruit (Isa. 5:2; Luke 13:7); the time of God's judgement had arrived.

Israel's profound problem was not its lack of political freedom but its deep ignorance of God's plan of salvation. The true enemy was not the Roman infidel, but the illusion about God that the people obstinately held to. The people wished to defend their national privileges, keeping God for themselves, whereas 'My house shall be called a house of prayer for all nations' (Mark 11:17). Instead of desiring to be saved from the Gentiles, Israel's mission was to be 'a light to the nations, that my salvation may reach to the ends of the earth' (Isa. 49:6).

There was also corruption at the heart of Israel's worship. The keepers of the temple, the Sadducees, operated a lucrative trade in animals for sacrifice. These had to be without blemish. They were being sold at four to five times their market value, and had to be bought using special coins which were exchanged for normal currency for a big commission. Extortionate prices were being charged in a monopoly trade. The temple had become 'a den of robbers' (Mark 11:17).

The people had proclaimed Jesus Messiah as he entered Jerusalem. Now he showed them what kind of Messiah he was. The cleansing of the temple was a powerful acted parable showing that the old order was passing away and that with Jesus all things were becoming new. From henceforth there would be a new temple; his crucified and risen body would be the place where God would be worshipped (John 2: 19–21; Matt. 26:61). Jesus' act of judgement did not spring from hatred, or desire for revenge. He wept over Jerusalem because it refused to recognise God's offer of salvation (Luke 19:41–4).

After this event, there was no way back for Jesus. He had challenged the present regime at its core. He had refused to interpret his mission in terms of a holy war for national liberation. He had predicted the destruction of Israel's most holy symbol and with it, by implication, the withdrawal of God's presence from his people. Forty years on the stone temple was dismantled, never to rise again. Five days later the temple of his flesh was destroyed to rise again after three days.

The cleansing of the temple was the beginning of God's judge-

ment on a people that had lost its way. The crucifixion was the
end of God's judgement on all who believed that through his death
and resurrection Jesus opened up a new era of salvation, a new
order, a new concept of peoplehood, a liberation from the destructive forces of political corruption, economic oppression,
nationalistic xenophobia, self-righteousness and trust in violence.
Significantly, in keeping with Jesus' whole mission, the last word
in the story is a call to the disciples to forgive: 'Whenever you
stand praying, forgive, if you have anything against anyone; so
that your Father in heaven may also forgive you your trespasses'
(Mark 11:25).

Jesus' mission and the disciples' mission

Assuming this brief outline of Jesus' public ministry to be a faithful
reflection of the events which took place, what may we deduce
about our mission in the way of Jesus Christ? No conclusions are
without dispute – but it is safe to make some affirmations.

Following

There is good enough evidence for Jesus' belief that those whom
he called to be with him would continue his mission of proclaiming
and performing God's rule on earth. It would be virtually impossible to imagine any other reason for the existence of the new
community of Christians in Jerusalem and Judaea and its survival
under the pressure of persecution.

The preaching of the nearness of the kingdom of God, the call
to repent and believe the good news (Mark 1:14–15) is now further
extended by the commission to proclaim repentance and the forgiveness of sins in the name of the crucified and risen Messiah
(Luke 24:46–7). It has been suggested that in the transition from
Jesus' mission to that of the disciples, the core of the message was
changed from the kingdom of God to the person of Christ. This
assertion arises largely from the polemical need felt by some to
distance themselves from the Christ-centredness of the gospel
message. It has minimal support in careful historical analysis.

The essential point of reference is that 'the time is (now) fulfilled'
(Mark 1:14). This statement is the 'good news of God'. What time?

The time of God's decisive action for salvation. The meaning of this good news was gradually unfolded. It involved God himself suffering because of the refusal of his people to understand his purposes for his world. Such was people's hostility that God himself was done to death. This is the amazing paradox of the drama: God was condemned for blasphemy against God: 'He sought total and complete liberation for humanity, and we condemned him as subversive of the established order'.[19]

The inauguration of the kingdom through suffering and sacrifice was vindicated in Jesus' resurrection from the dead and the testimony of those to whom he appeared alive:

> God integrated this injustice into the plan of salvation. God did not annihilate the murderers, but showed the final salvation of Jesus and his cause through his resurrection and followers. Without the resurrection our faith in him cannot be justified; without followers faith in him would be impossible.[20]

So following means witnessing, and following in the way of Christ means witnessing to the point of death (martyrdom):

> He said this [of Simon Peter] to indicate the kind of death by which he would glorify God. After this he said to him, 'Follow me' . . . This is the disciple who is testifying to these things and has written them, and we know that his testimony is true (John 21:19, 24).

Evangelism, justice, compassion and non-violence

Following in the way of Christ quite simply (and yet with many obstacles to overcome) requires communicating the good news of Jesus and the kingdom (Acts 28:30) (evangelism), insisting on the full participation of all people in God's gifts of life and wellbeing (justice), providing the resources to meet people's needs (compassion) and never using lethal violence as a means of doing God's will (the practice of non-violence as a means of change).

The Church's mission 'in the way of Jesus Christ' is thus to be an instrument of God's righteous and compassionate governance in the world. We can summarise this task briefly here under three headings (which we will expand in subsequent chapters).

(a) To create life

The Church is to be involved in every action that restores, even partially, wholeness to human life. In the area of physical healing it will share in the overcoming of illness by teaching and enabling a healthy way of living, and by providing, where not otherwise available, basic health care for all. Where people are suffering from mental distress, often caused by a lack of love and security, God's people will open themselves, their homes and their churches to the disturbed and abused. Where there is ignorance and prejudice, Jesus' disciples will challenge stereotypes and bigotry (images of the enemy), believing the best rather than the worst of people (1 Cor. 13:4–6). They will help to give people the dignity of self-confidence through appropriate education.

(b) To create welfare

Some may be called to the political task of ensuring the right kind of state provision for the welfare of all. All are responsible for seeing that wealth is so distributed through society that everyone's genuine needs are met (1 John 3:17–18). Priority will be given to the weak, defenceless and broken, those who need time and space to gain strength and proper independence. One of the meanings of 'peace' (*shalom*) (Luke 19:42) is 'fulness of welfare and health'.[21] This can be understood as a society where people are not disabled by circumstances and structures, but are enabled to live in the community by giving as well as receiving.

(c) To create non-violence

The Christian community is to be part of every effort to overcome the destructive spiral of 'an eye for an eye, and a tooth for a tooth' (Matt. 5:38–42). It will be involved in grass-roots efforts to build confidence between antagonistic groups, and to restore authentic democratic procedures where there has been a violent seizure of power. Mission means following Jesus in his response to violence, in an attempt to reach those who commit it. There was the frustrated violence of Judas, the 'holy' violence of Peter, the 'just' violence of the 'freedom-fighter' crucified alongside Jesus, and the official violence of the soldiers. All of these have been justified by their own logic, but each is ultimately futile as a means of achieving new ways of being human.

In these and many other ways still to be explored, God's people express their faith in Jesus the Messiah. They will not be deluded into thinking that, even counting on the immense power of God (Luke 24:49), they will be able to mend the world. Rather, they are to show by the testimony of word and action that God has *not* left a disordered world to its own devices, to reap the consequences of its obstinate decision to turn its back on his gift of life. He is still concerned to service and repair a broken-down version of the world, showing what even a partial restoration to life can be like; though eventually a new model will be needed. He is fulfilling his purpose through the consecrated hands and minds of those who know the grace of the Lord Jesus Christ (2 Cor. 8:9).

Exercises

1. Give your response to the person who says we cannot know what Jesus did or said.

2. Prepare a brief outline of Jesus' public ministry as recorded in one of the four gospels.

3. Write a short drama of Jesus' entry into Jerusalem and cleansing of the temple, drawing out lessons for discipleship.

4

Announcing Good News

Some of the discussion within the world Church about the meaning, purpose and methods of evangelism has been influenced by powerful catch-phrases. The very use of the words 'evangelism' or 'evangelisation'[1] has come to the fore in the Church's thinking roughly within the last 150 years.[2] To some extent this has followed the widespread use of memorable rallying-cries, beginning with 'The evangelisation of the world in this generation'.[3] In more recent times, the slogan 'The evangelisation of the world by the year 2000' has been used. These watchwords have captured a sense of urgency in the task of evangelism, though displaying an over-optimism in the ability to set measurable goals and achieve them.

Mission and evangelism

There is no consensus yet among people from different Christian traditions about the relation of evangelism to mission. Most separate the two, considering evangelism to be part of mission, i.e. an essential 'dimension of the total activity of the Church'.[4] This division has been resisted by some – mostly from the conservative evangelical section of the Church – who believe that the Church's mission *is* evangelism, whereas the Church's diaconal ministries must be seen strictly as subordinate, a consequence of its evangelising commission.

The main reason given for identifying mission with evangelism is the fear that, if evangelism is regarded as one aspect among many others of the Church's mission, it will gradually be eroded and lose its priority. The argument is that, whereas non-Christians can and do become involved in many worthy activities on behalf of oppressed and needy people, only the Christian community can

tell the story of Jesus Christ with conviction. That is its fundamental and obligatory task.

Others, while maintaining the distinction between the two, have
used the language of primacy or priority for evangelism.[5] So, if
Christians ever had to choose between evangelism and service,
between communicating the Gospel in words or manifesting its
reality in deeds, they would be bound to choose the first. So for
these people mission is wider than evangelism – it is 'everything
the Church is sent into the world to do'[6] – but everything it does
must be pervaded by the overriding commitment to evangelism.

Some of the disagreements follow from different emphases put
upon the meaning of evangelism. For the time being, I shall accept
the view of the majority within all parts of the Church (including
evangelicals) that mission is not synonymous with evangelism.
Interestingly, the main reason for keeping the distinction is the
same as that given by those who wish to merge the two: that if
evangelism is made to bear the full weight of the entire mission
calling of the Church, its sharp characteristic will disappear. In
other words, if everything the Church does is called evangelism
(because in some way it proclaims the reality of Jesus Christ), then
nothing is really evangelism. However, having made this point, it
will be necessary to stress (as I do below) that there can be no
authentic evangelism apart from a living testimony to the transforming power of the Gospel in action.

Reservations about evangelism

In 1988 the Lambeth Conference of bishops of the Anglican communion of Churches called for a Decade of Evangelism. The idea
was that in the final decade of the second millennium Christians
should concentrate in a special way on bringing men and women
into a living relationship with Jesus Christ. Many other Churches
did the same. However, the project has not found favour with all.
Some church leaders are suspicious of the concept for a number
of reasons: they complain that it looks too much like a strategy
imposed from above for recuperating membership lost by the
Church (mainly in Europe) during the last half century. In other

words, it could be interpreted as a means by which the Church simply promotes itself.

They also think that it may create confusion among Christians about the nature of the Gospel, emphasising the message as something which can be sold on the market by more imaginative packaging and more aggressive retailing. They are also conscious of the danger of increasing bigotry and intolerance by giving other communities of faith the sense that they are being 'targeted' by people with a crusade mentality. Those who had serious reservations about this kind of special programme counselled, therefore, that the whole project should be quietly buried, while the Church dedicated itself to a prayerful and thoughtful re-examination of its roots.

On the wider stage, there have been other objections. Evangelism, for example, has been closely associated in the minds of many with the imperial expansion of Western nations. This was particularly true of the Spanish and Portuguese conquest of Central and South America, when vast numbers of indigenous peoples were forced into baptism on pain of death. At the same time, their lands were seized and their treasures ransacked by the foreign Christians.[7]

Related to the colonial project is the protest that evangelism implies an arrogant claim to a monopoly on the truth. It is said to presuppose that the beliefs of non-Christians are either inferior, insufficient or perverse. The evangelist, it is assumed, often proclaims the message without much close knowledge of the faith, culture or circumstances of the hearers. As one native American once complained, when confronted with the Gospel, 'Why did God not reveal himself to our forebears?' Implicit in the question is the conviction that they too had a knowledge of God prior to the coming of the Christian missionaries.[8]

Finally, there has been a deep suspicion, particularly in nations that have been governed by unelected authoritarian regimes, that the evangelistic activities of some missionaries have been a cover for promoting conservative ideologies and agendas. The fact that these missionaries have not incorporated into their preaching any reference to people's genuine aspirations for justice, democracy and freedom, and have tacitly affirmed that, even under military dictatorships, there has been complete freedom to preach the Gospel, supports this claim.

On the other side of the argument, sections of the Church (largely within the formal ecumenical movement) have been accused of neglecting evangelism. In a famous challenge to the World Council of Churches, Donald McGavran (the father of the Church-growth theory of mission; see chapter 11, p. 221) anticipated that the Uppsala assembly of the WCC (1968) would betray those who had never heard the Gospel: 'By "betray" I mean planning courses of action whose sure outcome will be that the two billion will remain in their sins and in their darkness, chained by false and inadequate ideas of God and (humanity).'[9]

Following the Bangkok Conference of the WCC (1973), which seemed to reinterpret salvation in terms of God's liberating activity *outside* the Church and therefore to question the whole notion of the Church having a message to offer the world, Harvey Hoekstra censured the ecumenical movement for abandoning the traditional view of evangelism as communicating the good news of Jesus Christ to those who had not received it.[10] We see here, in part, a replay of the debate that followed the publication of the celebrated *Layman's Inquiry*[11] with its advocacy of a 'broader evangelism', meaning one that concentrated on social renewal in a spirit of cooperation with people of other faiths.

The WCC may have made itself a hostage to fortune by giving the impression of demoting the task of evangelism within its structures and by refraining from giving evangelism a sufficiently prominent place in its official pronouncements. Thus, for example, at the San Antonio Conference of the WCC's Commission on World Mission and Evangelism (1989), neither the moderator nor the director of the Commission nor the WCC general secretary mentioned evangelism in their speeches.[12]

However, there have been some strenuous defences of the ecumenical position. Thus, Eugene Smith rebukes the critics for maintaining a view of evangelism which appears to have nothing to say to nominal Christians who hold racist doctrines or which concentrates almost exclusively on personal decision to the exclusion of the creation of renewed communities:

Most traditional calls to individualistic evangelism are inadequate to our present challenge. There is nausea, widespread and justified, about the kind of evangelism which calls persons to an altar and tells them they have met Christ, but sends them out with segregationist racial attitudes unchallenged and unchanged . . . It is partly in reaction against such false evangelism, that many who are concerned with the biblical summons to justice become cold to programs labeled 'evangelism'.[13]

The meaning of evangelism[14]

No doubt one could give as many definitions of evangelism as there are people to devise them. Probably most of them would be correct in the sense that there is much that could be included in any description. However, as David Bosch argues, it may not be helpful to be too all-embracing.[15]

Clearly evangelism is a process that happens, and therefore can best be described by the use of a verb. If the underlying thought is *good news*, then what is normally done with news is to share it, publish it (perhaps as headlines in the media), spread it or announce it.[16] The primary emphasis is on communicating an exceptionally important piece of information, declaring it to be true and relevant. Probably the most famous definition of all bears out this sense of passing on a life-giving piece of news: 'Evangelism is witness. It is one beggar telling another beggar where to get food.'[17]

In the Orthodox tradition the words 'witnessing to' and 'testifying' are often used for evangelism. Thus: 'Evangelistic witness is here understood to be the communication of Christ to those who do not consider themselves Christian . . . a call to salvation, which means the restoration of the relationship of God and humanity';[18] 'Undeniably, their [the Orthodox Churches] common task is "to testify to the gospel of the grace of God" (Acts 20:24) to all people.'[19]

If evangelism is about witnessing to or making known good news, what is the news that is good? Most people would point immediately to actions which God has achieved through Jesus

Christ for the benefit of all human beings. David Bosch describes it in this way: 'Announcing that God, Creator and Lord of the universe, has personally intervened in human history and has done so supremely through the person and ministry of Jesus of Nazareth who is Lord of history, Saviour and Liberator.'[20] Likewise the Mission Affirmation of the Selly Oak Colleges' School of Mission states that: 'Through evangelism people are invited to accept for themselves the good news that, through Christ, their sin is forgiven, its power over their lives broken and they are restored to a life-giving fellowship with God.'

Along with the central reference to Jesus Christ, the kingdom or rule of God is quite often added (for reasons discussed in chapters 2 and 3). In this context it has often been pointed out that the Acts of the Apostles, the story of the early Church's evangelism, begins and ends with a declaration of the kingdom of God (cf. Acts 1:3; 28:31). Evangelism might be understood, then, as 'spreading the good news that in Jesus Christ God is establishing a new order [a new way of being human] and calling people to renounce all alternatives and embrace this reality'.[21]

If evangelism is essentially the declaration of the best news of all time – that God has found a way, which perfectly balances justice and mercy, of acquitting condemned sinners and making them free – it is also an invitation to them to believe their good fortune and leave their prison for good.[22] So evangelism has both an indicative and an imperative mode: it is both the conveying of a message and a challenge to act in a certain way in response to the message's content.

Hearing the news is not enough; positive action is required in order that its significance is personally experienced. There are various ways in which the invitation may be made, the one recorded in Matthew's gospel (11:28–9) – 'Come to me, all you that are weary and are carrying heavy burdens, and I will give you rest. Take my yoke upon you, and learn from me' – explains salvation in terms of receiving from Jesus Christ refreshment, liberation, a new direction and a new understanding of life. Evangelism is an invitation to people to hand over the direction of their lives to Jesus Christ, giving the reasons why this is such a supremely important action to take.

Implicit in the invitation is the requirement to turn one's back on a false way of life: what some baptism services call 'renouncing evil'. This corresponds to Paul's affirmation that the Christians in Thessalonica, on responding to the Gospel, had 'turned to God from idols, to serve a living and true God' (1 Thess. 1:8); or that he was sent so that people might 'turn from darkness to light and from the power of Satan to God' (Acts 26:18).

The content of the Gospel

The substance of the message may vary according to the circumstances in which it is conveyed. There is an enormous richness of material in the good news. It is inescapably about salvation, understood as God putting right a situation which has broken down or gone wrong. This situation may be described as *lostness*: the human race does not know what the problem is, or if it did would not know the solution. It may be described as *alienation*: being far away from, out of touch or in conflict with God, one's neighbour and the environment. It may be described as *helplessness*, the inability to overcome conflict, selfishness and self-assertion. It may be described as a *disease*: it destroys a person's ability to resist temptation.[23]

How then does God put right the failure of the world to function as he intended? In short, by 'bringing peace through Jesus Christ' (Acts 10:36). 'Peace' refers originally to the many promises recorded in the Old Testament that God would exchange his people's situation of oppression, violence and want for a community in which everyone contributes to the needs of all, where there is no scarcity and no brutality:

> The messianic peace, *Shalom*, wrought by Jesus Christ involves not only a new relationship to God but also a relationship between man and his neighbour. *Shalom* is not a gift that the Lord gives apart from himself; rather, he himself is *Shalom* (Eph. 2:14), and through his death he has brought all hostility among men to an end.[24]

The good news in the Old Testament

We can achieve a better understanding of God's work of salvation by looking first at what is promised to God's people by the prophets. For the sake of brevity, I will analyse the verse in Isaiah which is generally considered to include the fullest account of the good news prior to the writing of the New Testament:

> How beautiful upon the mountains are the feet of the
>   messenger
> who announces peace [*shalom*],
> who brings good news [*bashar*], who announces salvation
>   [*yashach*],
> who says to Zion, 'Your God reigns' [*malak*].
> (Isa. 52:7).

We shall consider the passage phrase by phrase.

1. *The announcing of peace. Shalom* is usually translated by the word 'peace'. However, the original is far richer in meaning than it is in English where its significance is often passive rather than active – conciliation, truce, composure, relaxation, calm, tranquillity. In each case there is the implied absence of conflict, hostilities, stress, anxiety or hassle. The root meaning of the original is 'completeness', in the sense of possessing a fullness of welfare and health (Ps. 38:3; Isa. 38:16–17), prosperity for the whole community (Job 15:21; Ps. 72:7; 37:11; 122:6) and security (Job 5:24). Above all it means being in a right relationship with the God of the covenant, when God, having no cause to judge or rebuke his people, is delighted with every aspect of the community's life (Isa. 54:10; 53:5; Jer. 29:11; Mal. 2:6). The Messiah is the agent of *shalom* (Isa. 9:6–7).

2. *The bringing of good news.* The messenger is sent on a journey to proclaim publicly glad tidings which will bring joy and excitement to the people. The content of the message is God's deliverance and care (Isa. 40:9–11), his faithfulness and saving health (Ps. 40:10), his victory over his enemies (Ps. 68:11) and his salvation (Ps. 96:2). Though the message is for all, those who will hear it with most delight will be the poor, the afflicted,

the broken-hearted, captives and prisoners (Isa. 61:1). The good
news is for both Jew and Gentile (Isa. 40:5; 49:6; 51:4). God
himself is the supreme evangelist (Isa. 55:11).

3. *The message of salvation.* The basic meaning of the original is 'to
create spaciousness' or, one might say, 'room to live'. From this
root, it comes to mean the people's freedom from whatever
confines or restricts their ability to flourish as God intends. It
also means 'to give victory to'. The supreme examples in the
Old Testament are the Exodus and the *New Exodus* (Return
from Exile), moments when God rescued his people from
exceedingly adverse circumstances and gave them a new
future. In many of the psalms (e.g. 9:9; 35:10; 82:3; 140:12; 146:7)
and in Zephaniah (e.g. 2:3; 3:12, 19–20), those who wait for
God's salvation are impotent in every sense – they are the
materially poor, the physically disabled, the persecuted and
oppressed. Salvation comes to mean deliverance, redemption
or release from all evil and wrongdoing, both collective and
individual (Ezek. 36:29; 37:23).The mediator is God's special
servant who bears the sins of the people in his own person
(Isa. 53).

4. *The proclamation that 'your God reigns'.* The God who has entered
into a special relationship with the people of Israel, who has
rescued them from forced labour in Egypt, who has given them
a liberating code of practice to live by and a fertile land to live
off, will exercise his legitimate rule. The authority of this God
extends over the whole universe, over all the nations, over
Israel and over individual lives. Nothing is outside his ultimate
control (Ps. 24; 47:8; 103:19; 145:11–13). However, God's rule is
not constraining, vindictive or discriminating, but liberating
(Ps. 145:14–20; 146:7–10).

This understanding of rule and authority is frequently misunderstood or misrepresented by people who cannot conceive how any
power-arrangements can be anything but exploitative.[25] Thus,
Mary Carroll Smith believes that all language that speaks of
'victory and success, triumph and conquering' repeats the ideology
of the group or class within society (most particularly the Aryans,

or Indo-Europeans) which justifies its hold on power by reference
to religious ideals.[26]

This criticism is heard frequently today and has considerable
historical justification. Nevertheless, it does not deal adequately
with a number of fundamental facts. First, there is the rampant
nature of evil in the world, which if not overcome will maintain
permanent structures of injustice in human society. How, for
example, does Smith see women's partial achievement of greater
equality in a number of societies, if it is not a 'victory' of justice
over bigotry or the 'success' of a movement of solidarity?

Secondly, there is a tacit acceptance of the apparent truism that
'all power corrupts'. In some circles, fortified by the writings of
those considered to represent postmodernity,[27] all pretensions to
power are seen as veiled claims to impose a particular interpretation of life on unwilling subjects. This is a dangerous half-truth.
Power is an inevitable reality of human life; it is exercised in all
sorts of ways, very often with extreme subtlety. There is no necessary connection, however, between power and oppression. If all
power were by definition repressive, freedom would be impossible,
for liberation requires the exercise of a superior power against
arbitrary subjection. The alternative is a quietism that allows injustice to reign supreme.

Thirdly (and this takes us to the heart of the Christian Gospel)
the way in which God exercises authority is the very opposite of the
corrupt use of power decried so often by those who idealistically
appear to be against all power. In his response to Mary Carroll
Smith, Orlando Costas sets the record straight.[28] He argues that
the language of Christ's authority 'is tied up with a radically new
order of life whose focus is the *reconciliation* of all things . . . and,
consequently the total *abrogation* of evil and alienation, of the syn-
drome of victor and victim'. He also argues that 'Professor Smith's
own proposal [the death-and-resurrection cycle in old European
religions] offers no real guarantee for a dynamic and radically
new order'. It has no place for judgement on evil and no way of
overcoming the fundamental distortions of human life. Moreover,
the return to the ancient pagan religions is but a variation on the
recurrent romanticism of Western 'liberalism' and its evolutionary
optimism. In Costas's opinion the whole package ends up inevi-

tably 'siding politically and economically with the established order'.[29]

Thus, although Christians in using or explaining the language of 'king', 'kingdom', 'lord', 'authority' and 'power' need to be careful, cautious and sensitive, they will also be aware that to abandon it is to strip the Gospel of its message of liberation and hope. Its use may be tested against the meaning of peace and salvation as outlined above. For what reasons, in whose interests and with what motives is power being used?

The good news in the New Testament

The essence of the good news as proclaimed by the first disciples of Jesus is that the restoration of broken relationships caused by human beings' selfishness, insecurity and will-to-dominate is achieved not through superior violence but through the power that breaks the chain of violence by suffering its full consequences. This is the historical reality of Jesus' death, caused by a struggle for power (John 11:50–2) to keep in place the old order of naked or covert violence of 'all against all'. Violence was used to defend and enforce perceived rights and privileges at all costs. Thus, Jesus had to die 'for the people'; the alternative, if people believed him sufficiently, was the end of the nation – the regime that enshrined exploitation and brutality.

In Jesus' own words, he came 'to give his life for many' (Mark 10:45). This action would establish a 'new covenant in my blood' (Luke 22:20), 'poured out for many' (Mark 14:24). So far is the old order of sin and death from being able to reform itself to be a proper agent of God's justice, mercy and compassion, that a new order becomes necessary. So virulent was the opposition of the old to the new, that it could only come into being through great cost to God himself. The abandonment of the Son by the Father (Mark 15:34) was not only a bitter experience for the Son but also for the Father. Such is the horror of the crucifixion of Jesus that many attempts have been made to tone it down.[30] But anything less than an understanding which makes Jesus the bearer of sin and all its consequences trivialises evil, weakens the importance of judgement and, therefore, has no grounds for upholding that justice of God which makes a moral universe possible.

In recent years, Jürgen Moltmann has powerfully captured the supreme seriousness of the death of Christ:

> On the cross the Father forsook the Son and hid his face from him, as the sun was hidden in the deepest darkness on Golgotha ... It is precisely this that is the cross in Jesus' crucifixion; the being forsaken by the God whom he called 'my Father', and whose Son he knew himself to be. Here, in the relationship between the Father and the Son, a death was experienced which has been rightly described as 'eternal death', the 'death of God' ... The Father suffers the death of the Son. So the pain of the Father corresponds to the death of the Son.[31]

This language may seem extravagant and risky but it is justified, not only in terms of Jesus' cry of dereliction from the cross, but by the use of the words 'surrender', 'send' and their equivalents in Paul's explanation of the Gospel:

> They are now justified by his grace as a gift, through the redemption that is in Christ Jesus, whom God *put forward* as a sacrifice of atonement by his blood [Rom. 3:24–5]; God ... by *sending* his own Son in the likeness of sinful flesh, and to deal with sin, he condemned sin in the flesh [Rom. 8:3]; He ... did not withhold his own Son, but *gave him up* for all of us [Rom. 8:32]; When the fullness of time had come, God *sent* his Son, born of a woman, born under the law, in order to redeem those who were under the law, so that we might receive adoption as children [Gal. 4:4–5].

Similar language is found in John's first letter (e.g. 1 John 4:8, 10, 14). It expresses the fact that the death of Christ which effects salvation for the whole world is the gift (2 Cor. 9:15) of the trinitarian God. In this one act of dying, God has found a way of breaking the spiral of violence without adopting the same procedure. He also succeeds in reconciling justice and mercy so that the absolute distinction between good and evil is maintained while human guilt can be removed: 'It was to prove at this present time that he himself is righteous and [yet] that he justifies the one who has faith in Jesus' (Rom. 3:26).

Elsewhere in the New Testament there are other ways of seeing the good news. There is the creation of a new humanity – Christ is the last Adam, the head of a new race which is freed from the power of sin by being raised to a new liberating life of obedience to God (Rom. 5—6). There is the gift of the Holy Spirit to inspire God's children to a spontaneous and joyful doing of God's will (Rom. 8:9–17). There is the promise that the whole of creation will be redeemed from frustration and decay (Rom. 8:18–25). Finally, in the creation of a new community, God reconciles the humanly irreconcilable – Jew and non-Jew, 'cultured' and 'non-cultured', male and female, privileged and exploited, people of every race, culture and class (Rom. 9—11; Eph. 2:13–22; 3:3–7; Col. 3:10–11; Gal. 3:28).[32]

The ends of evangelism

The purposes for which the Christian community undertakes evangelism should not be defined too narrowly. Undoubtedly there is a major emphasis on seeking a response from individuals to the offer of forgiveness and a new beginning with God, often called 'conversion' but this is only one aspect. Conversion is a decisive moment of turning from a self-centred life to one centred on God (Acts 26:18; Eph. 5:8; Col. 1:13; Gal. 4:8). It is also a continuing activity:

> The response to Christ's calling, conversion, is an ongoing experience, a growth process to Christian maturity . . . One is constantly being challenged to appropriate 'the unsearchable riches of Christ' (Eph. 3:8) to the realities of life in human community and society at large.[33]

In some people's understanding, conversion as an unrepeatable, personal decision to 'take Christ into one's life' is the main, if not the only, goal of evangelism. Such a view, however, confuses conversion with regeneration, human activity with God's activity. Regeneration is certainly a single event in which God brings to birth a new nature within the person who trusts Jesus Christ for salvation. Conversion, however, has both a beginning and many repetitions. Its meaning can be summed up by Paul's caution to the Christians in Rome: 'Do not be conformed to this world, but be [go on being] transformed by the renewing of your minds, so that you may know what is the will of God – what is good and acceptable and perfect' (Rom. 12:2). It is as if he were saying, 'Do not allow the world to form the person you are going to be' – to take an analogy, if you are like an unformed piece of wood, do not allow the world to be the furniture-maker. Rather, through the guidance of the Spirit, by centring all thoughts, ideas and opinions on the truth as it is displayed in Jesus (Eph. 4:21), allow God to determine the shape and form. That clearly is a process which only gradually touches every aspect of one's life.

The end of evangelism can be viewed from God's point of view as the creation of a whole new life in the image of Jesus Christ (2 Cor. 3:18) – the restoration of the glory lost as a result of sin (Rom. 3:23; Heb. 2:10) – or it can be viewed from the human perspective as a following after Jesus Christ. In the latter case, one may speak of a pilgrimage or race, in which one's steps are guided by the light of God's word (Ps. 119:105) and one's eyes are fixed upon Jesus, who both gives and perfects our life of faith (Heb. 12:2). In both cases evangelism has in view a total transformation which knows no bounds: 'The central aim of the Great Commission is making disciples, which includes simultaneously practising love and righteousness, that is upholding justice.'[34]

Following in the way of Jesus Christ is an integral aspect of evangelism and proof of its authenticity. There is no inward event which is, as it were, some kind of transaction between the soul and God, which does not also have an outward and visible sign. The disciple in action is guided by asking himself or herself, 'What would Christ *do* in these circumstances?'

Finally, it is the aim of evangelism that new communities of deep sharing, trust, integrity and humility should be built out of the debris of human failures, flaws and frailties; a task that would demonstrate beyond any doubt the existence of a living God! The fact that experience tells us so plainly that such communities are rare and struggle to live up to their high calling in Jesus Christ leads some to emphasise the inward and individual nature of evangelism. However, if the Gospel is about reconciliation, evan-

gelism must go on within the Church itself, not just from the
Church to the world.

Ion Bria sums up the goals of evangelistic witness in the following way:

> Conversion from a life characterized by sin, separation from
> God, submission to evil and the unfulfilled potential of God's
> image, to a new life characterized by the forgiveness of sins,
> obedience to the commands of God, renewed fellowship with
> God in the trinity, growth in the restoration of the divine
> image, and the realization among us of the prototype of the
> love of Christ. More briefly and succinctly put, the final goal
> of evangelistic witness is conversion and baptism. Conversion
> is a wilful turning from sin, death and evil to true life in God.
> Baptism is the reception of a new member into the life of the
> community of God's people, the church.[35]

Reasons for evangelism

The message of Jesus Christ must be passed on

General knowledge of 'the Story' can no longer be taken for
granted in many societies, and is still absent from many others.
Not only are people largely ignorant of the basic content of the
New Testament, but their limited understanding may have been
seriously distorted by startling and sensational views of Jesus
transmitted by a media more interested in controversy than serious
discussion.

Evangelism is a story-telling task[36] in which Jesus' life is
recounted against the background of first-century Judaism and the
geopolitical reality of the Roman empire. One powerful motivation
for evangelism is 'the positive conviction, born of the gospel, that
Jesus Christ is the centre and goal of world history'.[37] Perhaps, we
can claim that everyone born into the world has a *right* to know
why Jesus Christ came into the world and what he achieved. The
story has to be told by those who believe it is true:

> This right and duty of the Church to evangelize rejoins also
> the right of every *human being* coming into this world to know
> Jesus Christ and his liberating Gospel . . . The Gospel is not a

possession; it is a stewardship. Nobody can deprive us of this privilege or relieve us from this responsibility. Hence the urgency of evangelizing.[38]

Human beings are more than they earn and consume

There is a sense in which consumerism is a serious missionary enterprise – as the slogans put it: 'Shop till you drop', 'Shop around the clock'.[39] But in the light of the Gospel such activity confuses image and reality – it is like living in a shadow-land. The daily search for personal fulfilment, enjoyment, experiences and gratification is a perverted reflection of the messianic banquet. Life can either be seized as a right to be expected or accepted at every moment as an amazing gift from a bountiful giver.

This is why the story of the prodigal son (and elder brother) is probably the most powerful short story ever told. The younger son took his share of the estate by legal right and spent it all to satisfy his yearning for independence and pleasure (who said that modern Protestantism invented the solitary individual?). The elder brother was also isolated, caught up in his individualistic work ethic, believing that enjoyment was the rightful reward for hard labour. Both were wrong; only the former, however, came to realise where the true source of life lay.

Evangelism, then, is a liberating task, for the Gospel tells us what we may *be*, when the glamour and lure of *having* fails to satisfy or heal, or when there is little opportunity to possess anything at all. Irrespective of circumstances, character, achievements or social status, every single human being possesses an intrinsic worth. When an indigenous Christian leader from northern Argentina was once asked what the Gospel had done for his people, he replied that it had enabled them to look the white person fully in the eye.

Human beings are confused by the dynamic of sin

Many cultures tend to have a static view of wrongdoing, thinking of it in terms of failing to achieve a particular moral standard, like falling short of the pass mark in an exam. Sin is seen as something we do (commission) or fail to do (omission). Though this is a picture the biblical text uses, it also stresses that sin is an active force which is constantly devouring what is right, just, good, beautiful and wholesome. To use Paul's terminology, it is 'a power' (Col. 1:16; Eph. 6:12; Rom. 8:38).

Sin, in this sense, causes us to make wrong choices which then have further destructive consequences. So if a culture emphasises outward behaviour, offering a rational analysis of the violent side of human life and the power of education to reorientate individuals and communities towards a more wholesome way of behaving, it is likely to miss the subtle and deep-seated active power of sin. It then becomes confused about the real problems and naive about how to respond to them.

Evangelism is, then, a therapeutic task. The messengers of the Gospel are those who, by carefully listening to and experiencing both its message and life in the world, are able to diagnose the human predicament and prescribe the cure. Healing, however, can only take place once a person has properly heard the 'bad news' – that the problem of sin cannot be remedied by the human medicine of education, self-discipline or even the quest for spirituality: an aspirin is no cure for a cancerous growth.

The means of evangelism

The first principle in evangelism should be that the ends do *not* necessarily justify the means. However urgent the goals of evangelism may be and however noble the reasons, there are some methods which are unacceptable: 'No activity is admissible which in any way degrades or violates the full dignity of human beings'.[40] Unacceptable methods might include offering open or hidden inducements to believe or bringing cultural or psychological pressures to bear. They might involve concentrating only on the benefits of believing, omitting to mention the cost of discipleship. For example, a poster campaign in London advertising an evangelistic mission had this to say about the step of faith: 'All it will cost you is your frustration, anxiety, loneliness, sadness, insecurity, pessimism, dissatisfaction, instability, dependence'. Taken by itself (and that was all that was said) it is clearly untrue.

There has been in recent years a concentration on techniques. Methods which seem to work in one situation are applied in quite different ones. This has been particularly true of what is called 'mass evangelism', i.e. large concentrations of people who come together to listen to an evangelist or for healing or both. People have come to a genuine faith in Jesus Christ in this context. However, given the enormous outlay in time and energy, the difficulties in attracting thoroughly secular people to this kind of meeting, the dangers of manipulating people's emotions in a large crowd and the responsibility of every Christian to witness to his or her faith, there has been a move away from this method to a more personal approach.

If it is true that people need to see as well as hear the good news, then the messenger, as well as the message, is important. Indeed, research suggests that many people begin to take an interest in the message of Jesus Christ when they are attracted by the life of a Christian.[41] Evangelism is about persuading people to 'stop, look and listen'. What better way than the challenge of a transformed life? Only then will the evangelist have a chance of persuading a friend or colleague of the truth of the Gospel and answering objections and doubts.

Two further conditions must be fulfilled for evangelism to be authentic. First, it must proceed from a community that believes in evangelism and it must result in people becoming part of a community that knows how to welcome 'strangers' and make them part of its family. As John Wesley once wisely said, 'Faith that does not begin alone does not begin, but faith that ends alone ends!' Secondly, evangelism is God's work long before it is our work. The Father prepares the ground, the Son gives the invitation and the Spirit prompts the person to respond in repentance and faith to the good news.

It is appropriate to finish this chapter on evangelism by quoting a passage from the findings of the famous, but now much-maligned, Edinburgh World Missionary Conference (1910), which supports this last point. The Conference has been accused, in part justifiably, of emphasising the human agent in evangelism, for seeing it too strongly in terms of the Church's expansion from the Christian to the non-Christian world and for using an overabundance of military metaphors (sadly out of place in the light of the terrible slaughter of the 1914–18 war). Despite the unwarranted cultural

assumptions and spiritual triumphalism, this proper condition for
evangelism is also highlighted:

> It is the Spirit of God who alone has the power to convict
> men of sin ... The genuine fruits of the Spirit, as shown in
> repentance, conviction, restitution, and the making up of long-
> standing quarrels, have afforded convincing proof that God
> alone brings home the gospel with power to the hearts and
> consciences of men.[42]

Exercises

1. Draw out lessons you have learnt from any evangelism you
   have been involved in.

2. Describe to a sympathetic, but uninformed friend why you
   think the Gospel of Jesus Christ is good news.

3. If you had the opportunity, which questions about evangelism
   would you ask Paul? How do you think he might respond?

5

The Gospel in the Midst of Cultures

Significance of the matter

At first sight, to include the question of culture in a book about Christian mission might seem strange. Every other topic in this part of the book fits the description of mission as a task to be carried out: Gospel and culture is the odd one out. We can evangelise, engage in dialogue, work for justice and the care of the environment, be peace-builders and share in partnership with other communities. The relationship to culture is of a different order: one does not carry out any specific project aimed at culture as such.

Nevertheless, the matter of culture affects every aspect of mission. It is all-pervasive. If we ignore the influence of culture we run the risk of seriously misreading situations. It may, therefore, be helpful to begin by recalling some of the reasons why culture is central to mission at every point.

The Gospel is conveyed through culture

In the first place, the Gospel whose essential message I sketched in the last chapter, is always culturally mediated. This may be obvious – for example, in the way that I personally chose to emphasise certain features, showing how my own cultural background has influenced me to draw them out as the most crucial points. It is true (as we shall discuss later) that the Gospel is genuinely transcultural. However, it can only be expressed in terms of culture, and therefore has to be transposed from one culture to another in a rich variety of ways.[1]

This should not cause any surprise. The Gospel is made up of many pieces of good news – and to understand them, people have

to hear them in their own language (Acts 2:8). The message, though
having a divine origin, is conveyed through human channels (2
Cor. 4:7). Human beings are immersed in culture. The biblical
writers used culture to communicate the message. They sometimes
borrowed from other cultures: thus, for example, mention is made
of the Babylonian sea monster Leviathan (Ps. 104:26; Job 3:8; 41:1);
God's covenant with his people reflects the form of the Hittite
people's treaties with their vassals, and many parts of the book of
Proverbs have parallels in other cultural settings. More important
is the use Paul made of philosophical and religious terms current
in his time, such as *pleroma* (fullness), *apolutrosis* (the redemption
or emancipation of slaves) and *kurios* (lord, a title of dignity in
Greek culture), filling them with new meaning in the light of Jesus
Christ.

Supremely, the message comes from God in the most personal
form possible (John 1:18). God is born in a particular culture. God's
eternal word was born a baby through the normal process of
labour. The birth was marked by the ceremonies customary within
his community (Luke 2:21–4). Jesus Christ was born a Jew in
first-century Palestine, with Aramaic as his mother tongue (quite
probably he spoke Greek as well). He learnt a carpenter's trade,
presumably acquiring the skill to make objects in a way familiar
to the people of Nazareth.

Jesus was born a Jew, not a kind of universal man. Even though
they did not accept him, 'he came to his own people' (John 1:11).
He was educated in the law, he participated in the yearly festivals
(like the Passover), he celebrated his *bar mitzvah*, attended syna-
gogue, was steeped in Jewish history and, as a storyteller, showed
considerable artistic talents. God's becoming a human person at a
particular moment of history in a specific geographical location
(incarnation) is one of the keys to understanding the relationship
between Gospel and culture.

Cultural questions in the life of the early Church
Issues to do with culture in the expansion of the Church abound
in the New Testament. The early Church had to face some tricky
questions. By way of illustration we mention two. Early in his
letter to the church in Rome, Paul touches on the subject of the

moral condition of the Gentiles (Rom. 2:12–16). He argues that they are not bereft of moral standards. Their lives demonstrate that they accept a distinction between right and wrong. This is because, as human beings, they possess an innate conscience which, even if not a thoroughly dependable guide, points to the existence of a moral universe. The requirement to discriminate between good and evil is a fact of all cultures. Thus culture also shows up everyone's failure to live by his or her conscience and is potentially an ally in demonstrating the need of the Gospel (Rom. 3:9, 23).

One of the most powerful changes brought by the Gospel was the abolition of the distinction between 'clean' and 'unclean' (Mark 7:19; Acts 10:15). For many people living in a variety of cultural settings this separation is an integral part of their way of life. So it was for Jews of the first century.[2] Therefore, if Jewish Christians were going to eat with Gentile Christians they had to break with convictions that had dominated their lives from earliest times. However, Paul was convinced that 'table fellowship' was a matter of the deepest principle, in which the Gospel could not be compromised. The Gospel demanded a full and equal status for Gentiles and Jews. No cultural norm or practice should separate Christians. Eating together could not be compromised (cf. 1 Cor. 11:17–22, 33–4). The Gospel ended all ideas that some peoples were superior to others, whatever the basis for such ideas (history, customs, moral attainment or skin colour). Culture is a given fact of creation, but there are no grounds for it being a cause of division within the Church. Peter's action (Gal. 2:11–14), therefore, was a (cultural) distortion of the Gospel.

Spiritual dualism

There have been many other cases where culture has caused Christians to misunderstand or falsify elements of their faith. In the Church in the West, for example, there has been a strong tendency to accept implicitly a dualistic understanding and practice of the Gospel. This manifests itself in *fideism* (an overemphasis on right belief in comparison with right action), *subjectivism* (an overemphasis on a person's emotional needs in comparison with the call to radical change), *individualism* (salvation as personal reconciliation with God in comparison with reconciliation with fellow human-beings), and *prohibitionism* (the tendency to separate oneself from artistic life).

Ethnic and national identity

We are so immersed in our own culture that it is hard to see its defects – or to see the strengths and goodness of other cultures. What we are familiar with is often taken as the standard for judging what others do. We do not see the subtle, and perhaps insidious, influence of culture on our beliefs and behaviour. This has been particularly true in the area of national or ethnic identity. On the one hand, it is vital to human development and flourishing that each person has a settled sense of belonging to a particular group of people. Such inclusion is a gift of creation. This seems to be the meaning of the so-called 'table of nations' listed in Genesis 10.[3] The following phrase occurs three times: 'These are the descendants of . . . in their lands, with their own language, by their families, in their nations' (Gen. 10:5, 20, 31). Without giving to each part of this description the full weight it might have today, the phrase clearly affirms a value in belonging to the extended family of a people that share the same language and live together in a defined geographical area.

At its best, ethnic and cultural distinctiveness thus reflects the rich diversity of human life and allows people a sense of security in being able to identify with a group of people with its own history, customs and traditions. The loss of such association (rootlessness) can lead to a crisis of selfhood and eventually to personality disorders.

On the other hand, a stress on ethnicity can lead to vigorous tribalism and communalism in which belonging to one ethnic group entails hostility to others. This can become pathological, if the main way we affirm our own self is by despising others or rejecting their right to be different. At its worst, this manifestation of culture leads to the horrors of racism and caste prejudice, with their deceitful and perverted notions of cultural superiority and racial purity.[4] The reality is recognised in the pages of the New Testament, not only between Jews and Gentiles, but between Greeks, Romans and other races. The 'barbarians' (Col. 3:11) were those outside civilisation. They were considered to be wild (the original meaning of 'savage'): i.e. in a state of pure nature, uncultivated, primitive, unrefined and fundamentally uncontrollable.[5]

A society's attitude to cultural distinctiveness is shown in the interaction between majority and minority groups in the same territory. Either through immigration, the forced displacement of peoples or the arbitrary setting of national boundaries, most nations today contain a multiplicity of different ethnic groups with different histories, customs, religions, languages and traditions. This makes for uneasy relationships and potential instability. Real or sensed discrimination can cause deep mutual suspicion and can be used by opportunists wishing to exploit situations to gain power and influence in their community. A mature social community will allow as much difference as possible within the confines of a coherent political and legal system, and will investigate as dispassionately as possible all claims to wrongful treatment on cultural or ethnic grounds.[6]

A heightened awareness of the benefits and harm of cultural identity is fundamental for Christians seeking to live by the Gospel: their attitude to cultural and ethnic difference may be either a positive or negative witness to Jesus Christ. The Gospel offers salvation to every human being on exactly the same basis. It is by grace alone. No one has any cause to boast (1 Cor. 1:28–31). The Church has been created out of a place of deep humiliation and costly reconciliation: the crucifixion (Phil. 3:4–9; Eph. 2:14). It is in essence a universal fellowship: a new humanity, a holy nation, a kingdom (1 Pet. 2:9–10).

The final reality of history, in biblical perspective, is of this new community of peoples from every cultural and racial background together worshipping one God and one Saviour through one Spirit (Eph. 2:18, 22; Rev. 7:9ff.). The implication of this vision is, first, that the Church dare not risk identifying itself too exclusively with any one culture or nation and, secondly, that one group of Christians may not create barriers against others by the exclusive use of cultural symbols, such as language. So a Christian's primary identity is in his or her confession of Jesus Christ as Lord by the Spirit (1 Cor. 12:3); cultural belonging is a subsidiary means of understanding selfhood:

[The] universality of the gospel, which relativises all other
definitions of identity and claims to loyalty, does not replace
or suppress people's identity; neither is it a recipe for uniformity. It is meant to create a community marked by a
mutuality of relationship where people have to find their
identity in partnership with others who are different from
them.[7]

The Western nature of Christian faith

The Church in many parts of the world, and especially in Asia,
has had a hard time witnessing to a faith that has not been part of
the history and culture of its peoples until recent times.[8] One of the
effects of the modern missionary movement has been to bring
about a renaissance of other religions and cultures. The problem
of cultural estrangement has both a conceptual and practical
dimension. Conceptually, it is difficult to separate belief in the
Gospel from the values and institutions of Western society in which
the Gospel has been subtly shaped. It is also difficult to relate the
Gospel to societies moulded for so long by vastly different belief
systems. How does one commend a faith which has intersected
with local cultures only in recent times and is generally seen as
an intruder? The difficulties are associated both with a lack of
identification and with transplantation.

Practically, to become a Christian appears to be a betrayal of
loyalty to family, group or nation. Baptism in particular is seen as
a sign of abandoning one's cultural roots and joining a foreign
religion. Moreover, this religion is seen as inferior because it has
spawned a society (in the West) seen to condone lax moral standards, and to promote an indifference to spiritual values, the
defamation of religion, a lack of concern about vulnerable people
(like the old and the homeless) and economic aggression. It is a
religion seen to have no clear-cut message in the face of the moral
dilemmas of the day:

> The history of mission in China left Christianity discredited
> in Chinese eyes. It is labelled subversive. The taunt, 'One more
> Christian leaves us with one less Chinese,' in the anti-Christian
> May Fourth Movement revealed the resentment . . . The form

of Christianity which Chinese churches inherit ... is fragmented and does not possess a coherent understanding of the world. Theological concepts are often polarized. It regards grace and nature, ecclesiastical structure and personal salvation, evangelism and social concern, sacred and worldly as incompatible categories.[9]

Issues from the history of mission

The modern missionary movement has thrown up any number of crucial questions related to the Gospel and culture which make serious reflection vitally important. Perhaps none is more far-reaching than the extent to which the Gospel, brought by Western missionaries to Africa, Asia and Latin America, had an impact on indigenous cultures. There is a point of view that interprets the contact in almost entirely negative terms as far as the recipient cultures were concerned. In general terms the indigenous cultures were misunderstood, caricatured and humiliated, and the churches born as a result became subcultures alienated from the living traditions of the peoples. To 'civilise' was seen as an indispensable part of evangelisation.[10]

There is another point of view that states that this version of history is itself a caricature and may be due, in part, to a form of Western self-centredness. It appears to regard the indigenous peoples as passive objects of Western initiatives, whereas on many occasions they resisted the destruction of their cultures by all kinds of creative adaptations of the message and of the enforced customs of the missionary.[11] A number of people, most notably Lamin Sanneh,[12] have emphasised in this context the significance for indigenous cultures of having the Bible translated into the vernacular:

> The close connection between language and culture ... meant that language study and development, such as occurred under missionary sponsorship, touched off a ripple effect throughout society. One effect was the democratic levelling of Scriptural translation ... The vernacular languages that missionaries developed were, of course, the property of ordinary people, yet in making them the preeminent medium of religion,

missionaries detached these languages from the norm of
religious exclusivism, thus enfranchising men and women normally excluded in traditional religions.[13]

Charles Taber argues strenuously that the heavy dependence of
some missionaries on the functionalist school of cultural anthropology between the first and second world wars has distorted their
view of Gospel and culture. It has tended to take cultures as rather
static, harmonious, self-contained and unproblematic wholes. In
reaction to the accusation that cultures were dismantled by the
missionary movement, later missionaries made the opposite error
of believing that nothing in culture must be touched:

> Functionalism was strongly biased in favor of what is, because
> 'it works'. This led in missions to an overreaction against
> the older ethnocentric judgementalism and to an excessive
> readiness to approve almost anything and everything. It also
> led missionaries as it did anthropologists to be gullible in
> taking at face value the explanations and interpretations of
> those persons in each society who were privileged and to
> discount the perspectives of those persons who were not
> favored or rewarded by the culture, persons who might even
> be grievously oppressed.[14]

Cross-cultural communication

As soon as one concedes that the Gospel cannot be transmitted in
a culture-free or culture-neutral cocoon, but finds its own place
in the heart of many cultures, then some absolutely crucial missiological questions will have to be faced.

Is the Gospel the same in all cultures?

Is there a recognisable core statement which any Christian from
any part of the world would affirm to be true – a message about
God, Jesus Christ and the world that can be expressed in any
language and in different thought-forms in such a way that it is
recognisably the same? Practice would suggest that people believe
this is the case. It has become a truism that particular historical
and cultural perspectives distort our understanding of the Gospel.
It is quite common for one part of the Church to accuse another

of being unfaithful to the Gospel, either by omission (leaving out elements hard to understand or accept) or by the assimilation of beliefs and practices to cultural norms (often called 'syncretism').[15] A moment's clear thought indicates that, if the language of distortion is not to be meaningless, there has to be a clear core whose meaning, though expressed in different ways, does not change in substance. Otherwise it would not be possible to talk about false gospels and spurious evangelism. Deviation is always from a norm.

How is the language of the Gospel to be translated?

How far do different languages have words, phrases and ideas that correctly convey the meaning of God's actions and purposes in Jesus Christ as expressed by words like 'forgiveness', 'grace', 'love' and 'reconciliation'? Are current words adaptable? Can new words be invented, where necessary, perhaps as combinations of images? How are these words heard by people of different religious traditions and by secular people? What happens when the same words as are used for the Gospel, or similar words, are used in common parlance but with quite different connotations (e.g. freedom, justice, new age, enlighten).

How are true and false elements in the message to be distinguished?

How can we know that one way of confessing or practising the Gospel is purer than others? Might not our views be little more than echoes of our cultural prejudices or strategies for gaining and maintaining power? And if we allow a free-for-all multi-culturalism, what happens to the unity of the faith and of the community? Nobody, in practice, is a complete relativist.

When is the Gospel in harmony with culture and when does it conflict?

How far can some of the controversial matters where the Gospel touches culture deeply – such as patterns of worship, healing practices, leadership styles, family traditions and decision-making processes – be ruled by the Gospel? And who decides? How much change should one expect, and over what time-span, for people who are converted to Jesus Christ?[16] This is a deeply personal question that may have severe implications for people in tight-knit communities. The Japanese have a saying: 'If one nail sticks out, hammer it down'.

In this connection does it mean anything to speak of 'Gospel values' which are signs of the kingdom, and therefore valid for all cultures? Does the Christian faith itself presuppose certain cultural attitudes that, irrespective of the culture, cannot be altered? – for example, the place of women in society, the sanctity of life in the womb, the rightness of genuine participatory democracy, particular educational methods.

Being aware of culture

There is a tendency, in discussing the subject of culture, to assume that its meaning is understood by everyone in the same way. Up to now I have been using the term as if there were no problem about its use. However, some people have serious doubts about the usefulness of using an umbrella term to cover such a wide diversity of phenomena. For example, the Western world is characterised by a widespread fragmentation which makes talk about one moderately uniform and coherent culture somewhat dubious. Not only within Western nations, through multi-ethnic and multi-religious immigration, but also within the historically indigenous peoples there are highly significant differences of belief, attitudes and lifestyle. This is perhaps most notable between generations, and in particular between the group often referred to as 'Generation X' and their parents' generation, where differences in perspectives on life and in ways of doing things are at their sharpest.[17]

However, even granted a world in which change of all kinds seems to accelerate ever more quickly, there is continuity over time. It appears that each succeeding generation goes through a period of partial rejection of the values of the generation immediately ahead of it, only to adopt those same values at a later stage and then give birth to another group of temporary rebels. Whether one stresses the differences or the similarities between different expressions of culture may be a matter of perception, taste or

ideological bias. Once the choice has been made, it is not difficult
to find plenty of evidence to fit the alternative preferences.

Of course, there are many cultural expressions even among fairly
cohesive communities; but their ability to flourish depends to a
significant degree on there also being underlying structures and
institutions which bind societies together, thus permitting freedom
of experimentation. I am persuaded, therefore, that it is meaningful
to talk in general terms about the different components of culture
in such a way that similar tools of analysis can be used to understand each separate one. With this in mind, we will look at the
meaning of culture in more detail.

Definitions

Broad descriptions do not take us very far. One wag has called
culture 'what we do around here'. Though not intended to be
taken very seriously, there is much truth in the saying, for culture
is human life expressed in a variety of ways: 'It is a comprehensive
plan for living';[18] It is 'a society's complex, integrated coping mech-
anism';[19] 'It is the sum total of ways of living that shape (and also
are shaped by) the continuing life of a group of human beings
from generation to generation';[20] It is 'a more or less coherent set
of ideas ... which are created and shared by a group of people
and transmitted to their children, and which enable them to make
sense of their experience and to cope with their natural and social
worlds to their collective advantage.'[21]

Discerning the patterns of culture

The meaning of culture becomes much more precise when we start
looking at the details. Though using different terms and a variety
of categories, most students of culture find three fundamental
components: beliefs, values and outward forms. The interaction
between each level is so pervasive that one has to be careful not
to treat them as wholly distinct realities: what may be desirable
for the sake of careful description may not be so clear when looking
at actual practice. With this caution in mind, we will look at each
part.

Beliefs

These are often referred to as the world-view of a culture or society.[22] They comprise a more or less coherent interpretation of human existence that seeks to address the ultimate questions, making sense of experience, traditions, history and the relationship to the natural world. In particular, they deal with the major concerns of life:

- *Common humanity.* Those stages of life through which all human beings pass: birth and death; puberty; adolescence; sexual awakening; intellectual development.
- *Human differences.* Those characteristics which divide humans into separate groups: gender; race; economic inequalities; social status; natural abilities.
- *Suffering.* The variety of adverse circumstances through which most people pass, though some bear a much greater burden than others: sickness; disability; infant mortality; sudden death; incurable diseases; natural disasters; exploitation; violence.
- *Success and failure.* The division of humanity between those individuals and communities who seem to prosper and those who encounter adversity: the powerful and powerless; the wealthy and the deprived; the advantaged and the disadvantaged.
- *The meaning of life.* What could or should be the fundamental purpose for living? Is it given by God? Does it come through received tradition? Is it created by each individual or community? How do we explain the existence and the difference between good and evil? Are there two realities – one visible and one invisible – or only one? If there are two (however the second may be defined), how do we relate to it?

Human existence would be impossible without beliefs. It is a matter of how humans function.[23] They constitute the theoretical foundation on which our sense of what is legitimate and illegitimate, appropriate and inappropriate, is based. They help us to cope with the ups and downs of life. They give meaning both to routine and to strange and unexpected events. They lie beneath the symbols and rituals, however discreet or extravagant, which mark significant occurrences in the life of the individual or society.

Values

Values are the moral principles and standards which individuals or societies find acceptable or intolerable. They are used to justify particular ways of behaving or styles of life. They are usually derived, more or less closely, from the fundamental beliefs that dominate at any given moment in the life of an individual or society. They determine such diverse realities as the place of women in society, the ownership of property, whether to obey or break the law, patterns of sexual relationship, marriage, attitudes to the environment, views of work and leisure.

Increasingly in modern societies values are fragmentary and divergent, as belief systems become more ill-defined and uncertain. As there do not appear to be any provable or dependable answers to the major questions of life, the circle of values is in constant flux (for example, in the debate between law-and-order and libertarian views on managing crime or in the controversy between pro-choice and pro-life lobbyists regarding abortion). Perhaps the most that one can say, somewhat ironically no doubt, is that the supreme value is that society tolerates my *relative* beliefs and lifestyle as long as it does not affect my commitment to the *absolute* value of human rights.[24]

Outward forms

These are the components of culture which most people think of when the word is used. No doubt it is this level of reality that Hanns Johst had in mind in the celebrated saying (often attributed to Goering),'*Wenn ich Kulture hore ... entsichere ich meinen Browning!*' ('Whenever I hear the word "culture" ... I release the safety catch on my pistol').[25] The outward forms of culture are all those expressions of our beliefs and values which surround us and which we take for granted because we are immersed in them. Of these, the most fundamental is *language* (its vocabulary, morphology, syntax, proverbs and use of slang). Next comes the broad world of *art*, whether in its visual (painting, drawing, photography, cinema, literature), audio (music, speech), oral (storytelling, humour) or constructed (architecture, sculpture, landscaping, wood-carving) forms. Then there are the amazing variety of *customs* which a culture commends, tolerates or forbids, such as forms of hospitality, greeting, the naming of children, courtship, food. Finally, there are the *institutions*, the so-called backbone of society, like the family, law, the educational system and economic structures.

There are other ways of viewing the diverse segments of culture. Paul Hiebert, for example, speaks of the *cognitive*, *affective* and *evaluative* dimensions of culture. The first provides the source of our knowledge, way of reasoning and wisdom. The second directs our feelings and appreciation of beauty. The third influences our values and loyalties. Culture is manifested most obviously in the behaviour of people and in the products they create. It is cemented by particular symbols (notably flags, national anthems, uniforms, bodily gestures), patterns and systems (which are traits by which cultures are recognised as special entities).[26]

Cultural patterns in the contemporary world are so complex that easy categorisations should be avoided. Although at one level it may be useful to distinguish between small-scale (elementary or primary) societies with simple technology and uncomplicated social, economic and political structures, and urban literate, industrial and 'cybernetic' societies,[27] there is also plenty of evidence of mixed cultural patterns. Thus, if it is right to identify four main cultural components in two groupings – traditional/modern and religious/secular – a number of combinations are possible.[28] For example, it is quite common to find people who are 'postmodern' (in the films they watch or the rituals they adopt as football fans), 'modern' in their use of gadgets, means of communication and forms of medicine and 'traditional' in their adherence to conservative forms of religion. Or, they may be ultra-modern in their need to adopt the latest fashions in clothes and music and yet quite traditional in their views of punishment or of the best educational practices. The variety of possibilities is simply a reminder that a culture is almost as varied as the people who belong to it. To simplify may have educational benefits, but we should be conscious of the perils of being simplistic.

Intersections

Accommodation

In thinking through the intricate issues surrounding the expression of the Gospel in different cultures or the interpretation of the Gospel from the perspective of cultures, a number of conceptual tools have been developed. At an earlier time, people spoke about the 'accommodation' of the Gospel to culture. By this was meant, primarily, people deciding on the essential elements which distinguish the Christian faith from other systems of belief and adapting or adjusting these through the use of language, symbols and illustrations to the recipients of another culture.[29] It sometimes took the form of adopting the customs of the people to whom the missionaries went and adjusting the symbols of their religion to Christian forms, as in the celebrated cases of Mateo Ricci and Roberto De Nobili.[30]

Indigenisation

A second step, more common in Protestant than Catholic circles, was indigenisation. Russell Chandran understands the practice to mean 'the setting forth clearly of the Christian message, once for all revealed, and . . . the interpretation of this message in a manner "challengingly relevant" for each generation'. This means a reformulation and reinterpretation of the revelation, for no 'one formulation [can] exhaust the full meaning of revelation':

> In order to be able to use a people's language with power, we should have a positive appraisal of their religion and culture . . . It is, however, important to distinguish between the dialectics of indigenization and a kind of fancy-dressing of Christian theology with non-Christian terminology taken from classical forms of religions.[31]

The most famous expression of indigenisation has been the 'three selfs' – self-support, self-government and self-propagation – invented by Henry Venn and Rufus Anderson and developed by Roland Allen.[32] Indigenisation was intended to create as rapidly as possible a local church which was not for ever dependent on foreign assistance and upkeep. It has been suggested, however, that even this apparently impeccable motivation for appropriate mission has Western cultural overtones, in that it assumes a certain kind of entrepreneurial impulse and ability.

Gradually, mission agencies and local churches came to recognise that indigenisation as a model of cultural translation may have been too static: 'The danger inherent in all programmes for the "indigenisation" or "acculturation" of the gospel is that they involve the church with the conservative and backward-looking elements in society.'[33]

Inculturation

It seemed that culture was acceptable as it was, and all that had to be done was to find appropriate techniques of translation. In its place, therefore, the more dynamic term, 'inculturation' began to be used. This has been a concept particularly favoured within Catholic missiology: 'Inculturation works dialectically in a "marvellous exchange": the transformation of a culture by the Gospel, and the reexpression of the Gospel in terms of that culture'.[34]

The Catholic emphasis on the sacramentality of the whole of life means that that Church has tended to lay more stress on the embodied manifestation or the *presence* of the Gospel than on its verbal proclamation.[35] This has derived from the centrality in Catholic thought of the incarnation of the Word: 'The church is to be completely at home among each people in the same authentic way that Jesus was at home in Nazareth. This is genuine catholicity.'[36]

Inculturation, however, does cause problems for the Roman Catholic Church with its heavy emphasis on the visible unity of all local churches. A polycentric vision of Christianity could, from the viewpoint of the teaching authority invested ultimately in the pope as the 'chief bishop' (*primus inter pares*), mean that local expressions of the Gospel escape from control.[37] In theory at least, Protestants have less fear of a polycentric Church given their emphasis on the autonomy of local churches:

> The acceptance of difference means that the Christian faith can be at home in any culture. Consequently Christianity has as many centres as the number of cultures of its adherents.

This polycentric nature of Christianity may, in the eyes of some people, rob theology of the stability traditionally associated with it. Nevertheless returning to a Christianity with only one cultural centre is now an impossibility.[38]

Contextualisation

The understanding of the incarnational nature of Christian faith has developed further with the growing awareness, from the 1950s onwards, of the ways in which political commitments and social action affect the mission of the Church in particular cultures.[39] In general terms one might say that political and social analysis have joined anthropology as tools of discernment in the struggle of the Church to be faithful to the Gospel and relevant to the particular historical moment. Taken originally from Jesus' dispute with some religious leaders of his day (Matt. 16:2–3), 'reading the signs of the times' has become an additional task of the theology of mission.

Contextualisation recognises the reciprocal influence of culture and socio-economic life. In relating Gospel to culture, therefore, it tends to take a more critical (or prophetic) stance towards culture. The concept first came to prominence in the early 1970s in the arena of theological education.[40] It is intended to be taken seriously as a theological method which entails particular ideological commitments to transform situations of social injustice, political alienation and the abuse of human rights. José Miguez Bonino speaks of 'raising up the historic situation to the theological level' and of 'theological reflection in the concrete praxis': 'The inflexible will to act from the historical situation, analysed by means of socio-political instruments and adopted in a theological option, identifies . . . the starting point of the theological task.'[41]

Connections

The time has come to attempt some kind of assessment of this monumental debate. This assessment will be extremely tentative and limited, given the wealth of material, the diversity of standpoints and the continuing nature of the debate. I will endeavour to set down some markers which may help to guide us through the rugged terrain.

Within the WCC, the meaning of contextualisation has gone through a number of mutations: from a 'just, participatory and sustainable society', via 'peace, justice and the integrity of creation' to 'the programme to overcome violence'. These projects have sought to respond to urgent matters on the world stage. The accent on overcoming violence has arisen in part out of the 'programme to combat racism'. Thus, for example, in spite of the transition in South Africa from a white dictatorship to a multiracial democracy, intercommunal and other forms of violence have not diminished as was hoped. In part, the new programme is an extension of the 'Decade of Women' (1988–98) which has highlighted the pervasive nature of domestic violence against women, among many other causes of suffering.

It is right that the Churches should address theologically and practically the most up-to-date issues. However, they need to keep in mind two important considerations. First, the slogan of a former generation – 'the world sets the agenda' – is only partly true. What happens in the world is the setting for mission: it may influence strategic thinking and action, it may help to set priorities – but it can never define the ultimate goals of mission nor the specifically Christ-like means of achieving them. These are established through profound reflection on the significance of the apostolic message of good news. It is by means of a constant interaction with the fundamental affirmations of the faith that the Church can discern the particular ways in which the reality of Jesus Christ is good news in any particular context.

Secondly, the more contemporary a situation, the more difficult it is to achieve a measured response. Like most institutions the Church is affected by the culturally transmitted insistence on fast thinking and quick solutions. It feels itself under considerable pressure to be active, afraid that delay will be interpreted as indifference or distorted priorities. The Church seems to have a reputation for involving itself in yesterday's issues. This is a difficult balance to achieve. Perhaps different parts of the world Church can help each other to be simultaneously active and reflective. Certainly, strong and well-informed regional missiological 'think tanks' are essential, if the Church is to contextualise the Gospel adequately.

The fivefold typology for cultural engagement elaborated by Richard Niebuhr[42] – Christ *above, of, against, in paradoxical relationship to* and *transforming* culture – has been a helpful guide when considering just how Christians should express and live out their faith in changing circumstances. Though each aspect may represent a particular historical moment of the Church's life, there is no reason to believe that Christians should insist on any to the exclusion of others.[43] Given particular circumstances, the Church may need to emphasise one more than the others. Where, for example, it is under pressure to compromise with a particularly distasteful political regime or where it senses the abandonment of ethical norms given by God for human wellbeing, it may have to take a stance *against* culture. If, however, it is a persecuted minority, such a stance may have to take the form of being *above* culture. In such circumstances, the only way open to it to maintain its faithfulness may well be withdrawal. The *paradox* comes when Christians are constrained to say both 'Yes' and 'No' simultaneously to aspects of culture.

The Gospel, as we have constantly reiterated, is inevitably and rightly *of* culture. However, the Church's 'presence' or incarnation in the world may be such that it becomes compromised by cultural norms or political intrigue whose source is self-interest and whose consequences are oppression and inequity. The Church becomes an integral part of the power structures of society, or it is bought by the powers. It has slipped into its Christendom mode (i.e. its alignment with political and economic power for the sake of security or self-advancement). Again, to maintain a balance between the community's faithfulness to the norms of the Gospel (particularly that of non-retaliation) and its active involvement in political decision-making is an arduous task, as the history of this century has witnessed on numerous occasions.[44]

This leads us finally to what is perhaps the most effective check on a process of inculturation which is both fitting and proper, namely the universal Church. If different regional Churches can listen to one another, there is much more chance of preventing either the domestication (too local) or the abstraction (too general) of the Gospel. Las Newman from the Caribbean suggests the model of the Church as 'community in communion'.[45] Both aspects are to be treated with the utmost seriousness. The church is a local community. As such it possesses a mission mandate for its own particular situation. It has to identify with the people in whose midst it is set, called to meet their needs and bear their burdens.

The church also belongs to a communion of churches, with both great benefits and responsibilities. Somehow the local community has to commit itself to national, regional and international structures which make it accountable to the wider communions of which it is in a sense a representative. In this way it lives the permanent tension between the particular and the universal inherent in being Church:

> Every true community must live with differences which cause dissonance and tension. The goal of community must be health and wholeness from the discovery of what is truly held in common.[46]

> Inculturation of the gospel is a must in any missionary approach. Faithfulness to the gospel is our only contribution to the common treasure of humanity. To bring these two together in permanent and creative tension, to learn from each other, is the basic mission challenge ... We need to explore our belonging to a community of faith which implies an accountability that is not simply setting limits to diversity, but an enlarging of the horizons, and understanding that other diversities are signs of new possibilities that may challenge us.[47]

> Developing ecclesial communities, inspired by the Gospel, will gradually be able to express their Christian experience in original ways and forms that are consonant with their own cultural traditions, provided that those traditions are in harmony with the objective requirements of the faith itself. To this end, especially in the more delicate areas of inculturation, particular churches of the same region should work in communion with each other and with the whole church, convinced that only through attention both to the universal church and to the particular churches will they be capable of translating the treasure of faith into a legitimate variety of expressions.[48]

Exercises

1. Choose an example from your experience of how culture has distorted the Gospel and suggest ways of dealing with the situation.

2. Examine the conviction of some Christians that, irrespective of culture, the Church must be governed by democratic means.

3. Describe a situation in which you think the Church has been successful in making the Gospel relevant to a culture (or subculture).

6

Justice for the Poor

The scope of the study

One of the most decisive and pressing issues to confront Christians in all parts of the globe in the last 40 years has been what Gustavo Gutiérrez calls 'the irruption of the poor':

> This phrase means that those who until now were 'absent' from history are gradually becoming 'present' within it. This new presence of the poor and oppressed is making itself felt in the popular struggles for liberation and in the historical consciousness arising from these struggles. It is also making itself felt within the church, for there the poor are increasingly making their voices heard and claiming openly their right to live and think the faith in their own terms.[1]

In this chapter we will deal with those questions of Christian mission that relate to the situation of the majority of humanity who are unable to enjoy even the minimum of life's basic needs. There are both global and local issues which deeply concern Christians and challenge them to be actively involved in bringing about change. We will explore the meaning of justice, the identity of the poor, the effect of macro and micro development projects on changing situations of major need, what Christian faith can say about economic systems, how the poor are related to living and proclaiming the Gospel, the meaning of God's preferential option for the poor and the obligations present world poverty places on the Church.

The poor

The naked situation

'To be poor means that one belongs to a household which has access to a total annual cash income less than one half of the national average.'[2] Such a definition has the merit of being measurable and relatively objective: according to this explanation, some 60 per cent of all households throughout the world, and perhaps as many as 75 per cent of all human beings, are poor. On the other hand, it may create the impression that the poor are merely statistics. In order to put a human face on poverty further categories are used, the largest of which is known as 'the ultra (or vulnerable) poor'. These are the people who cannot work – the elderly, in some cases the disabled, those in poor health and children – those dependent on seasonal work and those who have no adequate productive resources to earn a satisfactory income – land, skills and tools.

The poor are often thought of as those who are deprived of the basic objects which sustain life – adequate nourishment, housing, clothing and healthcare. These criteria define poverty in terms of the *quantity* of goods and services available to people. The criteria which define life in terms of *quality*, realities which may be both the cause and result of material deprivation, are also vital. Among these are access to decision-making processes (which ensure that people are genuinely involved in deciding their own future), guaranteed redress in law against intimidation, violence and excessive bureaucracy, relevant and well-resourced education and training, useful and rewarding work and a healthy (pollution-free) environment.

Poverty is a reality of every day for the vast majority of people living in the world. Its extent is so great, and its eradication apparently so problematical, that those not affected become dulled to the suffering which it causes. In vivid terms it means precarious housing (frequently destroyed by fire, flooding or earthquakes), with large families sharing one or two rooms and sleeping together on the same bed (or adjacent piece of floor), no running water, no proper toilets, open drains, scanty health services (e.g. dental and eye care), unaffordable medicines and a meagre diet. Over one billion people go to bed every night hungry and undernourished. Poverty hits children particularly hard (and in many societies especially girls): they are prone to disease, stunted in their physical and mental growth and often destined for an early death. If they survive to their early teens they may be forced into prostitution or hard and monotonous labour in order to scrape together a miserable income for their families. It is not surprising that many people characterise the whole situation as one of death:

> Poverty means death. Death, in this case, is caused by hunger, sickness, or the oppressive methods used by those who see their privileges endangered by any and every effort to free the oppressed. It is physical death to which cultural death is added, because in a situation of oppression everything is destroyed that gives unity and strength to the dispossessed of this world.[3]

To complete the picture, those who are the object of serious discrimination in any society – such as the disabled, women and minority racial and religious groups – might also be listed among the poor. However, it is not so obvious that they would wish to refer to themselves in this way. A more accurate description might be disadvantaged or oppressed, in that because of birth or accident they come up against prejudice which affects their ability to find work or to enjoy the rights of full citizenship.

The emotionally and spiritually poor

There is another category of poor which, because of the high visibility of the materially poor, is often overlooked. As a group they are much more difficult to define, and the classification itself is controversial. However, in general terms, it covers all those who, even when enjoying an adequate or affluent material existence, are unfulfilled or depressed in their personal lives.[4] Their experience may be affected by an inability to sustain positive relationships with other people – either to make and keep friends or to keep alive a fruitful marriage partnership – because of a lack of any coherent purpose in life, a deeply pessimistic outlook, through pursuing objectives (wealth, status, power) which leave an inner emptiness or because of physical self-abuse (through excessive drinking or drugs).

The consequences of poverty

Rural poverty (the lack of access to sufficient land or employment to sustain life) drives people to the cities. This, along with an increased birth rate in some nations (also attributable in part to poverty), accounts for the phenomenal growth of cities like Mexico City, São Paolo, Lima, Nairobi, Lagos, Bombay, Bangkok and Manila. Needless to say, the existing infrastructure – sanitation, roads, transport and housing – is inadequate to deal with the influx. Among other effects, urban poverty increases certain forms of crime, the break-up of the family support network, the abandonment of children to the streets and an alternative economy (including a vigorous trade in drugs).

Poverty causes a waste of human resources. There is a sense in which, both literally and metaphorically, people are thrown on to the scrap-heap of society – or, to change the metaphor, are cast adrift as irrelevant flotsam and jetsam, the human equivalent of the rubbish that constitutes their life's work. They are the ones with, at most, a bare minimum of education and no training in skills.[5] It is not surprising that the word to describe the lot of these people has changed in recent years from 'marginalised' or 'peripheral', which still suggests that they belong to existing society in however negligible a way, to 'excluded'. It is more clearly seen now that, from the point of view of the way economies are run today, the poor are unimportant, if not irrelevant. Whether they are inside or outside the system is of little consequence.[6]

The causes of poverty

Whether the poor are wholly victims of their circumstances or also contribute to their own poverty is a matter of fierce debate. Those who opt for an analysis which casts the poor as the 'sinned against'[7] believe that poverty is to be seen mainly as the result of external forces which act permanently against the interests of the poor. They are systems and structures whose effects are to bring about and aggravate poverty. In the first place, a free-market economy operating through transnational businesses, with little accountability (beyond corporate shareholders) and ineffectually controlled, rewards the strong and punishes the weak (we look at this in more detail below).[8]

Secondly, there is the reality of international debt on an unprecedented scale.[9] This means that there is a massive reverse flow of wealth from the main debtor countries, who are already destitute of capital reserves. In turn this results in these nations having inadequate resources to invest in healthcare, education and job-creation. Their ability to move out of poverty through the creation of wealth is seriously impaired. The debt trap also leads to the overexploitation of natural resources, such as timber, and to the development of cash-crops for export (to the detriment of staple foods for the population) to generate foreign exchange for the debt repayments.

The present debt crisis was caused by the recycling of 'petrodollars', earned at the beginning of the 1970s by the sudden rise in the price of crude oil, as loans for the purchase of arms and for pharaonic schemes like the building of nuclear reactors, modern airports and state-of-the-art hospitals. Interest on the massive loans, often made to wholly undemocratic and corrupt regimes, rose steeply in the late 1970s and early 1980s.

Thirdly, the world trade systems operate to the disadvantage of those whose economies are weak through lack of diversification. Forced to a large extent to rely on the export of primary materials, the poor nations have never been strong enough to ensure a fair return for their crops or raw materials. The rich nations have also engaged in protectionist practices which erect trade barriers through tariffs and quotas against the poor nations. In spite of the rhetoric to the contrary, there are no level playing fields in world trade.

On the other side of the argument are those who minimise the external structural causes of poverty and emphasise the internal social ones. Thus Herbert Schlossberg writes:

> Commonly people are poor because of cultural factors which they choose not to change: that women not work outside the home; that animals not be killed; that it is more prestigious not to do physical work; that it is not worth taking risks.[10]

Ali Mazrui writes in a similar vein, though making different points:

> Many traditional societies, almost by definition, are cultures of
> nostalgia rather than anticipation. They value custom, ancestry
> and tradition – rather than making preparations for the day
> after tomorrow. Cultures of nostalgia are unlikely to monetise
> time as a commodity . . . Cultures which love ancestry tend to
> love kinship generally . . . kinship solidarity has effects on
> development capacity . . . Sometimes, they substitute a pres-
> tige motive for a profit motive among drives of behaviour . . .
> This fosters social ostentation and conspicuous consumption
> as part of the struggle for status . . . This may result in a
> combination of charity and solidarity with poorer members of
> one's broad, extended family.[11]

For people who tend to blame cultural traditions rather than economic structures, the relevant question is not so much why some
countries or communities are poor, but why some are wealthy. The
implicit reason for the latter is that, at a significant moment of
their history, they adopted cultural norms like thrift, a positive
evaluation of all work, the evil of nepotism and bribes and the
rejection of fatalism.[12] Put very starkly (and for many offensively):
'There can be no modernisation without Westernisation'.

Solutions to poverty

Needless to say, there are plenty of suggestions as to how the poor
can escape from the trap of poverty. These depend to a large extent
on how the causes are evaluated. In general terms, three kinds of
answer are given:

1. The political *conservatives* believe that poverty is mainly due
   to a nation's failure to sustain economic growth. This may be
   due to the inability to attract the right kind of foreign investment because of political instability and corruption. It may
   be due, as expressed above, to the absence of values which
   stress individual initiative and ambition, the right of private
   property, the legitimacy of profit-making and trust in business
   dealings.[13]

2. The political *radicals* believe that present economic structures can never solve the problem of poverty. These structures are, in their design (and quite probably by design), incapable of ever providing sufficient opportunities for everyone to be able to enjoy the basic necessities of life. At best, some crumbs may fall from the table of the rich ('trickle down'), but the system sustains and increases the affluent lifestyle of the small minority of the world's population most of whom happen to have been born in the highly industrialised countries of the North. The only solution is through a nation's proper control of the means of production, properly targeted investment, the reinvestment of wealth created locally and widespread redistribution to bring the majority of a population into the economy as consumers as well as producers, thus stimulating the economy from the 'demand' side.

3. Political *moderates* accept that structural changes are necessary, but believe that these have to be extremely gradual for fear of scaring off potential investors from overseas. Where possible, the centralisation of the economy should be avoided, though there have to be some political initiatives like land reform, fiscal benefits for small-scale entrepreneurs, control over currency speculation and price fixing and the assurance of minimally adequate working conditions and wages.

In macro-economic terms, the following proposals for reversing situations of endemic poverty would seem to make the most sense:

*   The one-off cancellation of the major categories of debt of the 'severely indebted nations' and the favourable rescheduling of the debt of 'the moderately indebted nations'; [14]
*   Trading terms in which prices for primary products reflect just wages and humane working conditions, and remain stable over extended periods of time;
*   The creation of stable democracies, which include free speech and action for opposition political parties and groups and which encourage local grassroots political action ('Civil Society');
*   A drastic reduction of the arms trade, which rarely has any

strategic justification and which benefits only the manufacturers – this may involve tough curbs on export licences by the
governments of the manufacturers' nations;

- The retention of a greater percentage of the wealth created
within the nation – this will entail some kind of control on
the level of both the dividends expatriated to foreign-based
companies and the location of locally generated wealth
overseas;

- A more equitable distribution of wealth within and between
nations through some kind of graduated tax-system which
would give preferential treatment to low earners thereby
encouraging their greater participation in the national economy.

The quest for justice[15]

From a Christian perspective the reality, causes and resolution of
poverty are inseparable from the call for relationships of justice
between individuals, communities and nations. Justice, alongside
freedom, has become the stock-in-trade of most commentaries on
contemporary economic matters. However, in the secular West
both the theoretical basis and practical meaning of justice constitute
contested ground. Morris Ginsberg, for example, argues that justice
is based on the supreme value of human personality. We all recognise, he states, that other people should not be used as objects or
means to our ends. Because they belong to the same species as
ourselves, we can see intuitively that we are all born with reciprocal
rights and obligations.[16] This argument depends for its strength on
personally sustained feelings of good will for the other, for it does
not contain a clear source for the acceptance of other people's
dignity, worth and value beyond our own sentiment. Once people
abandon the notion of a personal God who creates human beings
in his image and is the arbiter of good and evil, and is thereby
both the derivation of human worthiness and the one who
demands justice, the reasons for treating anyone as intrinsically
deserving of respect are tenuous.

As spontaneous goodwill is not something that can be guaranteed, secular societies have fallen back on some form of self-interest
as a motivating force for treating others fairly. The practice of

justice becomes the implementation of an implicit, unspoken social contract in which each is prepared to treat others as they would expect to be treated by them.[17] However, the social contract idea has two major problems. In the first place, it is purely hypothetical: in real life it proves to be insufficiently strong in many cases to persuade those with privileges to give them up. Experience shows that human beings are extremely adept at finding self-justifying reasons for not promoting equality. Secondly, inveterate gamblers will not be persuaded to abide by a system that spreads opportunities and goods in an even-handed way through the population. They may be prepared to take the risk of being disadvantaged by the system for the lure of 'the winner takes all'. They will play for the high stakes of considerable wealth in the hope of landing the jackpot (the essence of gambling).

In the absence of an ethic based on the will of God, secular society has to rely on the borrowed morality of the past – a deeply ingrained sense of the moral rightness of protecting the interests of people who are weak and vulnerable in economic terms. Even when, for example, a relative equality of opportunity has led to great disparities of wealth, there seems to be an appropriateness in redressing the extremes of affluence and poverty: thus, some people's needs are recognised as taking priority over others, and cut-throat competition in business and in securing jobs is considered morally objectionable.[18]

For a Christian who listens to the witness of the Old and New Testaments, the problem of finding an adequate basis for justice is solved. Both the basis for and the meaning of justice spring from the nature of the God who is. Justice is what God does, for justice is what God is. By definition he acts consistently with his attributes. So we know justice through God's acts of deliverance, through his laws and through the kind of relationships between human beings that he requires:

> He has told you what is good;
> and what does the Lord require of you
> but to do justice, and to love kindness,
> and to walk humbly with your God?
> (Mic. 6:8)

> Is this not the fast that I choose:
> to loose the bonds of injustice,
> and to undo the thongs of the yoke,
> to let the oppressed go free,
> and to break every yoke?
> (Isa. 58:6)

> Give the king your justice, O God . . .
> may he judge your people with righteousness,
> and your poor with justice . . .
> may he defend the cause of the poor of the people,
> give deliverance to the needy,
> and crush the oppressor.
> (Ps. 72:1–4)

The word of the prophet is addressed to the whole nation, not just to individuals. The whole community has a set of obligations which reflect God's character. 'To do justice' is to demonstrate that the corporate body of people belong to one another. Justice is an active concept. It is not the maintenance of a static state of equilibrium in which certain powers are kept in balance. It is an activity in which a disordered or disproportionate state of affairs is put right. To do justice is to enable the disadvantaged to escape permanently from the trap of deprivation in order that they may become full, responsible members of the community. This will happen as resources and opportunities in life are made available to all. Justice includes; injustice excludes.

Justice is also about checking the excessive concentration of economic and political power in the hands of a few, so that responsible decision-making may be an activity of the whole community. It is about ensuring that each person may own and enjoy the work of his or her own hands and be supported by the community when hit by adversity. It is not the same as legality. In an alienated world, aspects of the legal system may well reflect people's distorted sense of right and wrong. Or there may be a conflict between the proper procedures of the law and wrongful outcomes. Hence the quest for justice may well include the struggle for substantial changes in the law or in the processes of the legal system.

The quite specifically biblical view of justice is that of bringing

harmony to the community through the establishment of right
relationships. It is summed up in the legislation concerning the
year of jubilee (Lev. 25:8ff.). The purpose of the laws was to liberate
all those members of the community who had become alienated
from direct access to the means of livelihood (the land) and, therefore, permanently dependent on others (Lev. 25:13, 23, 35, 39–41).
The word for jubilee, *yobel* (*aphesis* in the Greek translation of the
Old Testament) means 'release' (cf. also Exod. 21:2–6; 23:10–11;
Deut. 15:1–18; Jer. 34:8–22; Neh. 5:1–13). Thus, in a sense, justice is
another word for liberation: the removal of the barriers which
prevent human beings from participating fully in the benefits and
responsibilities of the community.[19]

There has been considerable interest in and debate about the
possibility that in the so-called 'Nazareth Manifesto' (Luke 4:16–19)
Jesus was making a public declaration that the time had come for
the fulfilment of the jubilee laws.[20] The majority of commentators
think it unlikely that Jesus intended a literal year of jubilee with a
strict adherence to all the laws, intriguing and attractive though
such a hypothesis may be. Rather, he was using jubilee language
metaphorically to indicate the purpose of his own mission.
However, there is a consensus that jubilee points to the kind of
society that will be manifest when God fully reigns among his
people. In this sense, it is right to anticipate the purpose of the
laws, and echoes of the laws' objectives are to be found scattered
throughout the New Testament: for example, in the economic practice of the early Church (Acts 2:44–5; 4:32–7), the concern for the
poor (Acts 11:29–30; Gal. 2:10; 2 Cor. 8–9; Eph. 4:28; 1 John 3:17)
and the attitude of Zacchaeus (Luke 19:8) – a concrete sign of
salvation.

The new community called into being by Jesus Christ was to be
a 'jubilee' community not once every 49 years, but in its daily
practice. Here we find the typically evangelical dimension of justice
being worked out. Justice has often been defined as 'giving to each
his or her due'.[21] This is to cast it in the legal mould of ensuring
that rewards and punishments should be given without any bias
or favouritism; that each individual is treated with strict equality.
In this sense, the sign of justice is the scales in which carefully
measured retribution is weighed exactly. The emphasis is on the

requirements of universal fairness and an absolute separation of the judge from any relationship with the accused, except that required by the proceedings of the court. Upholding justice in this sense has its place. Disregard for the impartiality of the law through the giving and taking of bribes or through intimidation denies justice. However, in the light of Jesus Christ other factors come into play, principally those of mercy and generosity.[22]

Thus we might redefine justice as 'giving to each his or her due according to the circumstances in which they are placed, even when that may mean that others will have to forgo legitimate rights'. I think this meaning is illustrated in the tirade against the payment of unjust wages in the letter of James (5:1–6). The references to 'riches,' 'gold and silver', 'treasure', 'luxury', 'pleasure' and 'fattened hearts', in the immediate context of defrauding workers of their wages, suggest not just that the wages have not been paid, but that the employers have made excessive profit out of the wealth created in their agri-business by not paying adequate wages.[23] If it were not historically anachronistic, one might be inclined to believe that James here is anticipating Marx's discussion of surplus-value, the value added in the manufacturing process which is not returned to the worker but kept as profit, either to be reinvested in the business or paid to shareholders.[24]

However, the debate about theories of value is not the point I wish to make here. Rather, the issue is that of the just wage as an illustration of the biblical concept of justice. It might be argued that the minimum wage is a just wage for it is what the law requires. However, by consistently paying the lowest amount necessary, the employer is being unjust: first, for taking an excessive profit for himself and secondly for not considering the specific needs of the workers. The just wage is one that enables the worker to be respected as a member of the community, not dependent on further welfare benefits, and which does not create enormous disparities of wealth among people. In this concept of justice there is a strong element of grace: the requirements of compassion take precedence over the requisites of the law.

Economic systems

The reference to Marx brings us to the point of considering how the present global economic system affects the situation of justice for the poor. It would be an illusion to imagine that for the present there is likely to be any alternative to the capitalist world order. However critical one may be of both the justification and practice of capitalism, wishing that the economy were constructed on some other basis will not bring about the demise of the system. Therefore, as far as one can predict, justice for the poor will only be possible within the overall constraints of the global reach of the market economy.[25]

Nevertheless, a Christian must judge the system in the light of the kind of world order envisaged in Christ's mission. The kind of freedom envisaged, if markets are to work 'efficiently', militates against the Christian vision of the kingdom on a number of grounds:

1. Human beings are to be treated as having an essential value derived from their being created in the image of a personal God. This value is primary: it is neither given nor can it be taken away by human beings; it can only be recognised. It takes precedence, therefore, over the 'use value' that they may, or may not, command in the market. Unfortunately, the latter sees them as useful commodities, just one of the various elements which goes towards the creation of wealth and which, according to its abundance or scarcity, commands a certain price.

2. There is no absolute right of private property. The biblical view of creation means that human beings have been made stewards of what belongs fundamentally to God: 'The land [the basic means of production of the time] shall not be sold in perpetuity, for the land is mine; with me you are but aliens and tenants' (Lev. 25:23; also Exod. 19:5; Ezek. 46:18). Human beings have been set within creation to 'till it and keep it' (Gen. 2:15), that is to care for it with tenderness, sensitivity and sympathy so that it will yield enough for every living being (including animals). The idea that the material means of life

could be owned and used by some to the detriment of others is unacceptable. If they are not used satisfactorily for the benefit of all, they will be taken away and given to others. In biblical terms the unjust stewards will be sent away into exile, far from the inheritance they were meant to share with those in need.

3. Human beings are held accountable before God for the way they manage life in community. Justice for the poor is a matter of human ethical decisions for which people will be held responsible. There will be no excuse that they were just following impersonal market forces. In other words, responsibility for the welfare of people cannot be subordinated to the detached working of economic pressures: 'The economy was made for humankind, and not humankind for the economy; so the Son of Man is lord even of the economy' (variation of Mark 2:27).

The search for appropriate patterns of development

The Church has been involved in almost every conceivable kind of development project during its expansion across the world in the last two centuries. From the beginning of the modern missionary movement, the pioneers saw as part of their work the betterment of the social conditions of the people. It may be possible with hindsight to laugh at the incongruous notion of mission as building both churches and latrines, but the intuition was right that some scientific discoveries should be used to enhance the material life of people.

Questions of development today are more urgent and much more controversial. The Western Church has become a major donor agency in making available considerable sums of money and professional expertise to partner churches in the Third World in order to alleviate some of the acute deprivation there.[26] There is, however, considerable doubt in some circles that this is the right approach to justice for the poor. For some it is a dangerous palliative that masks the real causes of long-term poverty (outlined above). The Church's task in the West, beyond the supplying of humanitarian aid in emergency disasters (natural calamities, the effects of conflict), should be educative and political. It should be engaged both in raising awareness of the reasons why people are becoming more impoverished and in working for change. Development aid can easily prolong the culture of dependency, creating unhealthy relationships between different parts of the world Church and, in the name of the high moral virtue of compassion, fortify the Western Church's strong influence over the life of the Church in other parts.[27]

Part of the difficulty is that the Churches do not always examine and judge carefully the various secular discussions of development which, as one might expect, tend to see it in the *quantitative* terms of the latest technology, manufacturing capacity, gross national product, levels of income, balance of payments, financial reserves, strength of the currency and so on, as if each of these represents criteria which are objectively verifiable and universally valid.[28] Nevertheless, I believe that the Churches do have an immensely important role in modelling the right kind of co-operation between the more and less wealthy communities.

In addition to working for political and economic changes to existing structures, there seem to be two kinds of project in which the poor can be supported in their struggle to achieve a life where, at least, all basic needs are met. The first is designed to provide resources such as clean drinking water, primary healthcare (such as the immunisation of children), education in the prevention of common diseases, an understanding of sustainable agriculture, irrigation schemes, seed, technical skills and literacy campaigns. It is vital that these programmes are carried through in ways which are culturally appropriate and with the full support of the people themselves. The projects must encourage the development of a sense of self-worth in the local communities by generating resources internally whereby local people can keep them going. This is why emphasis has passed from *development projects*, in which the agents tend to come from outside only to be replaced by further outsiders, to *empowerment* (or *capacity building*) in which local people are enabled to carry through and sustain the work themselves.

The second kind of project is the setting up of small businesses through small low-interest loans. Such businesses have to be sustainable, must use means of production appropriate to the situation, generate sufficient income to support the business's owner and extended family and be capable of some growth, so that more workers can be employed. It has been shown in thousands of cases that such businesses are viable and can make a substantially positive impact on poverty in a variety of communities, both rural and urban:

> There is abundant evidence that investment in small scale enterprises run by and for the poor can have a positive impact upon income and job creation for the poor. Contrary to the myths upheld by traditional financial institutions, the poor are often good entrepreneurs and excellent credit risks.[29]

The Church's role in securing justice for the poor

It has often been pointed out that most of the members of Christian communities worldwide are themselves poor. The Church, therefore, does not stand over against the poor. It does not even stand alongside or in the midst of the poor. The poor are in the Church or *are* the Church. Thus the Church has an immense interest in the transformation of their situation. It is also a major player in the struggle for justice. I would suggest that in this struggle Christians have four major responsibilities that can be expressed in the following theological affirmations: to know God as the author and upholder of justice; to proclaim a gospel of justice; to make a preferential option for the poor, and to overcome materialism.

1. Knowing the God of justice

We said earlier that, because the Church's mission is a response to the mission of God in the world, it is supremely important to know who God is. As Christians living and ministering in situations of acute deprivation have constantly said, it is not easy to find appropriate language to speak about God in the midst of so much innocent suffering, thus Gutiérrez:

> From the viewpoint of theological reflection, the challenge . . . is to find a language about God that grows out of the situation created by the unjust poverty in which the broad masses live (despised races, exploited social classes, marginalised cultures,

discrimination against women) . . . A prophetic and a mystical language are being born in this soil of exploitation and hope.[30]

God has revealed himself – in the words of the prophets, the history of his people and the nations and supremely in the life of the Son – as a God who upholds justice and does not tolerate exploitation:

> Life in the promised land should be a life lived in the presence of God and marked by the fulfillment of the requirements of justice towards others. The land is the place and occasion for communion with God and communion among human beings. It should also be a place where God's commandments are observed, for it is a manifestation of God's fidelity.[31]

In the first instance, the prophetic message was a condemnation of idolatry, particularly that practised by the false prophets and priests in Jerusalem in the pay of wealthy landowners and traders. Their theology of peace, where there was no peace (Jer. 6:14; 7:1–20; 8:11; Isa. 57:21; Ezek. 13:10), was the consequence of an idolatrous view of God. It arose as the promise of a false liberation, to justify people's submission in the face of injustice and oppression. The idolatrous have to carry their idols, whereas those who know God truly are carried, lifted and liberated by him (Isa. 46:1–4).[32]

The implication of idolatry is the constant danger of a practical atheism among God's people: namely, the service of a God who tolerates evil in whatever form. The only God who can be known truly is the one who protects the weak and vulnerable. This is not a matter of superbly executed liturgies or fine theological insights, but a humble following of God's paths of righteousness and compassion.

2. Proclaiming a gospel of justice

One of the main dangers for those who have captured a vision of the God of justice and are outraged by the harsh and repressive situation in which millions of people live is self-righteousness. They may be so full of indignation and so busy condemning the sins of others that they forget that 'judgement begins with the household of God' (1 Pet. 4:17). Christians dare not preach the

Gospel to others before they have preached it to themselves. To what extent does the life of the Church show forth justice to the poor? What style of leadership is being exercised? Are the social and political views of Christians moulded by 'the good news of God'?[33]

Justice as we have been describing it is not only a question of ethics[34] – that is, the kind of action demanded of human beings in a moral universe – it is also a message of hope. In the Gospel there is a declaration of the situation that will be. It is a reminder to a cynical and indifferent humanity that suffering and exclusion are not the final word of the universe. It proclaims a judgement which is both the final verdict of absolute justice on all corruption and viciousness and a setting right of the situation. Sometimes the 'prophetic voice' is heard only as condemnation. But the announcement of judgement is also a word of graciousness, for the prophets always provide both a warning of the disaster that will happen if the people do not change and the opportunity to admit the fallacy of their policies, turn to God again and receive the blessing of doing his will.

3. Making a preferential option for the poor

Ronaldo Muñoz spells out what it means for God to 'be on the side of the poor'. He suggests four theses – two negative and two positive – which interpret a difficult idea:

- Oppression and deprivation cannot be attributed to God. The suffering of the poor is not God's punishment on them. God is not *against* the poor.
- Great discrepancies of wealth are not part of the natural order. God does not impose a situation of inequality like a remote despot. God is not *above* the poor.
- God's compassion is manifest in his being in the suffering of the poor, giving encouragement and endurance, and challenging the injustices. God is *with* the poor.
- God summons the poor to organise themselves to work for a new kind of society. God is actively *for* the poor.[35]

The idea that God has a preferential option for the poor causes dismay and is repudiated by many.[36] It is argued that God is impartial. He is equally the judge of all. To claim that he is particularly favourable to one group of people is to run the risk of giving a false sense of security. It may lead to a subtle form of idolatry which begins to equate human projects with God's will or to use God to legitimate particular perspectives or actions. It is particularly dangerous when the claim is made on behalf of the poor by those who can always walk away from their contact with poverty.

Further, it seems to suggest that the poor are always, inevitably and completely, the victims of their circumstances without at least some genuine responsibility for their plight. The consequence is to romanticise the poor, as if they were not sinners like everyone else, or as if their sin could be excused because of their suffering. It implies a false anthropology. Moreover, if the cause of poverty is always in external structures and actions over which the poor have no control, they become the playthings of circumstances. This is to dehumanise them. If, on the other hand, we believe that, given the right circumstances, the poor would act unselfishly in the interests of the common good, we make them into something more than merely human.

Finally, the objection is made that, given the continuing and worsening reality of poverty, the affirmation of God's preferential option has no 'cash value' – that is, it does not seem to bring about any change of the situation. Juan Luis Segundo asks where the 'power of the poor in history' is to be seen. Neither they, nor those who are advocates for their cause, seem to be any closer to achieving a significant breakthrough in freeing them from a social and economic reality which tramples on their human dignity.[37] There is a danger, due to the disappointments and frustrations at the lack of progress, of refining and repeating louder meaningless political slogans and theological rhetoric.

These points need to be carefully heard in order that a preferential option for the poor takes on a proper significance, rooted in the biblical vision of God. We might well begin with the laws concerning the widows, orphans and immigrants (Exod. 22:21–4; 23:9; Lev. 19:33; Deut. 27:19). For different reasons each of these groups was particularly vulnerable. They did not have any natural protection within the community. God therefore demands that the whole community should be specially responsible for them because of the precarious position in which they find themselves (Deut. 10:18–19).

Turning to the teaching of Jesus, we notice those whom he pronounces blessed. They are those who comfort the mourners, who show mercy, who work for *shalom*, who provide hospitality without any thought of reward (Matt. 5:4–9; Luke 6:30–6). The poor themselves are blessed, for in the coming of the kingdom there will be sufficient for all (Luke 6:20–1). In the parable of the good Samaritan, Jesus was affirming that the Samaritan truly acted as God would act, taking care of the victims of unprovoked and naked aggression (Ps. 146:7–9; 68:5–6).

Preferential option for the poor means ultimately the option to proclaim and live out all that is involved in God's new order, in which new relationships of fairness and equality, grace and forgiveness, responsibility for the neighbour and love for the enemy, become a reality. God's work of transformation implies a total conversion. Gross inequality is ultimately a spiritual issue. If we understand the goal to be 'the dignity of each being guaranteed by the dignity of all', then human beings need to be liberated from the desire to dominate, the fear of loss and the pursuit of their own security and happiness, all of which lead to the creation of structures in which power is abused. Liberation is God's work; it cannot happen outside a thorough conversion to the living God, followed by a life of trust and open accountability.

4. Overcoming materialism

The present world economic order, often called 'late capitalism', is driven by the requirement that people with disposable income be committed consumers. If, for example, enough people were to exert a freedom of choice not to follow fashions or be tempted by the lure of the newest products, the system might well collapse. In the short term this would have devastating effects on employment and investment. In the long term, it might result in a widespread debate about what kind of society is best for humans to thrive in.[38]

A radical change in habits is unlikely. Human nature, deeply flawed according to the Gospel message, continues with ever-renewed vigour the irrational pursuit of 'cracked cisterns that can hold no water' (Jer. 2:13). In spite of all the hard evidence to the contrary, possessions do not bring an abiding sense of fulfilment and contentment. The notion that happiness is the outcome of purchasing products – be they material goods, leisure activities, drug-related experiences or alternative spiritualities – is one of the greatest illusions of our age.[39] In the first place, it is based on an inadequate understanding of what it means to be human. If we do not know who we are or what we are supposed to be, we do not know what is worth choosing – every option and action is equally meaningful and absurd.

In the second place, consumerism can create a deep sense of insecurity. The ideal 'good life' is based on an imaginary image. Advertising persuades us to reach out for this image. In so doing, we go through the emotions of comparing what we lack with what others possess. All that is being promoted, however, are the stereotypes of success: the criteria which enough people are prepared to accept. But the image is a façade, it is skin-deep, it is external gloss. Meanwhile, the breakdown of communities endangers people's ability to achieve human relationships of mutual sharing. The 'other' may easily be seen as yet another product which we have a right to possess. The maximisation of external objects leads to what Christopher Lasch has called 'the minimal self', the person who withdraws from others in order to become emotionally invulnerable.

Apart from the idolatry of the modern 'captivity of Mammon', the Christian has other reasons for overcoming materialism. True freedom is experienced not in independence but interdependence. One view of life says, 'I take (buy, possess), therefore I am'; another says, 'I respond, therefore I am'. Freedom derives from an attitude of joyous reception from others (fundamentally from God), and is lived as a gift, not a right. To be human is to recognise and freely choose to accept one's moral responsibilities to others, not out of self-interest or a cold sense of duty, but spontaneously from the knowledge that all life is the gift of a Giver so generous that he has given himself.

Indeed the generosity of uncalculated giving is true freedom, for it expresses a liberation from the bondage of selfishness and false values (2 Cor. 9:6), and it is also spiritually enriching for it manifests the grace of God in the life of the one who believes. The cost is the loss of our lives – indeed, we must have them crucified in order that the life lived from self to self can be lived from Christ to others.

Exercises

1. Examine the merits of the various economic and cultural arguments used for the existence of poverty.

2. Write a letter to the chief executive of a bank which has made extensive loans to poor nations, saying why they should be cancelled now.

3. Design a leaflet for a Christian aid-agency which wants to present God's justice for the poor as a central aspect of the Gospel.

7

Encounter with Religions of the World

Basic questions

Of all the topics encompassed by the study of mission none is more fundamental and controversial than the relation between Christian and non-Christian faiths. David Bosch says that 'it is the epitome of mission theology'.[1] Carl Braaten wonders whether the issues are not so crucial that the Churches are faced with a new *status confessionis*. He argues that the radical relativism of some theologians has gone so far as to threaten the very heart of the Gospel.[2]

In trying to give a careful and coherent theological account of the diversity of religious life, let us begin by asking what sort of questions need to be addressed.

The nature of religious belief

There are a cluster of questions to do with the subject of religion itself. Our first task is to be able to agree a common understanding of the broad phenomenon called religion, particularly bearing in mind that many languages do not possess a word to cover it. Some commentators believe that all expressions of religion contain a common essence, i.e. that they are all basically motivated by the same kind of needs and have similar goals.[3] If such a core could be extracted, then it would make sense to compare the different manifestations. If not, and if the beliefs, symbols and rituals of the major religions do appear to be widely divergent, such a comparison seems problematic.

A related set of questions has to do with explanations about the significance of religions. Are they the means by which people experience God (or god)?[4] Or are they ways in which human beings try to understand the deepest issues of life? Alternatively, are they (as many people have suspected since the Age of Reason) symptoms of deep human alienation: illusions to compensate for emotional immaturity or ideologies to justify discrimination, injustice or servile mediocrity?[5]

The nature of God

It seems impossible to make common assumptions about the make-up of the divine. Some religious traditions perceive God in personal terms; others in impersonal terms. In yet others there is no reality that transcends human existence. Even where there is a measure of agreement about the legitimacy of using personal language to speak about God, as in the Abrahamic faiths of Judaism, Christianity and Islam, there are substantially different ways of explaining God's chief attributes or describing how God is active in the universe. Thus, for example, these three faiths do not agree about the conditions for knowing or pleasing God, how one should understand God's mercy or justice or what God requires of human beings.

Jesus Christ among the religions

In most varieties of Christianity Jesus Christ is central to faith, thus a number of questions thus arise about how other beliefs and practices relate to him. Does Jesus fulfil all spiritual searchings? Or, in contrast, does he contradict and nullify other faiths? How do they view Jesus? And, to what extent are their views to be taken as ways of building bridges? In particular, what is the significance of other people's opinions regarding the cross and resurrection?

Alongside questions to do with Jesus Christ as a figure of history and the initiator of the Christian faith, there are others to do with salvation. Do other religions provide authentic ways of salvation for their adherents? Do they perceive salvation in terms similar to those of Christian faith? Or indeed are they interested in 'salvation' at all?[6]

Christianity among the religions

As a monotheistic religion proclaiming the existence of only one living God, Creator and Redeemer of all things, Christianity is bound to ask itself questions about the existence of other religions in the providence of God. Are they, perhaps, the result of the failure of God's people to witness faithfully to his revelation of himself? Or are they partial revelations of God? Or expressions of God's 'common grace' at work (cf. Acts 14:17)? Do they display a genuine searching after God (Acts 17:23, 27)? Or, negatively, are they the creations of minds at enmity with God (Rom. 1:28; 8:7)?

Closely related to these questions is the vexed dilemma caused by different claims to revelation. Most religions appeal to sacred Scriptures as the foundation for their beliefs and practices. These documents stand in a special relationship to truth as they understand it. The Qur'an, for example, is for Muslims God's final testament for the whole of humanity.[7] In it God does not so much reveal himself as declare his will in respect of all aspects of life. If for Christians Jesus Christ is the measure for assessing all claims about God, how does a Christian account for these other claims? Do they represent a valid, if partial, glimpse of the truth of God? Or do they simply reflect the best of human wisdom cast in the form of divine revelation?

For Panikkar the challenge confronting the Christian Church in the third millennium is to lose its concreteness as a particular religion among many in order to enable the realisation of 'a more universal Christianness . . . the name for humanness as Christians understand it' among all religions.[8] Is it possible, however, for Christianity to lose its particular standpoint without at the same time losing sight of what it means to be human 'as Christians understand it'?

For some, most notably Karl Barth, Christianity is only true to itself when it ceases to behave like a religion. In one of his most celebrated passages on the subject of religion, Barth states:

> Religion is unbelief. It is a concern, indeed, we must say it is the one great concern, of godless (humanity) . . . From the standpoint of revelation religion is clearly seen to be a human attempt to anticipate what God in his revelation wills to do

and does do. It is the attempted replacement of the divine work by a human manufacture.

Thinking, perhaps, of the betrayal (as he saw it) of Jesus Christ by many Christians under the onslaught of Nazism, he adds the decisive words, 'In our discussion of "religion as unbelief" we did not consider the distinction between Christian and non-Christian religion. Our intention was that whatever we said about the other religions affected the Christian similarly.'[9] Is such a decisive separation of revelation from religion either feasible or advisable? Is Christianity essentially different from all religions? Does it belong to another order of things, such that it makes no more sense to compare it with the world's religious traditions as it would to compare roses with sparrows, or an oak tree with a chocolate nut sundae?

Where is the starting line?

Finally there is the complicated issue of justifying a particular set of assumptions as giving the right focus for the whole debate. Paul Martinson perceptively observes that the greatest challenge to Christians is not so much the pluralism outside Christianity but the pluralism generated among Christians by the impact of religious claims.[10] The different convictions, which we will explore below, spring in large measure from what is considered in each case to be the most decisive departure-point.

Classically, most Christians have believed that they are not at liberty to accept any view that appears to contradict the clear meaning of the Bible: here is *the* conclusive point of reference for all discussion of interreligious matters. Others, however, disagree: for some, given the necessity to understand each faith from its own point of view, the starting-point has to be the core experience or vision of each religion; for others, the starting-point is the fact of plurality indicating God's presence in the world; for yet others, extending this principle, it is the requirement laid on all religions to live in harmony or to combine forces to confront secular unbelief. Those who have developed theological thinking along liberationist lines begin with concrete praxis – an option for the poor combined with a critical historical analysis and search for justice.

It is not obvious that these different starting-places exclude one another. Nevertheless, the weight given in each case to the 'facts' on which they are based has meant, in practice, that substantial divergences happen quickly. In assessing different conclusions about both the significance and validity of religious traditions and the mission of those who believe in Jesus Christ, it is crucial to keep in mind these distinct points of departure.

Christian faith and other faith traditions

Before considering three broad options that Christians take towards the world's religions, we need to review some preliminary matters which bear directly on the discussion and should help to illuminate it.

Sounding out religion

Only the foolhardy or the audacious would attempt to define religion: a definition given is either too precise to encompass all legitimate manifestations or too general to be a description of anything. The matter is complicated by the fact that many languages do not recognise the phenomenon by assigning it a particular word. Moreover, having a word for religion, which distinguishes it as one part of a people's culture, is itself the result of a specific history. 'Religion' has come to mean a view of life in opposition to the secular. On the one hand, modern critical analysis divides the world up into manageable components like work, play, leisure, family, business, politics, civic duties, scientific investigation and social organisation. Religion is classified as a separate entity and can be studied, it is assumed, as a separate discipline. Within this study there are further subdivisions – for example, the study of particular religions, belief, faith, ethical attitudes, popular religion, civic religion, and nationalism and religion. On the other hand, religion is defined in contrast to a world-view that denies any reality beyond the visible. It is therefore an option for those not satisfied with a naturalistic account of the world and human life. Under the pressure of logical positivism and a strictly empirical account of natural phenomenon, religion has been put on the defensive.

In English and other European languages the word 'religion' comes from Latin. The root meaning is 'to tie up', and came to refer to that which binds a person or community to the gods, to divine powers or powers beyond the human. Ninian Smart identifies six dimensions of religion: doctrinal, mythical (the foundation stories and their interpretation), ethical, ritual, experiential (or mystical) and the social.[11] Others suggest a different division of a religion's component parts: for example, a message, an experience related to the message, a community which is both an expression of the message and expresses it, and a lifestyle which seeks to put the message into practice.[12]

These attempts to look at religious life by using broad categories have the merit of recognising the extraordinary diversity of expressions of religion even within the same recognisable family. It is open to question, however, whether they do justice to the wide differences between the religions in their 'classical' or 'orthodox' forms – i.e. based on a 'doctrinal' tradition recognised to be authoritative and delimiting for a particular community – and in their 'popular', 'heterodox' forms. Not enough recognition has been given to the fact that, when practised at a 'popular' level, *all* religions tend to converge around primal world-views: beliefs in spirits which directly cause events to happen which either prosper or damage fortunes in this life and practices which are designed to make sure that these spirits are well-disposed.[13] Thus, in relation to all the major religions, there are beliefs and practices which mix some of those religions' core beliefs with various forms of magic.[14] The result might perhaps be called 'popular religiosity' or 'indigenous spirituality'. The interesting point is the broad similarity, irrespective of the formal religious allegiance. In contrast, at the level of 'orthodox' belief and practice the religions tend to diverge.

There is also the phenomenon of new religious movements (usually variations on one of the major world faiths), which forms a recognisably distinct body of belief and practice and which is expressed by an independent group or community of followers.[15] In the discussion of the meaning of religion or of dialogue between different faith traditions, these communities seem to be largely disregarded. Is it because of their 'heretical' character?

The Bible does not help much in the discussion of religion. The word 'religion' occurs six times in the New Testament (Acts 17:22; 25:9; 26:5; 1 Tim. 5:4; Jas. 1:26, 27). In the first case, the word is used by Paul of the Athenians' devotion to the gods. In the second and third cases it is used of the Jewish faith by Festus and by Paul, the context being Paul's examination before the Roman governor and King Agrippa. In the last three cases, the word is used of the practical outworking of faith in the caring for widows and orphans and in controlling the tongue. Three different words are used, reflecting a variety of meanings. It would be unwise, however, to make too many distinctions on the basis of linguistic variation.

The passage in James does distinguish between true and false religion on the basis of how faith is, or is not, put into practice. The same distinction might hold for the traditions and customs being imposed on the Christians in Colossae (Col. 2:16–23) – though here it is not so much the particular regulations that are condemned as the insistence that they be followed.

Religion and the secular
Although many writers on interreligious matters acknowledge the negative elements in the actual practice of religion, not many have responded to the specific secular critique of religion as such. They tend to jump too quickly to the negative consequences of a secular mind-set, such as ethical relativism, purposelessness, spiritual alienation, materialism and a self-absorbing individualism. However, I believe that the secular suspicion about religious motivations, and the consequent atheism that seemed to be a necessary protest, should be heard in their full force. They can be a purifying agent which forces religious people to reconsider the authenticity of their beliefs and practices:

> Much of what goes by the name of religion today is little more than the religious mirror-image of the consumer-society. Human beings are considered as a consuming species in which religious products (like 'spiritual peace', 'salvation', 'eternal life', 'healing') are announced and promoted like any other good or service ... Does one exaggerate too much in suggesting that most religion, most of the time, is like flowers

adorning the chains, or like resentment against life, or like the infant's need of parental protection from the harsh rigour of the real world? It condemns itself unless it is willing to let go of all false securities, all illusions and all defence mechanisms.[16]

Religion in the eyes of the beholder

Speaking very generally, people are either positively or negatively disposed towards religion. Some see religious beliefs and practices as a natural part of culture – so belonging to a religious group depends on where one happens to be born. By and large religions have evolved to meet the needs of the communities which practise them. Therefore, attempting to persuade people to change their religion does not make sense: it would be the equivalent of destroying their identity, making them into cultural and spiritual orphans.

From an optimistic interpretation of a Christian point of view, religions are an authentic expression of people's desire to move closer to God. They all, to a greater or lesser degree, reflect the light of Jesus Christ which illuminates everyone's journey towards truth. Religion should, therefore, be affirmed as a necessary and positive aspect of human life. Individual criticisms simply confirm the seriousness with which religions must be taken. It is impossible to be fully human without espousing religious convictions. Those who seek to live without religion are humanly diminished; they are functioning on reduced power.

Others, as we have indicated above, believe that on balance religions are harmful, for they enable people to live on the basis of a false (ideological) view of reality. In secular terms, this would be described as either the justification of privileged power, or compensation for inferior power. In Christian terms, it would be described as either the justification of human-constructed laws and regulations to avoid the radical demands of God, or as compensation for a deep sense of unworthiness.

Religions and revelation

Various positions are taken on the revealing presence of God in religious beliefs. Those Christians who tend to take a negative attitude judge that other religions are too ambiguous to identify God's presence in them unquestionably. In fact, some would say that there are no good grounds for allowing other religions a privileged position as channels of God's will and life. In so far as they manifest elements of truth, goodness and beauty they are touching the reality of God from whom comes 'every good and perfect gift' (Jas. 1:17; 3:17).

However, it may be more accurate to speak of God's action in the lives of all people, whether or not they identify formally with religious beliefs. Sometimes they will dimly reflect God's nature by serving their neighbour, showing mercy, being peacebuilders and forgiving those who have caused them harm. Sometimes these characteristics will be displayed because of religious convictions; sometimes in spite of them. The verdict of history may, on balance, be against those who believe that people of religious faith understand and serve God better than those who make no such claim. Religions have so often caused people to live in the bondage of fear, fatalism, fanaticism, superstition and authoritarianism that to link them too closely with God may be unwise.

Those Christians who take a generally positive attitude towards other religions are convinced that people of other faiths are in touch with God – at the level of spiritual practices like *bhakti yoga* in Hinduism[17] or in the practice of ethical values like respect for nature, non-violence, tolerance and compassion taught by Buddhism. God's transforming life, they say, is clearly at work through practices in which God's will is being done, God's reign being brought about. This is sometimes expressed in terms of Christ, the Logos, finding expression in different forms:

> If Jesus is a treasure-in-vessel – even if he is the most important one – there is nothing that prevents us from assuming a plurality of vessels, for the treasure is not confined to Jesus alone . . . Jesus surely is unique. But Logos became incarnate in such traditions as Buddhism.[18]

Traditionally Christians have made a distinction between God's special and common revelations. The vehicle of the first is the word of the biblical prophet and apostle, and the person of Jesus Christ. The vehicle of the second is human conscience and the natural world. God is the author of both. They differ in content. Both mediate knowledge of God: the first in the most complete form, the second in a more diffuse way. Common revelation gives evidence of the reality of God and the reality of ethical norms of right and wrong. Human beings can, therefore, have an understanding of the world as God has created it and of themselves created in God's image. Knowledge of the way of salvation, however, only comes through special revelation. These are the main points, it is argued, that Paul is making at the beginning of his exposition of the meaning of the gospel – which is the revelation of God's righteousness 'through faith for faith' (Rom. 1—2).

In this understanding, religious traditions are responses to God's common revelation. They exhibit knowledge of God (Rom. 1:21), the practice of good (Rom. 2:10) and a search for truth, glory and honour (Rom. 2:7–10). At the same time, the knowledge is partial, confused and often corrupted by false ideas. It is not sufficient for salvation, for the more it displays God and God's requirements for life, the more it shows the inadequacies of merely human responses (Rom. 2:12, 15; 3:9–20).

Here we have seen a number of ways of interpretating the claim that God is at work in religious practices when they are undertaken out of a desire to follow the path of truth and goodness.

Questions of salvation

In discussing the relationship of Christian and non-Christian faiths it has been customary in recent years to distinguish three principal views: *exclusivism, inclusivism* and *pluralism*. Such a division is not wholly satisfactory since each includes elements of the others. As long as one is aware that the classification outlines three patterns of belief, each of which has its own variations, and that the boundaries between them are not always clearly drawn, then the three categories are useful in pointing out real, decisive differences of opinion.

There is a problem, however, in the words used for each group: 'exclusivism' gives an immediate impression of narrow-mindedness, even bigotry; 'pluralism' conjures up the image of relativism, even a lack of concern; 'inclusivism', however, appears to emphasise open-mindedness and tolerance – it is preferable to include than exclude, to be generous without being totally permissive. I propose, therefore, to experiment with three other headings – *particularity*, *generality* and *universality* – which represent the same positions, but which do not suffer from immediately negative connotations.

Particularity

Particularity is the belief that God's gift of salvation is available only through the atoning death of the historical person, Jesus of Nazareth, and is appropriated through explicit faith in Jesus and ratified by baptism and membership of the Christian community. There may be some difference among people who hold this view as to the means by which people come to faith. For most, faith must come through hearing the word of the Gospel (Rom. 10:17); but for some it may come through the less normal means of visions or dreams.

The assumptions behind this position are that God alone is the author of salvation, that salvation cannot be achieved by any kind of human merit, that God has provided only one way of salvation and that there must be a conscious response to the offer. Given the fact that human beings are naturally estranged from God, not to say yes to him implies saying no. Conversion – a turning from other objects of trust to the living God, who has sent Jesus to make salvation possible – is indispensable:

> Conversion involves commitment to a particular Person. On this follows self-dedication to a particular manner of life, in which every detail must be organised in relation to the central loyalty. Such a life can be lived fully only within a community in which every member is ideally inspired by equal loyalty to the divine Head.[19]

Generality

This position also affirms that salvation is available exclusively through Jesus Christ. However, it makes the means of appropriating salvation more general than the previous one. Whereas the best means may be through hearing the good news and responding affirmatively, there may be good reasons why this is not possible. For example, most people will never hear the Gospel in their own language during their lifetime. Even if they do, they may hear it in such a way that the message is obscured, either by the presentation or by the life of the messenger. It could be said, then, that millions of people will never have an adequate opportunity to respond to the offer of salvation in Christ.

According to this view, where people respond to the spiritual illumination they have, seeking in their religious practices God's mercy and forgiveness and attempting to live out a life of peace, reconciliation and justice, God's salvation in Christ is available to them. Or, to put the matter the other way round, those who do these things already demonstrate God's salvific grace at work in their lives:

> The universality of salvation means that it is granted not only to those who explicitly believe in Christ and have entered the church . . . Many people do not have an opportunity to come to know or accept the Gospel revelation or enter the church . . . For such people, salvation in Christ is accessible by virtue of a grace which, while having a mysterious relationship to the church, does not make them formally part of the church, but enlightens them in a way which is accommodated to their spiritual and material situation. This grace comes from Christ; it is the result of his sacrifice and is communicated by the Holy Spirit. It enables each person to attain salvation through his or her free cooperation.[20]

Universality

The major difference between this view and the other two resides in the little phrases 'one and only' and 'only one'. For the first two positions, Jesus Christ is the one and only Saviour, though opinions differ about how his salvation may be received. For the universalist, Jesus Christ is only one means of salvation among many others. God has devised not only different ways of attaining salvation through Christ, but a variety of ways of reaching him. Jesus Christ is one path among others. There has been a shift from a Christ-centred to a God-centred understanding of salvation.

God's salvation is universally available through many different channels: 'We have as much reason to think that the other great world religions are true and salvific as to think this of Christianity.'[21]

Questions about assumptions

These three convictions follow from certain basic premises which appear to be incompatible with one other. Particularists maintain that their position is the only possible way of interpreting the New Testament. The message is clear that, without the regenerating work of the Spirit of Christ, a person remains spiritually dead to God (Eph. 2:1–3; Col. 2:13), still a member of the kingdom of darkness (Col. 1:13; Acts 26:18), preferring darkness to light (John 3:19–20), at enmity with God (Rom. 5:10; Col. 1:21), still subject to a sinful nature and therefore unable to please God (Rom. 8:5–8; Gal. 5:19–21; Rom. 6:21; Gal. 5:24). This interpretation does not come from quoting a few verses scattered throughout the different books of the New Testament, but is (claim its adherents) the settled and unanimous stance of the Gospel. Before a person can live in a way which pleases God, he or she needs to go through a process of death and resurrection in union with Jesus Christ. This process is initiated by repentance and faith – a conscious renunciation of a self-centred life and a turning to God for forgiveness and new life.

   Particularists affirm that, as a matter of observation and analysis, whatever other religions may offer to their followers it is not salvation from sin understood as personal alienation from a personal God. Generalists are mistaken in believing that people following other religious traditions are likely to turn to the God of Jesus Christ, even in other acceptable ways outside conscious faith. Their culture and religious practice has conditioned them to a profoundly different view of the human predicament and its solution. They neither believe in sin as rebellion against God nor do they know of the possibility of forgiveness as a free gift offered on the basis that God himself has borne the just punishment for their offences. Their own religious beliefs have to be 'disbelieved' before they can experience God's salvation:

Contrary to much of the teaching we have reviewed, we have to insist that religion is *not* the means of salvation. The message of Jesus, of the unique incarnate Lord crucified by the powers of law, morals and piety and raised to the throne of cosmic authority, confronts the claim of every religion with a radical negation.[22]

Generalists would agree with much of the foregoing argument, but would insist that there is sufficient evidence in the Scriptures to suggest that there is more than one way of coming to God through Christ. The position of many people outside explicit faith in Christ may be likened to the Old Testament believers, whose faith (without knowledge of Christ) is highly commended (Rom. 4:9ff.; Heb. 11:4ff.). They received the limited, but nevertheless true, revelation that came to them. Cornelius stands for all God-fearing people who, because they pray to God regularly and give generously to those in need, are accepted by him (Acts 10:2–4, 34–5). Those who receive the messengers of the Gospel openly and generously, who attend to the needs of the weak and vulnerable, have, in one sense, recognised Christ in them; they will receive their reward (Matt. 10:40–2; 25:34–40). Not everyone loves darkness rather than light; there are those who live by the truth and who, as a result, receive more light for their path (John 3:21).

There will be many surprises: because God wills the salvation of all (1 Tim. 2:4), he will find as many ways as possible to bring them to himself. If God's grace is given in Christ before the *historical* coming of Christ (2 Tim. 1:9), should it not also be given in Christ before the *geographical* coming of Christ?[23] This view, common within the Roman Catholic and Orthodox Churches and among many Protestants, has given rise to the term 'anonymous Christians'. They are anonymous in the sense that, although they are united to Christ by his grace, this reality is hidden from them for they have not heard the name of Christ.[24]

Universalists make no particular appeal to Scripture, except perhaps for a reference to God's covenant with nations beyond Israel (Amos 9:7; Isa. 19:24–5), to the presence of true salvation and worship outside Israel (Isa. 19:19–22; Mal. 1:11) and to the absence of any concrete condemnation of other religions as such.[25]

This is not surprising given the assumption that the Scripture of each religion reveals God in different, complementary ways. There is no need to appeal to the Christian Scriptures, for they are meant primarily for Christians.

Universalists start elsewhere. John Hick, for example, believes that human behaviour, enjoined and inspired by other religions and equivalent to that demanded by the Christian view of God's rule of righteousness, is all the evidence required to show that these religions are true and salvific. There are no empirical grounds for believing that Christian faith produces people more just, loving, merciful or holy than other faith traditions.[26]

The core conviction of all *universalists* is that, behind different ways of conceiving God and a variety of visible expressions of religious phenomena, lies the same reality. They make the assumption that language is always tentative, fallible, contingent and generally an inadequate vehicle for expressing something as profound and mysterious as absolute transcendent reality. The core experience of every faith points hesitatingly to the same ultimate object. None can claim a superior understanding or be the norm for measuring the adequacy of any of the others. They will all equally find their fulfilment in God's final act of salvation to which they are pointing. It is idolatrous to pretend that God can be contained sufficiently in one set of symbols:

> As responses to the Mystery, the religions relate to each other within the Mystery and within our shared yet distinctly realized humanity, and within the complexity of our common history. To ignore the richness and promise of this diversity or to seek to reduce the religions to their least common denominator, or to judge one by the criterion of another would be great impoverishment, an act of aggression and a methodological mistake.[27]

Examining the responses

If these are, in broad outline, the major ways in which Christians conceive of other faiths and the assumptions on which their views are based, how should we evaluate them?[28] I would identify four areas that need to be thoroughly probed: the place of Scripture; questions about Jesus Christ; the issue of truth; and the matter of mission. It goes without saying, in my opinion, that in engaging in this task we should be careful

(a) to represent other people's views fairly, especially if we disagree sharply with them;[29]

(b) not to use *ad hominem* arguments, i.e. arguments based on the discrediting of some aspect of an opponent's characteristics, thereby refusing to listen to the arguments themselves.[30]

The place of Scripture

Where Christians give little or no special status to the Bible as the primary *locus* of God's self-revelation or do not find the language of foundation, norm, standard or rule acceptable or particularly helpful in deciding on Christian belief, there is little point in discussing the niceties of interpretation or hermeneutical methods. All one can ask them to do is to refrain from quoting Scripture at all, for that would appear to be a rather meaningless exercise. Understandably some people would want to hold that the usual way of interpreting Scripture requires the kind of mind that 'is alien to most Asian mentalities', or that the meaning of Christ is distorted if one confines him to the Christological expressions of the New Testament.[31] Then the debate is not about legitimate interpretations of the text, but about how one maintains a Christian identity having apparently abandoned the 'apostolic' witness to Jesus Christ.

For those who wish to take Scripture seriously as a definitive source for deciding what Christians believe or do not believe, even if they wish to engage in a radical rethink of the traditional interpretations, then two further presuppositions should be accepted:

1. The text must not be quoted selectively (not the same as saying that it should not be quoted at all!). It is inappropriate, surely, to refer to a medley of verses and passages which are divorced from their position in the text, because they seem to support particular ideas held on grounds other than that of the biblical message. It is even more lacking in credibility if at the same

time other verses and passages, which appear to say something quite contradictory to the ideas held, are ignored.

Selective quotation is, unfortunately, a habit which people of all persuasions tend to indulge in. On the one hand, particularists quite enthusiastically quote certain verses as if, on their own, they settled quite complex disputes – texts like John 14:6 and Acts 4:12; on the other hand, universalists do exactly the same with other texts – Matt. 25:31ff., Luke 4:18; 10:37. There can be no justification for such a practice, nor for the assertion of some parts of Scripture against others. Whenever Scripture is used to bolster previously held beliefs by people who have no intention of allowing Scripture to change those beliefs, the text is being violated and abused as a means to some other end.

2. When the text is quoted with a view to confirming a position it must be done according to normal rules of interpretation. Trying to make Scripture say what patently it never meant to say in the first place and has never been understood to say since is also to desecrate its integrity. In other words, verses like Acts 4:12 and passages like Matt. 25:31ff. have to be understood within both an immediate and wider context. They may not be explained away. Thus, *prima facie*, an interpretation of the words, 'There is salvation in no one else, for there is no other name under heaven given among mortals by which we must be saved', which refers it exclusively to Jews[32] or which restricts the scope of salvation in the context to healing,[33] must be suspect because they are quite plainly attempts to soften an otherwise absolute statement. Genuine interpretation faces the difficult and unpalatable verses head-on.

Though everyone may be guilty to some degree of selective quoting or question-begging exegesis, generalists and universalists are more prone to it. One quite generalised practice involves taking an isolated verse from a passage and using it in a way which the rest of the context would not allow. An example of this is Colossians 1:20: 'Through him God was pleased to reconcile to himself all things, whether on earth or in heaven, by making peace through the blood of his cross'. This is taken by some generalists to validate the belief that at the end of time all will be reconciled to God, whatever their present relationship to him may be, and that this will happen through Christ. However, the following verses (Col. 1:21—2:7) make clear that the reconciliation refers to those who have heard the Gospel (Col. 1:23), who have received Christ (Col. 2:6), who belong to Christ's body the Church (Col. 1:24) and who continue steadfast in the faith (Col. 1:23) until they reach maturity in Christ (Col. 1:28). It is not speaking about anyone else. From this practice a general principle can be deduced: the more one has to resort to dubious interpretation, the weaker is one's position, always granted that the apostolic Gospel is the indispensable bench-mark for identifying valid Christian beliefs.

Questions about Jesus

The most disputed of all issues to do with the Christian encounter with people of other faith traditions centres on the uniqueness and universality of Jesus Christ. There is a clear and sharp dividing line between those who say that Jesus Christ, as he is presented in the New Testament, is the one and only Saviour and Lord of all people, irrespective of their religious affiliation or their agnosticism, and those who say that unconditional and unlimited claims for Christ have to be reinterpreted. This is the substance of the debate in the volume, *The Uniqueness of Jesus*: most of the significant arguments about Christ and the religions are well set out in the various essays, and most of the well-known protagonists share their views, so a summary of the book's main points will cover most of the ground.

Paul Knitter, generally known as a universalist, has set out and explained a number of theses concerning Christ's uniqueness as he would like to advocate it. He believes that the meaning of uniqueness when applied to Christ *can* and *must* be reinterpreted. It can be reinterpreted because, even in the New Testament, there is a wide variety of Christologies. It must be reinterpreted because the traditional understandings of uniqueness do not lead to productive dialogue and harmonious relations with people of other faiths. He is convinced that dialogue is 'hamstrung from the start if one of the partners insists that he or she has the God-given full, final, and unsurpassable vision of truth'.[34]

Uniqueness is then explained in terms of Christ being a true and decisive revelation of God, but not a full, definitive, unsurpassable or only revelation. The view expressed here is familiar: all that we can learn about God and salvation through Christ is true, but it does not exclude the complementary truths found through other religious traditions. Jesus Christ is indispensable, but then so are the core beliefs of the other faiths: 'The uniqueness of Jesus contains Christianity's essential and distinctive contribution to the inter-religious dialogue.'[35]

At the end of the debate, Knitter expresses his preference for the adjective 'correlational' rather than 'pluralistic', 'to describe the kind of dialogue or theology of religions that many Christians are searching for'.[36] This does not mean, he claims, that Christians have to abandon their commitment to Jesus as divine Saviour. But, in his estimation, real dialogue becomes problematic when Christians make Jesus into the final norm for judging all other truth-claims. He is advocating the distinction made by Kajsa Ahlstrand between 'subordinating inclusivism', 'which means that other traditions are seen as less perfect forms of my own tradition', and 'egalitarian inclusivism', 'which means that I may interpret other traditions through categories and images in my own tradition but also accept having my own tradition interpreted in the same way by believers from traditions other than my own'.[37]

In the course of the discussion a number of important points are made. Ahlstrand believes that 'the claim that Jesus is unique is not necessarily a significant theological statement', for in one sense everyone is unique. She prefers to speak about the special significance of Jesus. She does not wish to smooth out the contradictions between traditions. Panikkar thinks that the uniqueness of Jesus only becomes a problem in interreligious dialogue when it is linked to the universalising of particularity: 'Either we defend the universality of Christ above, behind, or through all cultures, or we bestow universal and absolute value to one single culture or group of cultures, namely, that doctrinal world for which the statement makes sense.'[38] Kenneth Cragg thinks that unique should be understood to mean 'wholly', 'entirely', 'completely', in the sense that 'if God is revealing, then God is revealed'.[39]

Those who maintain that Christians cannot any longer pretend that Jesus Christ is God's final and definitive means of salvation base their arguments on two assumptions:

- The empirical observation that any kind of exclusive claim will frustrate a genuine exchange between people of different religions;
- The view that, as a matter of fact, exclusive claims do not lead necessarily to lives of higher quality.

There is the additional philosophical conviction that all human descriptions (especially of divine realities) are inevitably partial and open to correction. Therefore Christian claims for Jesus Christ must allow new insights and fresh revelations to aid our understanding of his significance for all peoples.

These (generally universalist) views do not go unchallenged in the book. The major complaint is that all the attempts at reinterpreting Jesus Christ end up in reductionisms. The content of Jesus is diminished and impoverished. Thus Michael Amaladoss states that, 'If Jesus is reduced simply to one way that mediates the saving presence of God to some people, then he is not the redeemer Christians are talking about.' The problem with these Christologies, according to Amaladoss, is that they 'reduce the role of Jesus to mediating God's presence, communicating God-experience, or revealing the truth about God'. The Christian understanding of redemption is much more.[40] Denise and John Carmody believe that the reinterpretation of Jesus' uniqueness to mean *truly* but not *only* does violence to Christian faith. Unless one is going to scrap the traditional Christian convictions about the full divinity of Christ within monotheism, then no salvation occurs apart from Jesus.[41] Clark Pinnock believes that Knitter has transformed Jesus into 'a unique saint for the world rather than the only saviour of it'.[42]

As we have already suggested, there is a widespread disagreement about the epistemological status of the various starting-points. On the question of dialogue, the conviction that a true meeting of hearts and minds can only take place on universalist assumptions can be challenged by counter evidence. Certainly in Christian–Muslim dialogue, in my experience, Muslims would no more expect Christians to find ways of making acceptable their confession of the trinitarian nature of God or the sonship of Christ than they themselves would redefine *tawhid* (the unity of the one God) to include plurality in the Godhead, or the Qur'an as the 'seal of the prophets' to allow for the New Testament confession of Jesus Christ. Experience proves that dialogue can remain fruitful and enriching, even when (especially when?) both sides come with incompatible beliefs.

The real lines of battle between the universalists and all other Christians are drawn up on the two fundamental issues of the right handling of the New Testament and the question of truth. Even John Hick recognises that 'If Jesus was God the Son, Second Person of a divine Trinity, incarnate, then Christianity is the only religion to have been founded by God in person and must be superior to all others.'[43] Leaving aside the emotive word, 'superior', those who wish to resist this conclusion are obliged to adopt one of two strategies: either to show that the high Christology of the fourth century creeds is an unnecessary and unfortunate development not demanded by the New Testament witness to Christ,[44] or to suggest that the New Testament can no longer determine what can and ought to be said about the Christ. Both procedures have been adopted.[45]

It is easier to discuss the first alternative than the second. If one believes that there are other sources of valid knowledge of Christ outside the original apostolic testimony, then there is little common ground for a fruitful conversation. One can only ask that the grounds for such knowledge be clearly spelt out and justified. The conversation would have to begin at that point. The first alternative should be a matter of historical and exegetical investigation. Even though Christians are not necessarily committed to defending the language of the creeds,[46] it is hard not to interpret the Christological language of the New Testament as implying an extremely exalted view of Jesus Christ.

Most attention has been focused on John's Gospel, and particularly the Prologue (John 1:1–18). If the author was Jewish (a plausible assumption), he makes astonishing claims: 'the Word was God' (John 1:1); 'all things came into being through him' (John 1:3); 'in him was life' (John 1:4); 'the true light was coming into the world' (John 1:9); 'grace and truth came through Jesus Christ'

(John 1:17); 'No one has ever seen God. It is God the only Son . . . who has made him known' (John 1:18). These claims are born out in all sorts of direct and subtle ways in the rest of the gospel. The writer's intention throughout the gospel is to convince the readers that Jesus is the Messiah and he is the Messiah in this particular way (John 20:30–1).[47]

If this was the main testimony in the New Testament to an exalted Christology, one might perhaps say that it represents a marginal tradition. However there many others; two of them at least seem to have anticipated the contemporary Christological debate in a pluralist context – the letters to the Colossians and to the Hebrews.[48] Both speak about Christ against the background of attempts to reinterpret him in ways that harmonise with other religious convictions. It is difficult to identify precisely the kind of teaching which Colossians is addressing, though it appears to be an amalgam of speculative ideas about the planets (Col. 2:20), ascetic practices related to Judaism (Col. 2:16) and dualistic notions of salvation. The author counters it on the basis that it is speculative, not based on the true revelation of God in Jesus Christ but on human wisdom and traditions (Col. 2:8, 18). He denies that people are naturally open to the spiritual world. God's presence is closed to them because 'they were dead in trespasses' (Col. 2:13), guilty of breaking God's moral law and subject to enslaving spiritual powers (Col. 2:15–23).

The basic conflict between Christian faith and the religious systems of the ancient world, as reflected in Colossians, centred on true knowledge of God. The philosophers speculated about the nature of reality and how human beings should come to terms with it. Christian faith starts from the history of one human person. Precisely in this one person (to echo Kenneth Cragg's understanding of 'unique') the completeness of God is publicly manifest: 'He is the [visible] image of the invisible God . . . In him all the fullness of God was pleased to dwell . . . In [him] are hidden all the treasures of wisdom and knowledge . . . In him the whole fullness of deity dwells bodily' (Col. 1:15, 19; 2:3, 9).

The claim is that all which can be known about God is explicitly or implicitly contained in Jesus Christ. It is a response to an incipient gnosticism which started from the same kind of assumption as is often advanced today, namely that God cannot be contained in particular expressions. The gnostics believed that the real divine being could only be reached through a series of mediators (perhaps the angels of Col. 2:18), ranks of lesser beings of whom Jesus would rank as one. Among universalists the ultimate reality is beyond all partial manifestations. To claim otherwise is to be guilty of idolatry,[49] possibly even blasphemy.[50] The point at issue, however, is the remarkable parallel between the beliefs being combated in Colossae and those being advanced by Paul Knitter and others:

> In the Christian tradition a shift of emphasis gradually occurred from the God of salvation history (*oikonomia*) to the abstract being of God in Godself (*theologia*) . . . The 'correct' understanding of the divine nature continued to be derived from metaphysics and the biblical revelation made to conform to it. Hence, instead of allowing the biblical message to critique the prevailing plausibility structure, the God beyond God was allowed to stand, which led to the Hellenization of the gospel.[51]

It might be said that here we are dealing with two incompatible approaches, not only to the New Testament but to the concept of truth. The universalist theology of religion does not so much represent an alternative interpretation of Christian faith as a wholly distinct religious system. However, even the notion of 'alternative', 'incompatible' and 'opposite' is itself disputed. We must conclude, therefore, with a brief discussion of the different views of truth which ultimately, I believe, undergird the whole debate.

The issue of truth[52]

This is not the place to enter into a general discussion of the concept of truth; we can only touch here the dispute about the distinction between appearance and reality, which first appeared in philosophical debate (in the West) in the writings of Immanuel Kant. Kant believed that it was useless trying to know 'things-in-themselves' (that is, as God knows them) fully and exhaustively. All our knowledge of reality is filtered through our senses and through our perspectives. Hence any claim to an

absolute knowledge is only an ideal projection; it does not corre-
spond to any actual or even possible knowledge. We can have
partial knowledge of *phenomena* – that is, objects as they impinge
on us through our senses. But our knowledge is always contingent,
open to doubt, criticism and modification. Absolute, undoubted
knowledge belongs to *noumena* – objects of pure thought which
are inaccessible to us.[53]

Kant's view has had an immense influence on all subsequent
thought. Designed to combat the scepticism which arises from the
inability of reason alone to provide an assured access to objective
reality, it ends in the relativisation of all knowledge. More impor-
tantly, in the context of a theology of religion, it drives a wedge
between objective and subjective truth: 'No longer is truth outside
of us, something we discover and receive and submit to; it is
something inside us, private, subjective. No longer does it shape
us; we shape it.'[54]

This epistemological revolution has led to a number of consequences: an enormous weight is put on the function of experience;
a division is created between the methods of discovering the
natural and the supranatural worlds; a separation is made between
reason and faith; and the importance of historical evidence for
what we believe is weakened. Thus in the matter of the resurrection
(to give one example), a fundamental reinterpretation takes place
which profoundly alters the Christian faith's credal belief:

> If we say 'Jesus rose from the dead', we are not making a
> statement about a physical event in the ordinary world at
> a specific point in history; we are stating a higher truth, some-
> thing theologically true that has no relationship to history, fact
> or physics.[55]

All of this has challenged the basis on which the Christian faith
has been based hitherto – namely the faithful apprehension of the
truth that God has communicated reliably through Jesus Christ
and his apostles. The New Testament as the divinely inspired
interpretation of 'God's mighty acts' in a specific locality can now
be viewed only as the (sometimes) 'inspired' insights of exceptional
people on the basis of an overwhelming encounter with a remark-

able spiritual teacher. The 'insights' are paralleled in other religious traditions.

It would be ridiculous of me to try to resolve such a fundamental difference of outlook at this juncture. For our purposes, it is important to realise why there is such an immense divide between those who hold to the basic tenets of historical Christianity and those who wish to interpret the whole body of belief in a totally new direction. It rests on two radically different epistemological traditions – the 'idealist' and the 'realist'.[56] If there is to be any resolution of the differences, this is where we have to begin. Inter-religious dialogue may be much easier than inter-Christian dialogue.

Exercises

1. Find out the views of one or more people from another faith tradition about secular society. Compare them with your own.

2. Discuss the relevance of one of the follow passages to the subject of religion: Acts 10; Acts 17:16–34; Rom. 2:6–16.

3. Outline what you would say to a follower of Hinduism or Islam about why you believe Jesus Christ is unique.

8

Overcoming Violence and Building Peace

Preliminary remarks

Curiously, the subject of this chapter is rarely, if ever, mentioned in any of the major works on mission.[1] Peace is often coupled with justice, but then largely ignored, and reconciliation (the over-coming of violence) is usually associated with Christ's atonement. This does not mean that Christians have disregarded the challenge of pursuing peace in the context of actual or threatened conflict at local, regional and international levels. Indeed, in recent years, Christians have been actively engaged in finding ways of ending fighting and other forms of strife in many of the trouble spots of the world (e.g. El Salvador, Bosnia, Rwanda, Sudan, Somalia, Sri Lanka, East Timor). However, this has not usually been related to the mission calling of the Church.

There may be reasons for this omission. Justice, as the major political and social objective in situations of hostility and warfare, has been the overriding concern of Christians. It has been fashion-able to interpret the main cause of inter- and intra-state conflicts as the abuse of people's rights by ruthless political groups. Such an explanation implies that violence can only be terminated once the justice of people's grievances has been recognised and addressed. It is almost a truism of political ethics to assert that any cessation of hostilities which does not bring about a more just situation is not worthwhile. Unless peace is built upon the righting of social and economic wrongs, it is quite simply an illusion.

This approach to overcoming violence is based on the assump-tion that conflict is fundamentally the result of an animosity engendered by a strong sense of injustice, discrimination and the frustrating of legitimate aspirations. This is true in many cases, but it is not the whole truth. The causes of conflict are multiple: it may, for example, be equally due to the unrelenting pressure of fear (real or imagined) which one community has about the intentions of another. Likewise, it may arise from the seemingly universal human desire to exact retribution or wreak vengeance for bloodshed or for the experience of military humiliation, cultural degradation or personal shame. Finally, conflict may be the outcome of a very primitive urge to dominate others or to expand one's influence and power.[2]

Given the diversity of causes, it would also be true to say that peace is a prerequisite for justice. It is possible to conceive of situations where the roots of injustice have largely been tackled, but where, as a direct result, conflict has intensified. Justice (of a sort) may be achieved by using means so brutal that continuing violence appears to be the only way of ensuring that the gains are not lost. This has been the reality of many so-called revolutions, where power has been seized on behalf of the dispossessed and downtrodden. In circumstances where violence is still actual or latent in society, to talk of bringing about justice is empty and worthless.

An integral part of mission

There should be no need to justify the Christian's role in overcoming violence and building peace as an indispensable aspect of his or her calling to mission. Already in chapter 3 we have referred to the direct political implications of Jesus' refusal to use violence as a mission strategy. We talked also of the rejection of violence, the practice of non-violent policies, the refusal to be drawn into accepting images of 'the enemy' and the rejection of retaliation as both consistent with mission in the way of Christ and as the most assured means of bringing about real change.[3]

In chapter 4, we emphasised that peace through the genuine reconciliation of hostile parties is a fundamental aspect of the good news of Jesus and the kingdom. Jesus' own ministry, culminating in his death by crucifixion, is based on the reality that broken relationships entail deep distress and cost a lot of pain to restore. The gospel of peace is a message of costly reconciliation in which the injuries caused by alienation are mended. Evangelism is incomplete unless it addresses the problem of violence and points to Jesus' sacrifice as the means of recovering harmonious relationships.

Chapters 5 and 7 reminded us that the causes and intransigent nature of violence may have deep cultural and religious roots, and that peace may be understood rather differently according to cultural variants and religious convictions. In chapter 6, we mentioned the danger of false theologies of peace elaborated by deceiving prophets who sold to the highest bidder their spurious theories about an indulgent God who did not really care about injustice. In chapter 9 we will use the language of peace to speak about the right association between human beings and the natural environment. And in chapter 10, the theme of worldwide partnership in mission assumes the ability to work through frictions and contentious issues to reach consent and concord.

In all these ways, and many more, overcoming violence and building peace is an indispensable part of Christian mission. It is pleasing to see that many parts of the Church are now recognising that this calling is essential to sharing and living the Gospel. We will attempt to think through some of the missiological implications of a difficult, often complex and sometimes dangerous task.

Aims and objectives

In general terms it is quite clear that Christians aim to follow in the way of Jesus Christ in a ministry of building conditions of reconciliation and peace. The disciple is blessed in so far as he or she engages in making peace (Matt. 5:9). Those who wish to follow Jesus are challenged to exceed conventional ethical standards, whether those practised by Jewish religious leaders or by the Gentiles (Matt. 5:20; 5:47). This entails the renunciation of the normal human reaction to intentional injury (Matt. 5:40ff.) and to the concept of enemies (Matt. 5:43ff.). Peacemaking is linked to non-retaliation, to a carefree generosity and to love for the enemy by the promise that those who demonstrate such a lifestyle will show themselves to be genuine children of God (Matt. 5:9; 5:45). Despite what human wisdom might believe, the Father in heaven cares equally for those with whom we identify and those whom we find objectionable (Matt. 5:45). The child proves the relationship with his or her parent by doing as the parent does (Matt. 5:48).

With regard to overcoming violence and building peace, mission in the way of Christ is quite explicit.[4] Peace is the fruit of breaking the spiral of retaliation and vengeance – of 'An eye for an eye and a tooth for a tooth' – it is the result of refusing to join this logic of reciprocity. This ethic of repudiation seems to have been standard practice for the first Christians:

> Do not repay anyone evil for evil . . . If it is possible, in so far as it depends on you, live peaceably with all . . . Never avenge yourselves, but leave room for the wrath of God . . . No, if your enemies are hungry, feed them; if they are thirsty, give them something to drink . . . Do not be overcome by evil, but overcome evil with good (Rom. 12:17–21).

However, the apparent unambiguity of these verses is not obvious to all. Down the ages most Christians have tended to interpret this teaching as an ideal which may be applicable in some circumstances but cannot be consistently carried out. In particular, the ethic of non-retaliation has been understood at most to refer to personal injuries suffered. If anyone attacks me personally I am enjoined not to strike back. However, it does not apply to my responsibility to use force to defend a third party against unprovoked aggression. In other words, I may not 'turn the other cheek' on behalf of someone else. Such a stance, if consistently carried through, would promote injustice in that evil people determined to carry through their plans by violent means would go unpunished. To refuse to restrain the violent would be an affront to moral sensibility. It would demonstrate a very naive attitude to the nature and extent of evil in the world.[5]

Given divergent understandings about the meaning of overcoming violence and building peace in the way of Christ, Christians aim to discover what it means in practice to live under the authority of Jesus Christ. A first step is to sort out in their own mind the relative strengths and weaknesses of the pacifist and non-pacifist positions. Otherwise they are likely to be swayed by arguments or circumstances that have not been submitted to the mind of Christ – e.g. secular views of justice, natural passions or spurious nationalisms. Although we cannot begin to do justice to the many complexities of the issues, we will try to give a brief summary of the main claims made in the debate before looking at the chief matters of contention. This will lead to a discussion of how Christians may fulfil their mission calling to overcome violence and build peace.

Approaches to the use of violence

It is generally agreed that Christians did not participate in military operations of any kind for at least the first 200 years of the Church's existence.[6] Some time after that period we learn of Christians enrolled in the armed forces of the Roman empire. Subsequent to the official recognition of the Christian faith by Constantine, the legitimacy of Christians' participation in war was recognised theologically in the development of the theory of the 'just war'.

There are divergent interpretations of this early period of the Church's history. Some historians believe that non-participation in the military was simply the consistent outworking of Christian discipleship which demanded the repudiation of all recourse to force. Others believe that the main objection to service in the army was the taking of an oath to the emperor – both the nature of the oath and the taking of oaths as such were objectionable to the Christian conscience. It has been suggested that gradually Christians were conscripted into the army in roles that did not involve killing. The transition from army service being a rare exception to being more commonplace has been understood either as the failure to live consistently by the norms of Christ or as exercising responsible citizenship.[7]

The witness of history is not conclusive in the debate between pacifists and non-pacifists, as each side tends to view historical developments from within the basic stance they take on other grounds. However, it does appear that the theory of the 'just war' as elaborated by Augustine was an attempt to respond to the assumption that the burden of proof for participation in war lay with those Christians who believed that it could be justified.[8] This

therefore suggests that after Constantine the main conviction of
Christians concerning the legitimacy of killing others changed.

The 'just war'

Contrary to a common misconception, the theory of the 'just war' is
not an attempt to sanitise the general use of lethal violence, but to
show how *unjustified* it is in most circumstances. As a theory
intended to guide the relationships between peoples on opposite
sides in a conflict, it intends to lay down precise and restrictive
criteria for deciding when force, which is likely to entail killing,
may be used legitimately. Because war can only be sanctioned as
a last resort, and rarely if ever as a first strike, many are unhappy
to speak of a *just* war; at the most it is permissible to speak of a
justified war. This is not a matter of semantics but of indicating
that war always expresses failure; it is always evil, though it may
be the lesser of two evils.

The criteria for justifying war in carefully defined circumstances
are very explicit. They may be divided into three groups:

- The cause must be righteous;
- The means must be controlled;
- The outcome must be predictable.

The first of these is known technically as *jus ad bellum*. It is a theory
of ends which 'defines the conditions under which it is permissible
to resort to war'.[9] War may be justifiable in self-defence against an
aggressor, to remedy a situation of injustice (e.g. to aid another's
legitimate self-defence), to protect the innocent (e.g. against the
threat of genocide), to defend human rights (e.g. in the overthrow
of a tyrannical regime). War must be the last resort after every
possible attempt to resolve conflict by non-violent means (e.g.
negotiation) has been exhausted. It must be preceded by due warnings to the aggressors that they will be responsible for war if they
do not cease their belligerence. Finally, for a war to count as just
it must be fought without hatred for the opposing forces and
without any desire for revenge.

The second and third of these criteria are known as *jus in bello*
and have to do with the means by which war is pursued. Here

three further considerations have to be brought into the equation. For a war to be just requires:

- *The use of minimal force.* The amount of force used must not exceed what is needed to achieve the aim of the war. There must therefore be a reasonable expectation that the goal of justice can be achieved without escalating the conflict by drawing in other agents or by prolonging it beyond a tolerable time-limit.
- *Proportionality.* The violence inflicted must not be greater than that which it intends to end. The good consequences of the war must outweigh the bad.
- *Discrimination.* Force must be directed only against legitimate targets of attack – namely, opposing combatants, military installations and other military objects. The intentional killing of civilians is outlawed and the unintentional must be kept to the absolute minimum.

According to these criteria, a war would be unjust if it were waged as an instrument of national policy, to promote religious or ideological ends, to defend national pride and (probably) as a pre-emptive strike against the threat of violence. It would be unjust if fought using a scorched-earth policy, saturation bombing of towns and cities or weapons of mass-destruction (nuclear, biological or chemical).[10] Finally, war is unjust if it stimulates further aggression by giving an excuse to the defeated to seek revenge at a later date, or if it brutalises those engaged in combat.

Justifying the theory

Fundamentally, the criteria as set down are not intended to make war appear acceptable, but to limit it and eventually to make it untenable. If the conditions were strictly adhered to, there would be no war for no one would be justified in *initiating* violence. However, given the reality of evil in the world, Christians have justified using lethal violence.[11] Two main grounds are usually given – the arguments from justice and from citizenship.

1. The argument from justice

God requires justice to be administered in society (Deut. 1:15–17). This entails judging and punishing the guilty (Deut. 16:18–20) and defending the poor and oppressed (Prov. 31:8–9). In particular circumstances, justice may require the penalty of death (Deut. 19:11–13) or the waging of war (Ps. 149:6–9). In the scales of justice, although the lives of individuals are to be highly respected, they are not ultimately inviolate. With enormous regret and sorrow, sometimes lives are forfeit in order to achieve a greater good.

However, justice cannot be executed by individuals on their own initiative or according to their particular whims. The Lord's way of seeing justice done (Rom. 12:19) is through government (Rom. 13:4): 'Authority . . . is the servant of God to execute wrath on the wrongdoer'. Justice in a fallen world requires the use of force to ensure compliance with its demands. Those who use force are ultimately accountable to God, and they must be duly constituted authorities in society for God to have given them this responsibility.

2. The argument from citizenship

God has designed human life to exist within a network of relationships (the extended family, the local community, the nation). Within each set of relationships there are both rights and responsibilities: 'Give to the emperor the things that are the emperor's' (Mark 12:17). A Christian is therefore required (as a citizen) to be a responsible member of society in the defence and propagation of justice, even to the taking of life in extreme circumstances.

The Scriptures seem to recognise the logic of this position. Thus John the Baptist tells soldiers to repent of dishonesty, greed and extortion, but not to leave the army (Luke 3:14). This is a clear case of accepting a particular end and yet outlawing illegitimate means for achieving it. Jesus appears to concur with Pilate's claim to use force rightly (John 19:10–11). He only refuses it as a means of realising the aims of the community of the kingdom (John 18:36). As far as we know, on believing in Jesus Sergius Paulus did not cease being proconsul of Cyprus and commander of the army there (Acts 13:6–12).

To remain a coherent community, any society of human beings must promote both *retributive* justice (punishment for wrongdoing) and *distributive* justice (rewards for honesty and integrity). A Christian as a member of society must take part in this task and can do so with a good conscience.[12] It is only in personal relationships that Christians may not use force for personal reasons. Here the law of mercy, forgiveness and forbearance takes precedence (1 Cor. 6:7; Matt. 18:21–2, 35).

Criticism of the theory

As well as the question of whether following in the way of Christ demands an unconditional refusal of the use of lethal violence, Christians have always had other difficulties with the concept of a just war. The main objection is that it is no more than a (neat) theory. As a proposal, it is clearly conceived and well-balanced. Its problem is that it is quite impractical. It expects standards of conduct and a dispassionate attitude towards aggression which fallen human nature is incapable of. In the heat of the moment people do not act in the temperate and unprejudiced way that the theory demands. This is born out by the fact that only in very rare cases have ordinary citizens (let alone Christians) refused to participate in a particular war on the basis of its being unjust. The test of the theory ought to be its ability to promote dissent in some circumstances.

However, even by its own standards the theory is judged to be defective. If it is wrong for an individual to take the law into his or her own hands, it is equally wrong for a collective entity to do it on a larger scale. There is no difference in principle (only in extent) between individuals who, in deciding what course of action is legitimate, act as both judge and jury in their own case, and nations who do the same. It is conceivable that an 'independent' agency (like the International Court of Justice or the Security Council of the United Nations) could act as a court of appeal to decide whether or not response to a particular act of aggression was just. It would be difficult, however, to arrange the decision-making process in such a way that all sides accepted the verdict as disinterested. International politics, as practised, is self-serving and hypocritical.[13]

At all levels, the 'just war' criteria are unrealisable. The outcome cannot be predicted with any degree of accuracy at all. Was

Saddam Hussein's invasion of Kuwait any more evil than his
continuing persecution of the Kurds or Shi'ite Muslims in Iraq? It
is arguable that the Gulf War was partly responsible for inten-
sifying and enabling the second violence. How many of those who
have not been party to the conflict would argue that the violence
used to set up the state of Israel was justified in the light of half a
century of continued bloodshed and suffering for all sides? Wherever weapons of mass destruction could be used, if the stakes
were raised too high, the three requirements of controlled means
(minimal force, proportionality and discrimination) are bound to be
denied – the indiscriminate and mass killing of innocent civilians is
unavoidable. But what theory of justice could possibly put this on
one side of the balance and decide that there are other considerations which outweigh it ?

The usual response to these criticisms is to concede that, taken
one by one, the 'just war' criteria are difficult to defend in the
context of modern warfare but that, nevertheless, there is a fundamental ethical intuition that brutal, dangerous and unprovoked
aggression must be halted by powers that have the means to do
so, acting on the basis of generally accepted principles of justice
and compassion. As we shall see, given the perils of modern weaponry, governments and other agencies have in recent years
redoubled efforts to find creative ways of defusing potentially
violent situations. Notions like 'common security', 'civil society'
and 'the culture of non-violence' are being advanced as the
ordinary means of coping with conflict. At the same time, war is
marginalised as a possible necessary affliction in very exceptional
circumstances.

Issues to be faced in overcoming violence and building peace

Nationhood and citizenship

Assuming that every citizen has duties towards the nation of which
he or she is a part, one of these is participation in the realisation of
justice. However, the citizen also has the responsibility to exercise a
critical conscience with regard to all obligations that the state may
seek to impose. There is no such thing as a wholly righteous nation.

The Old Testament tends to divide nations into the repentant and unrepentant. In the first category come Israel under Josiah and Nineveh confronted by the preaching of Jonah. In the second category Tyre and Egypt represent nations that seek arrogantly to defy the just will of God (Ezek. 26—32).

Although Christians, as a general rule, are to 'be subject' to the governing authorities (Rom. 13:1), this is a matter of a fine-tuned conscience (Rom. 13:5). Therefore, 'subjection' cannot mean unquestioning obedience, for in such a case conscience would be in abeyance. The implication of Paul's discussion of civil society is that the authorities act as God's servants, *in so far as* they distinguish correctly between good and evil, upholding justice and punishing evil-doing (Rom. 13:3–4). Whereas it is wrong to resist authority (for example, by declaring oneself free of a government's right to enact laws), it may be right to resist a particular authority over particular issues – 'the things of God', where they conflict with those of Caesar, take precedence (cf. also Heb. 12:4).[14] According to the Pauline reflection on power and authority, 'all thrones, dominions, rulers and powers' have been created through and for Jesus Christ, so that 'he might come to have first place in everything' (Col. 1:16–18). He is not only the Lord of the Church, but the judge of the nations (Rev. 19:11–16). The nation is held accountable to the 'Lord over all authorities'.

Somehow Christians have to maintain a proper tension between their dual citizenship – members by birth or naturalisation of the secular realm and members by new birth and adoption of the divine realm. They may not so interpret one membership that it rules out the rightful obligations of the other. They have to be alert to the possibility of a state making idolatrous claims for itself, or of the Christian community misunderstanding what is entailed in freedom in the Spirit. All the models of Church–state relationship that have been tried in the past – 'Constantinian', 'pietist', 'reformist', 'liberationist', and 'Anabaptist' – are defective to different degrees.[15] There are times when one of the models would be more appropriate than the others. The mission of the Church is to discern these times.[16]

Democracy

The kind of attitudes we have been suggesting as part of Christian mission are more easily realisable in a democratic society. Democracy entails representative, elected, open and accountable government. It means that the economy and the institutions of the state are administered on behalf of all the citizens, and in particular that the legitimate rights of minorities are protected. It requires a spirit of service, the strict control of any financial gain obtained by virtue of governing and the willingness to admit failure and wrongdoing where it happens. Above all, in the global market economy, it implies distancing the executive and legislative responsibilities of government, and the legal processes from the powerful interests of big business. Walter Wink suggests that 'in significant ways, democracy is nonviolence institutionalized'.[17] What he means is that the more democracy is functioning as it ought, the more change can be effected by peaceful means (e.g. voting, signing petitions, lobbying individuals).

Security[18]

There is nothing more likely to promote conflict and violence, both within nations and between them, than real or perceived threats to security. Aggression seems to be a basic reaction to the fear of losing rights, privileges, means of livelihood, symbols of identity, supporting networks and other aspects of life which give and maintain a sense of security and wellbeing. To recover this sense of self-preservation and protection, peoples may be willing to amass huge arsenals of arms, threaten massive destruction and even initiate hostilities in a bid to crush the real or imagined source of their anxiety.

These were the issues behind the escalation of the nuclear deterrence into weapons systems of mutual annihilation in the early and middle 1980s. On one side were people who argued that defence was a matter of securing a nation from military attack or invasion by an external opponent – as something which a nation does on its own or in alliance with trusted friends. Security is to be achieved, according to this view, by withdrawing behind a raised drawbridge and ensuring that one's parapets are bristling with arms. The ultimate conclusion of this approach was the nonsensical 'Star Wars' project, which epitomised the belief that all and any act of aggression (first strike) could be repelled infallibly if a sufficiently sophisticated system of weaponry was put in place.

On the other side were people who argued that only 'common security' – i.e. treating perceived antagonists as potential friends and partners – could secure a lasting peace and guarantee real safety. The notion of security through deterrence was rejected because its *spirit* is to divide people simplistically into friends and enemies, its *logic* is the arms race based on a worst-case analysis and in its *practice* it diverts huge financial and creative resources away from meeting chronic human needs. It is built on the illusion that somehow peace can be secured through technology – 'Star Wars' is really an idolatrous search for invincibility. Even the idea of minimum deterrence – i.e. the retention of sufficient weapons of mass destruction, and the ability to deliver them, to make the risk of all-out war unthinkable – is inherently unstable, for other powers are encouraged to acquire their own nuclear deterrents, thereby creating even greater insecurity.

Common security implies treating the perceived hostile power as a potential ally and friend. In turn this involves a major shift in attitude away from distrust, stereotyping, self-righteousness and distorted images – all of them created by distance. By its very nature, security cannot be achieved by means of the threat of massive destruction. It is obvious that an escalating supply of arms is more likely to provoke than prevent a conflict. Common security implies that peoples belong together, irrespective of the policies of their governments,[19] that they are interdependent and that co-operation, not confrontation, is always in their best interests. For Christians there is the added consideration that one of the most frequently recurring themes in the prophetic and liturgical literature of the Old Testament is the call to God's people to find their security in God and not in military alliances (Isa. 30:1–5; 31:1–3; Ps. 118:8–9; 146:3; 108:12–13). Trust in weapons to secure freedom from the fear of violence and war was a manifestation of human independence of God.

The Church's mission to overcome violence and build peace

Given both the all-pervading reality of violence and the Gospel message of peace and reconciliation, the Church must play a role in breaking the spiral of violence and creating conditions of peace wherever it can. For effective action three preconditions are necessary.

1. Getting its own house in order

The Church itself must be an example of how to solve conflict. Internally, within its own structures, it must ensure that principles of democracy are in place which allow for processes of open consultation, the encouragement of initiatives by its members and policies of conciliation when individuals or groups of Christians strongly disagree about important matters (Matt. 5:23–5; 18:15–17). The themes of reconciliation, peace and fairness must feature prominently in its teaching and preaching ministries and in its liturgical practice (e.g. the sharing of peace). It must evolve procedures for dealing firmly and equitably with autocratic leadership and minority pressure groups. In particular it must learn how to resolve the threat of division, knowing the proper limits for allowing dissent, and when and how discipline has to be exercised.

Externally, the Church must distance itself from partisan involvement in conflicts caused by national, ethnic or communal strife. The picture of different branches of the Church taking sides in the ethnic conflicts unleashed in the former Yugoslavia is a cause of shame.[20] The inability of the Church in Rwanda and Burundi to extricate itself from some complicity in the horrendous slaughter of defenceless civilians was a major scandal for the Gospel. The use made by some Church leaders in Northern Ireland of Christian motifs to suppress genuine aspirations for change is unacceptable to the Church at large.

However, in seeking to understand the delicate and complex relationship between issues of justice and peace, the Church must not necessarily and always opt for the latter. There will be situations where conflict is justified until certain situations of injustice have been put right. These situations are likely to involve asymmetric relationships between the parties – i.e. where 'financial, political, military and other resources are unevenly distributed'.[21] The conflict is likely to continue until the asymmetry has been righted, for fruitful dialogue can only take place once legitimate aspirations for a share in power have been recognised.

2. Understanding the causes of violence

The Church can engage both with its own theological tradition and with the many insights which have come from contemporary peacebuilding efforts. The Church should not be surprised by the extent or depth of violence which exists in the world, though it should always be distressed by it. It knows that the human situation is abnormal. The problem may be described as one of *estrangement*: human beings are *strangers* to one another and to God. They are alienated from other people who are often seen as competitors to be feared. Estrangement may turn inwards, so that individuals are strangers to themselves, with no understanding of themselves – their uncontrollable passions, their illusions, their confused sense of what is worth pursuing in life. This may lead to unresolved internal conflicts in which a person despises himself or herself. In a number of cases, this can lead to self-inflicted violence (such as attempted suicide, excessive drinking or drug abuse), to depression or other forms of mental disturbance, or it can lead to violence inflicted on others (such as child abuse or violence towards one's marriage partner).

Another major cause of violence is the will-to-power. Human beings have a bias towards using other human beings as means to further their own ends. In acute circumstances they may seek to 'eliminate' them (not necessarily in a literal sense, but metaphorically by ridicule, stereotyping, isolation and misrepresentation).[22] We possess an innate tendency towards protecting and advancing our own interests before those of others. We find it easier and more satisfying to use the language of rights than that of duties and responsibilities. A self-centred view of life often leads to violence. One example of this is abortion, as the following quote illustrates:

> All killing requires justification, and it is somewhat more difficult to justify the deliberate destruction of a sentient being

than of a living thing which is not (yet) a centre of experience;
but sentient beings do not all have equal rights. The extension
of equal moral status to fetuses threatens women's most basic
rights. Unlike fetuses, women are already persons. They
should not be treated as something less when they happen to
be pregnant. That is why abortion should not be prohibited,
and why birth, rather than some earlier point, marks the beginning of moral status.[23]

The argument has the merit of being ruthlessly honest in its justification of violence, even when the assumptions are false at a
number of points. In particular, we may note the amazing view
that the full personhood of women can only be realised through
the freedom to choose to end the existence of a 'living thing' which
causes inconvenience. Why should not personhood be fulfilled
through protecting and caring for another ? Behind the right to
the termination of pregnancy lies also the implicit belief that personhood can only be guaranteed if the woman has the unrestricted
freedom to choose as a solitary individual the destiny of the foetus.
This an astonishing view of freedom, rights and moral values.

Lest one be accused of a sexist bias in selecting this example, let
me emphasise my conviction that, on the whole, men have a far
worse record than women in seeking to justify their own self-
interests. In a general sense, all manifestations of patriarchy are
attempts to maintain men in positions of power and privilege –
not least the maintenance, across all cultures, of the sexist myth
about a woman's particular duties in the family (coinciding with
those activities that men find least congenial).[24] Within the context
of family life, the Bible, at least, seems to give to both parents
equal authority and responsibility in bringing up children (cf. 2
Cor. 12:14; Eph. 6:1–3; 1 Tim. 5:4), and no division of responsibility
for domestic chores is apparent.

It has often been pointed out that violence is self-engendering.[25]
Much violence is a response to violence suffered. This is true at a
personal level, as in the case of the neglect and sexual abuse
of children, often (though not invariably) carried out by those
themselves abused in childhood. It is true at a local or national
level, when people decide to resist the violence of oppression or

discrimination by force of arms. There is a circle of violence which becomes part of the structures of human minds and emotions, or a method of achieving social and political ends, when non-violent means all seem to have been thwarted. In these cases one cannot deal with isolated instances but must look for the historical development of conflict in order to be able to deal with the root causes, which may lay buried in a past that still needs to be discovered and confronted.

3. Learning to apply principles of conflict transformation

Both the Church as a body (it may be through specific departments, boards, voluntary agencies or local churches)[26] and Christians as individuals or as members of informal groups will build on the growing experience of many organisations in the area of peacebuilding. In addition, they will call upon the distinctively Christian resources at their disposal. The task may be said to contain three levels of operation: the prevention of conflict, the resolution of conflict and the establishment of peace.

(a) The prevention of conflict

There are two levels at which strategies for preventing conflict may work: the *structural* and the *direct*. In the first place, there will be sustained attempts to create a general culture of non-violence. The objective will be to persuade any party to a conflict that the use of violence is not a solution to conflict but an aggravation of it. This is in line with the observation that violence can only be ended when its self-propagating nature is cut. But the likelihood that only non-violent means will be used to end conflict depends on such means being available, workable and effective. Thus there must be in place legal and institutional frameworks which support conflict resolution: skilled people using well-respected mechanisms and backed up by sufficient financial resources to intervene when and where appropriate:

> In order to flourish, peace, respect for human rights and democratic governance all require a fertile cultural base which nurtures them and a framework of institutions which protect and sustain them ... The base comprises the cultural values

of nonviolence, mutual tolerance and respect, co-operation
and equality, which are the bearers of justice and human development.[27]

In the second place, there will be direct intervention by third
parties (trusted by both sides in a potential dispute) to provide a
service of conciliation. The Church, with all its experience in education and training, may have much to offer in the field of
communication – the production of literature, the organisation
of workshops, the use of different forms of media, the development of professional skills – all designed to lessen tensions and
to promote alternatives to violence.[28] Overcoming violence and
building peace should be part of the Church's theological education
programmes at all levels.

(b) The resolution of conflict

Where violence has already broken out between antagonistic
groups, or where a generalised campaign of terror is in operation
(as in the case of 'war lords'), techniques designed to end death
and destruction are needed. These include securing an early cease-
fire, bringing in emergency aid, setting up medical centres to deal
with the injured, calling together conferences between the fighting
parties in which mediators seek to interpret to the other side
the reasons given for conflict, building grass-roots pressure on the
leaders to agree terms. Absolutely central to the resolution of conflict is the building of trust. Mediators have not only to be
impartial, in the sense of having no self-interest in any particular
outcome of the peace process (beyond a sustainable end to
hostilities), but must be seen to be impartial. Their role is the
creative one of looking for and suggesting alternative ways of
interpreting the situation, and trying to find outcomes in which
both parties gain benefits ('win–win'). One of the most difficult
tasks in mediation is to balance confidentiality with transparency.[29]

In situations of personal or domestic violence, the first requirement may be to remove the violated immediately from contact
with the violator. The Church must therefore either support
existing refuges or, where they do not exist, must contribute to
their creation. The same applies to counselling services. It is beyond

the scope of this chapter to enter into the complexities associated with child abuse and how the best interests of children who have been brutalised can be served.[30] It is clear, however, that the willingness to foster such children is both a gift and calling for some Christians.

(c) The establishment of peace

Peace may be said to have arrived, not when hostilities are over, but when the causes of the conflict have been resolved and the consequences of the conflict have been dealt with. Peace requires reparation for damage, the re-establishment of agriculture and industry, the repatriation of refugees, the judicial processing and punishment of war criminals, the re-establishment of representative democracy, the disarming of combatants, the reduction of stockpiles of military hardware and the reintegration of soldiers (tragically in many cases including women and children)[31] into civil society. When hostilities are over, there has to be some kind of recapitulation of the history of the conflict. In recent years, following the massive human rights abuses in countries like South Africa, Chile, Haiti and Rwanda, Truth and Reconciliation Commissions have been set up. Their general purpose is to exorcise the demons of the past, to create the possibility of a new beginning for the nation.

Who can doubt that in some respect the motivation for setting up these Commissions responds to the proclamation of the Gospel of Jesus Christ that forgiveness, the cleansing from sin and guilt, reconciliation and new life are dependent on repentance? Repentance is a central theme in the Christian faith. Without it new relationships are not possible. In political contexts it is extremely problematical, not least because it is a very personal decision of the will. Repentance is not remorse or shame: it is more than feeling regret for a situation that has gone badly wrong. It includes, but goes beyond, a public apology. True repentance involves admitting the truth of the accusations laid against one, one's responsibility in doing wrong, a deep sorrow for the hurt that has been caused, the giving of compensation or restitution where appropriate and the resolution not to return to the same behaviour again. Reconciliation happens when the repentance is accepted by the grieved party (in many, if not most, conflicts wrongs have been committed on both sides) and forgiveness offered.

In many ways repentance is beyond the natural capacities of human beings. Most of us are prone to defend our innocence, excuse our shortcomings and justify our evil deeds to such an extent that we are incapable of facing the real truth about ourselves. Perhaps we are only pushed to it when we have nowhere else to go – i.e. when we can no longer hide from the facts of our guilt, either because we know that others know or, more significantly, because we recognise that God knows. It is a hard path to take, and if we are right to believe that repentance and forgiveness are preconditions for reconciliation which is itself a precondition for peace, then peace is no soft option.

With regard to the political arena, Walter Wink concludes, from a survey of the aftermath of the despotic regimes of Namibia, Uruguay, Guatemala, El Salvador, Brazil, Argentina, Chile, South Africa and a reference to Eastern Europe, that the restoration of peace after conflict requires at least the following procedures:[32]

- The truth needs to be told.
- It needs to be told completely.
- If the threat posed by the old regime and its forces prevents full disclosure, then as much should be revealed as is possible.
- The truth needs to be sanctioned by an official body. If the new government is too weak to do it, then it should be done by the Churches (or other non-governmental organisations?).
- The leading architects and executors of the policy of disappearances, murder and torture should be prosecuted.
- If they cannot be prosecuted, they should at least be publicly exposed.
- Amnesty should not be offered until the truth has been told and, if possible, at least some of those most guilty have been prosecuted.

Maybe this is the most (and it is considerable) that can be expected as a process towards reconciliation; real repentance may have to remain a distant ideal, but one still to be striven for.

Exercises

1. Discuss the view that under no circumstances may a Christian deliberately engage in an act which may result in someone's death.

2. Compose a speech you would make at a Church assembly questioning the Church's support for a nation preparing for war.

3. Devise materials you would use for training Christians in the non-violent resolution of either community or family conflict.

9

Care of the Environment

Setting the scene

Looking in a south-easterly direction from a high building in the centre of Mexico City it is possible to see the majestic twin snow-covered peaks of the volcanoes Popacateptl and Ixtaccihuatl. There can be few if any cities in the world that have a more magnificent backdrop than Santiago, the capital of Chile, with the awe-inspiring Andes towering away to the east. Unfortunately, neither of these two vistas is common as the mountains are obscured for long periods by heavy smog. This tale of two cities can be repeated in many other locations across the globe.

The unregulated emission of toxic fumes by traffic and heavy industry is one of many examples of the accelerated deterioration of the natural environment in recent years. Three major areas – pollution, environmental instability and the depletion of natural resources – have been causing disquiet to the world community during the last 30 years. As well as high levels of air impurity, *pollution* also includes acid rain caused by sulphur dioxide from coal-burning plants – the cause of respiratory diseases, a variety of allergies and damage to buildings – the contamination of fresh and sea water through waste disposal, leakage from nuclear plants and disused oil wells, the seepage of fertilisers and pesticides from the land into river systems and the break up of the atmosphere's ozone layer due to the vast increase in the emission of chlorofluorocarbons (CFCs) (used especially in refrigerators, air conditioners, aerosol propellants and foam production). There is also a permanent danger of highly poisonous substances escaping from industrial complexes (as happened in the high-profile cases

of Bhopal, Chernobyl and Seveso in recent memory) and of permanent, damaging changes to the climate.[1]

Environmental instability is caused when the equilibrium of biological systems is upset through the use of fertilisers and
insecticides in intensive farming techniques, by the destruction of
natural habitats (such as hedgerows and woodlands) for wildlife,
the rapid expansion of deserts and deforestation. Deforestation in
particular brings about changes in climate, massive erosion of the
soil and the destruction of vegetation.[2]

The *depletion of natural resources* is also highly disturbing. The
actual or threatened extinction of many species through over-
hunting or changes to the environment often hits the headlines.
The cases of some much-publicised mammals (like certain species
of whale and the tiger) are perhaps the most notorious. Over-
fishing in many parts of the world also permanently endangers
stocks. Farming land is permanently destroyed to make way for
roads, industrial plants, leisure complexes and housing schemes.
Non-renewable fossil fuels are consumed at disturbing rates, as if
there were no tomorrow.

The immense human pressure on the delicate balance of the
world's ecosystems is further increased by the exponential growth
of the human population in the last few decades. This hugely
controversial topic was highlighted by the celebrated Brandt
Report[3] and has been the subject of fervent debate in subsequent
UN conferences on population. It raises fundamental questions
about culture, human rights, democracy and the relationship
between government and family units. Needless to say, there are
significant differences of opinion about the impact of growing
populations on such matters as food supplies, global warming and
the disappearance of animal and plant life.[4]

The issues

Some of the issues which emerge directly from the actual or potential ecological disasters listed above are the needs for the
maintenance of the highly tuned interdependence and rich diversity of ecosystems (such as food chains), for the reduction in the
amount of energy used from non-renewable resources and for

the sustainability of other resources (air, water, land and wilderness areas). There are also indirect concerns which arise from the discussion of the nature of the relationship between the environment and its fiercest predator – the human being.[5]

We will be discussing delicate questions relating to the rights of human, animal and other living organisms, the dispute about whether the human race is inclined to 'speciesism' (i.e. privileging its own position within nature), the debate about 'limits to growth' and the argument about appropriate lifestyles. Most immediately, however, there is a doubt about whether the whole topic should be included under the heading of mission. Some will suggest that care for the environment is stretching the scope of mission too far. They may observe that the sight of Christians 'turning green' is but another example of their trying to jump on a secular bandwaggon that has begun to roll and roll. It might seem like another illustration of the strongly contested opinion that, as far as mission is concerned, the world sets the agenda.

Slightly cynical commentators might seek to show how some Christian enthusiasts have moved, more or less in step with the changing emphases of Western middle-class altruists, from focusing on issues of social revolution to general human rights, to the concerns of feminists, to the protection of minorities and latterly to ecological matters. I believe that a strong case can be made, irrespective of what may or may not be the most current ethical fashions, for holding that the Church's mission does include a measured response to all matters to do with the environment.

Part of Christian mission

As in the case of peacebuilding, environmental matters have not received a high profile in studies of mission. Jongeneel's almost exhaustive survey of mission studies over the last two centuries does include a short heading on ecology, linked to the ethics of culture. However, the paucity of the bibliography cited, in comparison with that given for culture, perhaps bears out the impression that environmental matters are seldom linked to mission.[6]

The main reason for including care of the environment as a part of the Church's mission calling is its intimate link to other topics already reviewed. The strain on the environment is clearly related to matters of economic and political justice. Deforestation, intense agricultural practices, over-grazing, soil erosion, the greenhouse effect on the climate and many forms of pollution are the direct result of current economic relations between rich and poor nations. Situations of violence can arise because of the deterioration or disappearance of land suitable for sustaining human communities. Some liken the abuse of nature to the abuse of vulnerable humans: nature has neither voice nor vote; although it has the capacity to hit back (through human-created natural disasters), it is powerless to influence the way it is treated. Environmental mismanagement is the equivalent of the way some parents and societies violate the sensibilities of children and old people. Finally, the way nature is treated depends to a large extent on the cultural norms of any given society. The environment is not merely an illustration of how culture functions but an integral part of a society's cultural values, and these (as we have discussed at some length) are intimately bound up with its religious beliefs and practices.

Hence the conviction of the World Council of Churches, whatever may be the motives or the results, is correct: that peace, justice and the integrity of creation belong together.[7] I believe the Church at large has to endorse the finding of the San Antonio Conference of the WCC's Commission on World Mission and Evangelism that 'mission in Christ's way must extend to God's creation. Because the earth is the Lord's, the responsibility of the church towards the earth is a crucial part of the church's mission.'[8]

Approaches to the environment

Accompanying the transition of Western societies from a pre-modern to a modern perspective, quite novel attitudes to nature began to arise. Ian Barbour has noted three in particular.[9] In the first instance, the workings of nature were compared increasingly with those of a *machine*. This view was linked with a belief that non-human life was devoid of minds and feelings, part of a mechanistic world of necessity in which human beings could exercise their freedom of choice as fancy took them. In the second place, following the industrial revolution, nature was seen primarily as the *source of raw materials*. And with the development of capitalism, with its heavy emphasis on the private ownership of the means of production, nature was seen as one element in the creation of wealth and a *means of profit*.

These utilitarian or instrumentalising attitudes came to dominate human relations to nature. People assumed that nature was a given which could be exploited for an unquestioned and unlimited growth in production. It was immediately disposable in exchange for cash. The only sense of accountability was in making the most efficient use of the goods in terms of the value added. This approach was part of a much wider sense of cultural destiny shared by the peoples of Western Europe. Theirs was the task of conquering the unknown – distant lands, scattered mineral supplies, unknown peoples, the hidden mysteries of the natural world, markets in the process of being created, eventually space. Jürgen Moltmann has summarised the approach aptly:

> The modern aggressive ethical attitude towards nature is a product of the European Renaissance and of European Imperialist expansion in America, Africa and Asia. It was the Renaissance which for the first time stripped nature of its rights and declared it to be 'unclaimed property' which belonged to whoever took forceful possession of it. It was the same aggressive spirit of conquest which took possession by armed force of inhabited America, Africa and Asia, turning them into European 'colonies'.[10]

The burgeoning scientific endeavour which was both the cause and result of the technological changes of the modern era was based to a large degree on the rigid distinction between subject and object. Nature was there (like America, Antarctica, Everest, the Amazonian basin, the tribes of Papua New Guinea) to be 'discovered' and then brought into order ('civilised') and harnessed for human use. Scientific research was often motivated by a utilitarian ethic that saw experimentation as legitimate as long as it could be justified to the smallest extent as being of benefit to humanity.[11] The collusion with big business has also meant in a number of cases that science will engage in what may be or become commercially profitable (e.g. the use of animals for research in the 'beauty industry').[12]

Langdon Gilkey has called this modern approach 'scientific positivism and anthropocentric pragmatism'.[13] Needless to say, there have been significant challenges to the mechanistic and manipulative approach to the environment. The Romantic movement, the early American 'sacralisation' of nature,[14] modern feminism and indigenous cultures have all emphasised that human and non-human life makes up one seamless robe. They, and others, have stressed interrelatedness, organic wholeness and the reciprocity of relations. It has been pointed out that the rediscovery of harmony with nature is one major means whereby people deal with the stress of a depersonalised and automated existence. There is all the difference in the world between one's relationship to a computer and to the exquisite beauty and delicate perfume of a rose.

Environmental ethics

One of the major expressions of the development of postmodern ideas is the re-evaluation of the bond between the human species and the rest of creation. Until the 1960s, as a result of the apocalyptic upheavals of two world wars, the holocaust, decolonisation and the cold war, intellectual attention was given to history – the processes by which evolved civilisation had plunged to such 'primitive' depths of barbarity. Later, however, people began to notice the detrimental effects of the massive and precipitate expansion of the economies of the advanced industrial nations. Commentators started to turn their attention to nature.

The decline of the observance and influence of Christianity in the West – a thoroughly historical religion – and the search for alternative spiritualities – mainly among the religions of the East, with their emphasis on reverence for all forms of life, may have predisposed this trend from historical processes to the natural order. It has also been affected by the decline of Marxist ideology with its firm historical pretensions, the onslaught on rationalism, the acceptance of the equality of all races and cultures and the censuring of all forms of hegemony.

Three issues have been at the forefront of ethical debate with

relation to the environment: the status of human beings within
nature, the question of animal rights and the moral basis for
restricting the human exploitation of nature.

1. Humans and the non-human world

The discussion continues between those who believe that only
human beings are 'morally considerable'[15] and those who believe
that the equal interests of all living organisms should be equally
treated regardless of species:

> A life-centred ethic counts all living things as morally con-
> siderable, although not necessarily of equal moral significance.
> So it might be better to save a Pig-nosed Turtle than a waratah
> shrub, even though both are morally considerable. The former,
> however, might be more morally significant because it is a
> more complex living thing.[16]

Here biological complexity is deemed morally important.

Those who wish to advocate a human-centred ethic argue that
only humans, by virtue of their linguistic capability, capacity to
plan, and ability to choose and accept responsibility for their
actions, can function as members of a moral community. Only self-
conscious beings, who can conceive the future and choose goals
for themselves or others on the basis of beliefs and rational reflection, are moral subjects.[17]

On the other hand, it makes little sense to hold animals to
account, since they have no perception of moral values. It is only
in children's stories that we ascribe to animals the human capability of distinguishing between right and wrong. In the real world
they behave according to experience and instinct, avoiding pain
and the threat of others and fulfilling their basic needs for survival and propagation.

Others believe that a rigid distinction between the human race
and all other living organisms is 'speciesism' – a self-centred bias
towards privileging its own kind – parallel to other forms of discrimination. At the very least, if human beings are able to feel
sympathy towards other beings which clearly suffer pain and distress, the latter are 'the proper recipients of moral concern'.[18]

2. Animal rights?[19]

Discussion of a code of conduct regulating the treatment of animals would be easier if it could be generally agreed that the rights of animals are a meaningful concept. Moltmann, for example, takes it for granted that they exist, though he gives no basis for his general statement: 'An animal is not a thing and not a product. It is a living being with its own rights.'[20] Unfortunately, the final point he makes does not necessarily follow from the others. The notion of rights is notoriously difficult in the case of humans; how much more in the case of animals. To have any meaning, rights must be based on the absolute equality of all members of the same group and their identical intrinsic worth. However, animals belong to any number of species and their moral equivalence to human beings is strongly disputed.

Peter Singer argues for animal rights on the basis of the suffering experienced by all animals: 'No matter what the nature of the being, the principle of equality requires that its suffering be counted equally with the like suffering – in so far as rough comparisons can be made – of any other being.'[21] There are two problems with this reasoning. First, how can we possibly know the level of suffering of different members of the animal kingdom so that we can apportion rights accordingly? The nature and intensity of a fish's suffering on the end of a line or a fox's when chased by hounds is immeasurable by members of another species. But then, secondly, how do we know that experiencing pain is the same as suffering? A human's suffering of pain is accompanied by sentiments we presume are absent in animals, such as a sense of moral outrage, guilt or rational perplexity (why am *I* suffering?), which puts it on a different plane and makes the notion of like suffering between species inappropriate. Thus, the 'principle of equality' in this context is extremely uncertain.

If Tom Regan is correct in assuming that rights only belong to beings which have intrinsic value – namely a value which is independent of their moral attainment or utility[22] – then to speak of animal rights is quite simply to beg the question. Kant's famous categorical imperative – never to treat other beings as means to your ends but only as ends in themselves – applies without qualification only to humans. As humans alone are moral beings, 'knowing right and wrong', it is much more satisfactory to talk about their responsibilities towards animals and the rest of the natural world than to talk about rights. The next question then becomes: on what basis can we satisfactorily discover what those responsibilites are?

3. Moral foundations

Apart from the Christian faith, which we will consider in the next section, there are four other grounds for taking a considerate, non-exploitative approach to the environment.

(a) Ecological holism[23]

This is an attempt to move away from the individualism of trying to balance the rights and responsibilities of different species by advocating the supreme worth of the ecosystem as a whole. The advantage of this view is that it includes insects and non-sentient members of the biosphere which play enormously important roles in maintaining equilibrium, advancing conservation and furthering the fertility of the earth (e.g. trees, worms and some bacteria). The difficulty with this approach is the problem of differentiating between life-forms on the basis of their usefulness to the whole. To concede an equal right to life[24] would mean paralysing just about all forms of agriculture and horticulture and threatening the security of human beings and other higher forms of human life: 'If the welfare of the biosphere is the only criterion, are there any limits on the methods one might employ to reduce the human population? . . . Human values seem precarious if they can be over-ridden when there is a conflict.'[25] And what use are dogs when kept as pets? Can the killing of malaria-carrying mosquitos or disease-infected rats only be a matter of a self-centred attitude to survival by humans?

(b) Reverence for life

Reverence for life is a variant on holism which emerges from monistic religions and philosophies.[26] They teach that the whole of life is sacred and that the chief goal of life is to achieve and maintain harmonious relationships with all that exists, whether animate or inanimate. In the case of Buddhism, this is to be achieved by an attitude of non-violent deference to the natural world, accompanied by an attitude of detachment to material things. The exploitation of nature is due to human avarice which identifies fulfilment with the possession of things. True fulfilment (enlightenment) is, however, achieved through a gradual disengagement from the ego which craves the pleasures that come through material objects:

> On the most concrete level the search for wealth and possessions leads either to envy (if unsuccessful) or to possessiveness and fear of loss (if successful) . . . Compared with the higher achievements to come, the sensual is inferior even as a source of pleasure and happiness. The mind preoccupied with it loses contact with its own central nature . . . We continue to try to force experience into a false mould, by our craving . . . So our likes and dislikes generate attachment and rejection, forming a more or less fixed pattern made rigid by habitual desires and prejudices. These form the prison of our future. Yet understanding the nature of the process makes possible an escape from that prison.[27]

So in a sense the domination and exploitation of the natural world by human beings is one of the main sources of suffering. It manifests a profound disease.

(c) Anthropocentric utilitarianism

Utilitarianism is an ethical theory which attempts to define right and wrong actions in terms of their welfare consequences. Usually understood as 'the greatest good of the greatest number', utilitarianism would measure humanity's treatment of the environment according to whether it produced greater wellbeing or greater suffering. Thus, efforts to curb pollution, arrest soil erosion, protect the ozone layer, check global warming, maintain optimum stocks of fish and so on, contribute to human beings' (enlightened) self-interest. It is to their advantage to be ecologically sensitive and prudent.

The difficulties with utilitarianism are well-known. The major questions concern the concept of 'the good' or welfare. How is this to be defined? Who defines it? And who decides whenever a conflict of 'goods' is perceived by different groups of people? To judge the moral worth of an action by the goodness of its outcome is simply to beg the question. Bernard Williams relates these difficulties directly to the handling of the environment:

> Objections to utilitarianism may focus on its welfarism: the attempt to reduce all human values and objectives to something like preference satisfaction has been reasonably argued to be implausible and at the limit unintelligible. Apart from questions of whose preferences are at issue (a matter of particular importance when utilitarianism addresses problems of population control), it seems notably false to certain aesthetic and (differently) environmental values to reduce them to matters of what people happen to like or prefer.[28]

Some people may prefer goods at a price that does not have to absorb the cost of cleaning up the environment; others may prefer a clean environment.

(d) Responsibilities to generations to come

According to an African proverb, 'We have borrowed the present from our children'. It might be put the other way round: 'Our children have lent us the present'. How, then, are we going to hand it back? It is, to say the least, irrational to give birth to children knowing that we bring them into a world where their health will be increasingly endangered, their likelihood of starving enhanced, the possibility of dying from radiation progessively more likely and their enjoyment of the natural world diminished.

By what right does this generation take unalterable decisions (such as genetic engineering) on behalf of those not yet born, even though they will be directly affected? Utilitarianism is particularly unfitted to make this consideration a priority, because the further into the future the consequences of our actions are projected, the more impossible it becomes to calculate their likely outcome: 'Events of low probability or great uncertainty are assigned low weights in cost-benefit calculations'.[29] Serious doubts about the side-effects of genetically modified foods (such as the weakening of immune systems) are beginning to be aired.

It is a general moral principle that people should not benefit from short-term gains at the expense of long-term losses, when they personally will not be around to care. Like the injustice caused by the present generation having to shoulder the burden of massive debt incurred by unelected, unaccountable governments of the past, so future generations may have to bear the burden of our massive environmental follies.

A Christian view

The Judaeo-Christian world-view is often accused of being the main cause of Western societies' abuse of the natural world. The aggressive exploitation of the environment to gratify human beings' insatiable desire for pleasure is said to derive from the command in Genesis to 'subdue the earth and have dominion over . . . every living thing that moves upon the earth' (Gen. 1:28). Nothing could be further from the truth. Neither Judaism nor Christianity can be held responsible for the misapplication of one solitary verse. If the whole of their respective views of the environment was based on one verse that would be proof-texting indeed!

The Judaeo-Christian tradition has nothing to be ashamed of with regard to its teaching on humanity's relationship to the environment. It does not need to borrow from other traditions to supplement its own shortcomings, though it may listen carefully and respectfully to the views of others. It has all the resources necessary, in the words of Jan Jongeneel, 'to pursue a middle course between the Scylla of the divination of nature by traditional religions . . . and the Charybdis of the modern desacralized exploitation of it'.[30]

In the beginning God . . .

The Christian faith follows the Bible in focusing on God rather than on the universe; on the Creator before the creation. It is decidedly not a nature religion, though it holds nature in high esteem. Its view of the natural world stems from confessions like: 'The earth is the Lord's and all that is in it, the world, and those who live in it' (Ps. 24:1); 'The heavens are yours, the earth also is yours; the world and all that is in it – you have founded them' (Ps. 89:11).

The universe exists solely because God wills it. Psalm 104 suggests that God imagined the universe, turned his thoughts into words and everything came into being (also Ps. 33:6). There is no word for nature in Hebrew; even the noun for creation is not very common, only the verb. Creation depends entirely upon God's eternal power sustaining all things. If this were to be withdrawn even for a moment, all would disappear, as it were, into some cosmic black hole (Ps. 104:27–30). The first reason for creation is to show the 'greatness, the power, the glory, the splendour and the majesty'[31] of God: 'O Lord, how manifold are your works! In wisdom you have made them all; the earth is full of your creatures' (Ps. 104:24).

Let us make humankind according to our likeness

God wished to share this beautiful, fertile earth with someone like himself. He created us human beings, and alone of all his creatures gave us specific responsibilities. God's first word to his image-bearers concerns nature (Gen. 1:28). The words used here – 'subdue' (*kabash*) and 'have dominion over' (*radah*) – are forceful images, meaning 'cut a path through' (dense undergrowth) and 'stamp flat' (e.g. an anthill or a tin can). It is not surprising that, taken out of context, they have been understood as words of aggression, suggesting an energetic subjugation of creation.

Two observations can be made. First, the command is certainly intended to convey humanity's responsibility to control and bring order to nature. Human beings are of a different order of creation from all the rest (Ps. 8:5–6). The biblical account of creation does not teach that all objects are of equal worth or sacredness, or that all things are united in an indissoluble whole. It teaches that God also makes distinctions: the genus *homo sapiens* is quite different from all other kinds of being. This seems self-evident to observation and experience. The philosopher Roger Scruton speaks about the 'enormous gulf in the world of organisms: the gulf between us and the rest'. He goes on to specify the features of this distinction: 'We have capacities that we do not attribute to animals, and which utterly transform all the ways in which we superficially resemble them. Two in particular deserve a commentary: rationality and self-consciousness.'[32] He then goes on to elaborate how

these capacities put us into a different situation in comparison
with every other existing thing:

> Our use of concepts like truth seems precisely to separate us
> from the world of our experience, in a way that casts doubt
> on the thesis that we are subservient parts of the natural
> order . . . The presence in nature of creatures that gain and
> respond to information about their environment is a great
> challenge to science. But it is not, as such, a challenge to
> philosophy. The problems begin, however, when we acknow-
> ledge the presence in nature of a first-person point of view.[33]

The Christian view of creation is opposed to all forms of nature
religion, which tend to incorporate nature into the divine, and to
pantheism, which does the reverse.[34]

Secondly, Genesis 1 is not all that the Bible says about creation.
It takes a wide view. 'Subdue' and 'have dominion over' are qualified by two further verbs: 'to till' (*abad*) and 'to keep' (*shamar*)
(Gen. 2:15). The root of the first means 'to serve' and the root of
the second 'to preserve'. These notions are very far from exploitation. Thus, in a Christian framework, care for the earth is not based
on either a pantheistic belief that we are all part of the same stream
of life, nor on a holistic view that affirms an equal worth to all
living matter, nor on a pragmatic belief in the supreme value of
survival. It comes rather from the respect and honour due to a gift
that needs cherishing. Because creation belongs to God, it comes
to us as a bequest (Gen. 1:29 says, 'I have given you . . .')
entrusted to us. The world contains enough to sustain life for all
(Acts 14:15–17), as long as it is managed wisely and justly. Work
is the means given by God for people to enjoy the fruitfulness and
enhance the beauty of the gift.

The corruption of the earth

Unfortunately, things have not gone according to plan. In the book
of Proverbs we find a view of life which accepts that human beings
can discern the truth by careful attention to the world around them
(Prov. 1:1,4). Hence the scientific task of acquiring knowledge about
the workings of the natural order flows from the responsibilities
that God has given humans for the world. However, Proverbs also

makes clear that the task is not just to gain knowledge of *how* the world works, but to acquire the wisdom necessary to discern *what it is for.*

There is a difference between the *task* of mastering life, bending it to our wills, and the *art* of steering through life to goals that God has set. 'Ecology', understanding and living sympathetically with the whole inhabited world, has the same root as 'economics', the management of material resources. Unfortunately, under the impact of modernity, management (the task) has taken over from understanding (the art); knowledge and subjection have displaced wisdom and caring (particularly evident, perhaps, in the conversion of farming into big business).

The major reason for this deviation from God's original plan is that the creature has rejected accountability to the Creator; the tenant-farmer has demanded to be the sole owner. Worship of the Creator and wonder at creation have been turned into admiration for the brilliant intelligence of the creature's production – namely, technological innovation and profit-making. There is little humility in the face of the devastation which our enterprise cultures cause. Significantly, the story of the Tower of Babel, constructed with new technology to 'make a name for ourselves' (Gen. 11:3–4), ends the Preface to the History of Humanity (Gen. 1—11).

Ultimately all corruption springs from idolatry: arrogating to ourselves the position that is God's alone. This has led to the belief that natural resources belong to us, that they can be exploited for our gratification, that what is scientifically possible (embryo research, animal experimentation, gene modification) should be allowed, that we are responsible only to ourselves (and our shareholders). There is all the difference, however, between freedom *from* God and freedom *before* God.[35]

The first stage in idolatry is to lose our sense of preoccupation with God, relating every aspect of life to his loving concern. The second stage is to pursue our own imaginations, 'following our own devices' (Isa. 65:2). Either we orientate the whole of life to God's wisdom or we rely on our own (called in today's jargon 'rational planning'). Of course, human wisdom does touch the truth of the universe at a number of points, but in the debate about the environment it is in serious danger of becoming hopelessly unbalanced. Nature begins to take the place of God and become the really real.[36] Then rites and beliefs akin to the worship of creation begin to flourish. It is but a step from this to the use of nature to influence the course of history through astrology, charms, rituals, talismans and other objects of magic (Isa. 65:11).[37] Such an approach not only underlines the belief that the universe is godless or made by an arbitrary god, but it undermines the scientific enterprise which depends on the reliability of an ordered cosmos.

Healing the brokenness

Following the healing of a man crippled from birth, the apostle Peter tells the crowds gathered in the temple precincts that the restoration of physical integrity is due to the power of Jesus Christ (Acts 3:16). He continues to explain that the healing process will extend to the whole created order: 'Jesus . . . must remain in heaven until the time of universal restoration that God announced long ago through his holy prophets' (Acts 3:20–1). Peter also refers to Jesus as 'the author of life' (Acts 3:15) who, paradoxically, was killed by evil men. The universe 'came into being through him' (John 1:3) and 'for him . . . in whom all things hold together' (Col. 1:16–17).

In his earthly life, Jesus recognised both the essential goodness and life-sustaining capacity of creation, and its ability to destroy and be destroyed (Matt. 5:45; 6:26; 13:7). In calming the storm, he shows his power over hostile nature. In feeding the crowds, he shows his ability to overcome scarcity through the willingness to share. In turning water into wine, he points to the rich quality of life when touched by God's hand. His ministry was fulfilled in the transformation of his broken body in the triumph of life over death. The resurrection is a sign of the total re-creation of all things and proof of God's will to eliminate all destructive forces from the earth: 'Nothing accursed will be found there any more' (Rev. 22:3).

The 'universal restoration' invokes a new creation, the fullest picture of which occurs in Isaiah 65 (17–25). All that corrupts and has been corrupted will be eliminated: premature death (20); lack of food (21); the expropriation of what belongs to another (22);

miscarriages or stillborn babies (23). In contrast, there will be fullness of physical life (20) (could this mean that those who die young
have a chance in the resurrection to grow to maturity?), security
(21) – freedom from exploitation and violence means everyone can
enjoy the fruit of their own work – and the peacefulness of the
whole creation (25) – fear will be removed from the animal world.

Mission

It will be obvious that the Christian faith, rightly understood, does
not support a careless and reckless approach to the environment.
On the contrary, it advocates a restrained attitude compatible with
the meeting of every person's basic needs for food, shelter, healthcare, meaningful work and education. So close are many of the
'green' issues to those of justice for the poor that much of the same
kind of action is needed. In addition to the reasons given in chapter
6 for overcoming materialism, care of the environment necessitates
a limiting of consumption. Christians have good reasons for considering a self-indulgent lifestyle both immoral and immature:
conspicuous consumption is often an attempt to cover over a deep
sense of personal inadequacy, which should be dealt with through
the restoration of broken relationships (God, friends, family) and
a discovery of self-worth. Even when consumption is legitimate,
it may be right to renounce perfectly justifiable expense for the
sake of witnessing to the truth that life does not consist in
the abundance of the things possessed, but in generosity to others.
Paul tells Timothy that being ready to share is a means of 'taking
hold of the life that really is life' (1 Tim. 6:18–19). Paul had himself
learnt the secret of contentment – the readiness in all situations to
give thanks to God whether having little or having plenty (Phil.
4:10–13).[38]

Perhaps some kind of health warning should be issued about
the dangers (physical and psychological) of over-consumption. The
problem is that the global economy is based on the ability to
stimulate consumption, rather than on its ability to meet the needs
of all as a first priority. Apparently humanity is caught in the
deathly alternative of permissive spending, with its accompanying
waste, and the threat of unemployment. The economy is not only

immoral in being profligate with limited resources; it is also irrational in not being able to solve this equation.

The matter has been greatly debated, not least in the controversy stirred up by the report *The Limits to Growth*.[39] The contributors argued, with a wealth of statistics, that a continuously upward curve in the growth of economies was not sustainable over a long period of time because of the strain on both resources and quality of life. Others have contended that the prediction is too pessimistic. With the advantage of hindsight, it may not be necessary to advocate zero growth. The warning itself has stimulated scientists to discover ways of producing more abundant yields of food and governments to make industry carry the cost of cleaning up its pollution of the oceans and rivers. Little optimism, however, can be gained from the ability of unregulated market mechanisms to treat the environment with consideration. Time and again in UN conferences on the environment – Rio de Janeiro, Copenhagen, Kyoto – we have witnessed the success of the lobbying power of multinational companies and the electoral expediency of (mainly Western) politicians in diminishing and postponing strategies for sustainable living announced by governments on behalf of their citizens.

Christians must press for legislation sensitive to carefully planned sustainability, which challenges both technology (for its own sake, or on the basis of who can pay) and the 'profit motive' as sufficient reasons for destroying ecosystems. Modernity has led the human race into a wave of expanding expectations. In modern medicine, for example, people are caught up in the rising prospects of being cured through the development of ever more sophisticated medical techniques (machinery, drugs, gene modification). This anticipation is led by some truly remarkable scientific breakthroughs. However, demand far outstrips supply in the sense that a welfare healthcare system does not have infinitely expandable sources of wealth to call upon. The result, therefore, is either that additional resources are given to the technologically spectacular and removed from other healthcare provisions – illness is seen as an affliction that needs to be cured rather than prevented – or resources are allocated to those who can pay for them (in private medical schemes).

Christians are already extensively involved in supporting those who practise good farming methods in all parts of the world. For example, the 'sabbath principle' of rest (Exod. 20:10; Lev. 25:1–7) indicates the natural process of fallowing, often replaced today by the use of fertilisers to squeeze maximum production out of the land:

> The weekly sabbath is not a day of rest for human beings alone. It is also a day of rest for the animals who belong to the family community (Ex. 20:10). This is the day on which human beings are supposed not to intervene in nature, either through work or harvest, but are meant to perceive nature as God's creation and respect it accordingly.[40]

Alongside this, Christians must constantly press for land reform, which allows care for the land to be exercised by those who have a personal or community stake in it.[41] They alone – not absentee landlords, sometimes living on the other side of the world – have an interest in what the Rio Conference called 'sustainable agriculture': that is, agriculture that enhances rather than depletes resources, is not dependent on outside inputs, is diversified for local sustenance and allows people to stay on the land by ensuring a source of stable income for local people.[42]

Finally, the biblical notion that creation exists pre-eminently to reflect the glory of God, and only secondarily to be used by human beings, suggests that Christians must support all initiatives to preserve, extend and open to human enjoyment the 'wilderness' areas of the world, including the migration routes of birds and other species, and to keep these inviolate. The movement to create national parks (for the equal benefit of all) and to protect sites of outstanding natural beauty from human constructions is in some ways the environmental equivalent of designating certain buildings as part of a national or international heritage. They belong to the collective history and inheritance of the human race and should be handed on intact to coming generations, allowing them to experience the same joy in visiting them. We return to where we began. Human-fabricated pollution, whether smog, pylon lines or refuse, or the human-caused depletion of plant and animal life, lessens our sheer wonder and awe, which should be our first response to nature, at the imposing mountains and other majestic landscapes.

Exercises

1. Give your reasons for considering care of the environment to be a matter of particular concern for Christians at this time.

2. Discuss the arguments for and against the notion that the environment, particularly animals, have 'rights'.

3. Prepare a paper for your church to inform its response to a national consultation on a transport strategy which will reduce reliance on the motor car.

10

Sharing in Partnership

A fashionable idea

Here we touch on a crucial but perplexing aspect of world mission. How should different Churches and mission agencies relate within and across national boundaries? What are the optimum conditions for churches belonging to different denominations and traditions to work in close co-operation? How far is unity among Christians a prerequisite for mission? How much is it the fruit of mission?

In recent years it has become fashionable and common to speak of relationships between different groups of Christians in terms of 'partnership'. Though not free of ambiguities – in some societies its meaning has become cheapened by being used of couples living together without the public commitment of marriage[1] – 'partnership' has a positive and reassuring ring about it, denoting a sense of equality, collaboration and a public commitment to share in common endeavours.

Within world Christianity, 'partnership' expresses a relationship between churches based on trust, mutual recognition and reciprocal interchange. It rules out completely any notion of 'senior' and 'junior', 'parent' and 'child', or even 'older' and 'younger'. It is a term designed to show how different parts of the Church belong to one another and find their fulfilment through sharing a common life. It implies a relationship in which two or more bodies agree to share responsibility for one another, and in which each side meaningfully participates in planning the future of the other. Put in this way, partnership is an ideal to be aimed at. In practice, as we shall see, there are real difficulties in the way of a truly equal relationship. However, before we come to the problems, it is worthwhile seeing what partnership can mean.

A short history

As early as the Jerusalem conference of the International Missionary Council (1928), John Mott was calling for an end to the notion of 'sending' and 'receiving' churches.[2] The creation of the World Council of Churches in 1948, the result in part of a recognition that all Churches were engaged in a common witness, spoke of the acceptance of all self-governing Churches, in whatever part of the world they existed, as full and equal members of a consultative assembly.

Within the Communion of Anglican Churches, a process of partnership between provinces and dioceses was set in motion in the 1960s, called 'mutual responsibility and interdependence'.[3] It is not surprising that such a mouthful should become 'partners in mission' at a later date. Nevertheless the wording recognised the importance of a mutual bonding that carried with it responsibilities for the life and witness of other Churches. As might be expected, following the period of decolonisation (from the 1947 independence of India and Pakistan onwards), it became increasingly common to talk of 'independent' and 'autonomous' Churches, meaning those which had formerly been established by Churches and mission agencies from the West.[4] It should, however, be remembered that many new Churches came into existence in Africa, Asia and Latin America which were independent from their inception.[5]

Though it might seem a contradiction of the spirit of partnership, the debate (in the late 1960s and early 1970s) about a 'moratorium' of missionaries from the West was intended to cement a proper understanding of partnership on a solid basis. The question of a moratorium was first launched by Ivan Illich in an article in the Jesuit magazine, *America* (January 1967). He argued that the enormous flow of Catholic missionaries from the USA to Latin America was impeding the Church in the south from engaging fully in the social and political upheavals of that continent. The North American Church's best missionary commitment at that time, he argued, was to confront the political and economic powers in the USA with their complicity in suppressing the rising aspirations of the poor in Latin America.

In 1971, a Philippine Christian, Nacpil, wrote an article in the *International Review of Mission* (which two years earlier had dropped the 's' from Missions) entitled 'Mission but not Missionaries'. He echoed the strong feeling among many Christians in the Third World that missionaries from the West stifled and inhibited the growth of a truly indigenous faith.[6] It was also observed that the Churches which did not receive missionaries (such as those in China and Burma) were the fastest growing.[7] Here was a call for a period of missionary 'abstention', so that the younger Churches could sort out their own life and strategy without having to look over their shoulders or give an account to the older Churches. The relationship would then become genuinely mature, and the younger Churches would have a real say in what kind of person they wanted to come from elsewhere to share in their work. Nacpil wrote:

> The most *missionary* service a missionary under the present system can do today in Asia is to go home! And the most free and vital and daring act the younger churches can do today is to stop asking for missionaries under the present system.[8]

Perhaps the expectation that Churches and mission agencies in the West would stop sending missionaries for a period of time (however short) was not realistic, although it did happen in a few cases.[9] The fact of the matter (seen by many as a sad reflection of an inadequate view of mission) is that without at least a token number of missionaries going overseas from the West it would have been hard for Churches and agencies to maintain financial support at acceptable levels. The understandable desire to put a personal face on support for mission is only slowly extending beyond the country where the Church or mission agency is located to include people of other nations.[10]

The essence of the Church

In spite of a continued failure of the Church in the West to adopt the structures and style of a body geared to mission, at least in theory it has been conceded that the Church has no rationale apart from its calling to be part of God's mission wherever it is. Writing of the period up to the Mexico City conference of the WCC's Commission on World Mission and Evangelism (1963), Wilbert Shenk says:

> Two centuries of worldwide missionary exertions sponsored by Western churches had largely failed to effect a fundamental reorientation in their ecclesial consciousness. In terms of that consciousness, Christendom remained a self-sufficient and insular reality. Church history and theology continued to be taught in the West as a Western affair. What happened out 'there' was missions and therefore of no immediate consequence: what happened in the West was 'church'.[11]

Following on from the Mexico City conference, the CWME initiated a study into the 'missionary structure of the congregation', thereby recognising the Church's essential missionary nature.[12] It was indeed an attempt to reconceive the Church as owing its existence only to mission. It has to be said that the historic Churches in Europe in particular still have not grasped the difficult lesson that, from a sociological point of view, they are a minority cult in a cross-cultural situation, and from a theological perspective they are a pilgrim people crossing an unfriendly terrain from Babylon 'to the city . . . whose architect and builder is God' (Rev. 18; Heb. 11:10; 12:22).

It may therefore be even harder to lay hold of the notion that 'partnership in mission' also belongs to the essence of the Church: partnership is not so much what the Church *does* as what it *is*. Churches (theologically) belong to one another, for God has called each 'into the fellowship (*koinonia*) of his Son, Jesus Christ our Lord' (1 Cor. 1:9). However diverse may be patterns of worship, methods of evangelism, styles of leadership, involvement in society and ways of expressing faith, there is 'one body and one Spirit . . . one hope . . . one Lord, one faith, one baptism, one God and Father of all' (Eph. 4:4–5); 'in the one Spirit we were all baptised into one body . . . and we were all made to drink of one Spirit' (1 Cor. 12:13). Partnership is therefore not a nice slogan that some clever committee has dreamt up; it is the expression of one, indivisible, common life in Jesus Christ.

The foundation in Scripture

Perhaps the nearest word in the New Testament to partnership is
koinonia. Its most basic meaning is 'partaking together in' a group
which has a common identity, goals and responsibilities. Its most
perceptible use might be in the sharing of a solemn meal together,
such as that which Jesus Christ shared with his disciples on the
night he was betrayed – 'dipping bread into the bowl with me'
(Mark 14:20) – and which subsequently became a meal to celebrate
his death and resurrection (1 Cor. 11:20ff.). It has often been pointed
out that the term 'companion', with a similar significance to partnership, means literally 'one who eats bread with another'. We are
not talking here of a casual snack together, but the recognition of
an express union solemnised in sharing the same table. It is not
possible to stress too much the importance of this table fellowship
in actively declaring that the participants belong together.[13]

In the New Testament we can find four aspects of this partnership.

1. Sharing in a common project

At the beginning of his letter to the church in Philippi, Paul thanks
God for the Christians' partnership with him, 'sharing in the gospel
from the first day until now' (literally 'fellowship for the sake of
the gospel') (Phil. 1:5): 'They are partners (*sunkononoi*) with him
in the defence (*apologia*) and confirmation (*bebaiosis*) of the gospel'.[14]
The church in Philippi was a body in partnership with Paul in
many different ways: 'You Philippians indeed know that in the
early days of the gospel, when I left Macedonia, no church shared
(*ekoinonesen*) with me in the matter of giving and receiving except
you alone' (Phil. 4:15). Paul envisages the partnership in terms of
a giving and receiving on both sides. No doubt in different ways,
both parts benefited from the mutual sharing that took place.

Then there were Paul's 'co-workers' (*sunergoi*). These are people
he singles out for special mention, either because they travelled
together in the work of evangelism or because he had received
particular help or encouragement from them when he visited the
local churches (among them were women as well as men, slaves

as well as free) (cf. Phil. 4:2–3; 2:25; Rom. 16:3,9; 2 Cor. 8:23; Col. 4:11; Philem. 1–2).

2. Sharing of gifts

Partnership in the body of Christ is emphasised in those passages which speak about the gifts (*charismatoi*) given by the Holy Spirit to each member of the body. In the passage in Corinthians, Paul is constrained to stress that to each is given the manifestation of the Spirit 'for the common good' (1 Cor. 12:7), because the exercise of the gifts was bringing serious dissension into the body. It may well be that those who had the more spectacular (or extraordinary) manifestations – such as 'the working of miracles', 'various kinds of tongues', 'gifts of healing', 'the utterance of wisdom and knowledge' (1 Cor. 12:8–10) – were despising those who possessed what they considered 'lesser' gifts. There is a hint of this in Romans as well, where Paul says, 'Do not be haughty . . . do not claim to be wiser than you are' (Rom. 12:16).

Only by the exercise of all the gifts as necessary for the health and wellbeing of the whole body can there be growth into mature adulthood: 'The gifts he gave were . . . to equip the saints for the work of ministry, for building up the body of Christ, until all of us come to . . . maturity, to the measure of the full stature of Christ' (Eph. 4:11–13). Here is a picture, based on the organic growth of a body, of how each person is dependent on the gifts given to all the others. It describes partnership as participating in the life of one another in such a way that the needs of all are met (Rom. 12:6–13).

3. Sharing of material resources

In his second letter to the church in Corinth, Paul touches at some length on the requirement for the church to share what it has with the Christian community in Judaea in its hour of need.[15] In the first place, he commends the example set by the churches in Macedonia (no doubt that of Philippi in particular) which, even when they could least afford to do so, were exceptionally generous in responding to a crisis in another part of the body of Christ (2 Cor. 8:1–5). In the second place, he exhorts the church in Achaia, at least, to match the liberality and dedication of those churches further north (2 Cor. 9:1–4). He reminds them of the self-giving act of Jesus Christ which was the means of their receiving enormous spiritual riches (2 Cor. 8:9). He argues that the collection which Titus is making will enable the needs of other Christians to be met and will thus bring about a situation of equality:

> I do not mean that there should be relief for others and pressure on you, but it is a question of fair balance between your present abundance and their need, so that their abundance may be for your need, in order that there may be a fair balance [or as many translations have, 'equality'] (2 Cor. 8:13–14).

The elements of partnership abound in Paul's discussion of this matter. The churches of Macedonia and of Achaia are sharing together in a particular ministry on behalf of the church in Judaea (2 Cor. 8:4). The churches in Judaea, who will receive this token of love and allegiance, have also given them the Gospel itself:

> Macedonia and Achaia have been pleased to share their resources with the poor among the saints at Jerusalem. They were pleased to do this, and indeed they owe it to them; for if the Gentiles have come to share in their spiritual blessings, they ought also to be of service to them in material things (Rom. 15:26–7).[16]

They also share in a ministry of prayer for them (2 Cor. 9:14). Finally, all the churches are not only in partnership with one another but also with God. On the one hand, God will provide them with much more than they could ever hope to give (as long as they go on sharing – 2 Cor. 9:8–10). On the other hand, God will also receive praise and thanksgiving (2 Cor. 9:12,13). This is another example of partnership in the Gospel: 'Through the testing of this ministry you glorify God by your obedience to the confession of the gospel of Christ' (2 Cor. 9:13).

4. Sharing in suffering

At the beginning of the same letter, Paul speaks about the Christians in Corinth sharing in his and Timothy's sufferings (2 Cor. 1:7). In reality they are all sharing in the sufferings of Christ, which continue in the sufferings of his body, which is the Church (Col.

1:24). This particular kind of sharing is a deep participation in the broken body: 'the fellowship (*koinonia*) of his sufferings' (Phil. 3:10; Gal. 6:17; 2 Cor. 4:8–12). The suffering has many causes – persecution, hardships while travelling, hunger, thirst, sleepless nights, exposure to cold, sheer hard work, misrepresentation, insults, anxiety for the wellbeing of the churches (2 Cor. 6:4–10; 11:23–9). Because it is also the suffering of Christ, every member of Christ feels the suffering of every other member (1 Cor. 12:26). In many ways this is the most profound and difficult of all manifestations of partnership. When the Church has learnt to share in this way, it has truly learnt what it means to be a *koinonia* in the Holy Spirit:

> Participation in suffering and struggle is at the heart of God's mission and God's will for the world. It is central for our understanding of the incarnation, the most glorious example of participation in suffering and struggle. The church is sent in the way of Christ bearing the marks of the cross in the power of the Holy Spirit (cf. John 20:19–23).[17]

The foundation of partnership is the model provided by the drama of the incarnation of Jesus Christ. 'God with us' is partnership or, as some people would prefer it, 'solidarity':[18]

> Since, therefore, the children share flesh and blood, he himself likewise shared the same things, so that through death he might destroy the one who has the power of death, that is, the devil . . . Because he himself was tested by what he suffered, he is able to help those who are being tested (Heb. 2:14,18).

Obstacles to partnership

Partnership is a wonderful idea; pity about the practice! Truly equal sharing will remain problematic across the world Church as long as material resources are so unevenly owned. All too often Western Churches and mission agencies use either financial inducements or veiled threats of withdrawal to promote their own concepts of mission and evangelism, church growth, development and social struggle. Sometimes a cloak of respectability is given to

Western programmes and strategies by ensuring that indigenous leadership from the Third World has a high profile. Yet the most important decision-making and long-term planning are still done outside the situation.

As long as economic relationships are not changed, dependency rather than full interdependence is built into the situation. There can be no genuine partnership. To be able to exercise responsibility, people must have the freedom to make decisions. This means owning resources so that decisions can be fully acknowledged and not imposed. Both money and the personal gift of one's life can only be shared when two groups of Christians have a genuine (not conditional) say in the activities they engage in. The ideal would be for resources to be pooled and mutual decisions taken about how they are used. There are a number of substantial difficulties in the way.

Demand outstrips supply

Where there are many more requests than there are abilities to meet them, discrimination is inevitable. By what process are criteria adopted for deciding between the requests? Who decides on the criteria and binds themselves to abide by them? Who interprets them in specific situations where there may be genuine differences of opinion? This is a minefield where there is potential for very damaging accusations of preferential treatment, partiality and even nepotism.

Past guilt

A bad conscience about former patterns of relationship inclines sensitive Western mission agencies to respond by giving without accepting the responsibility of genuine consultation with the recipient. Are resources going to be used to further coherent mission objectives? Is there any hidden rivalry or competition between groups of Christians? Getting partnership right may mean that for a time no resources flow in any particular direction. It may also be a painful process that causes misunderstanding.

Different perceptions of mission

The availability of resources depends upon people being willing to release them. Images count for a great deal. In vogue at present in some sections of the Western Church is the house church or base community model of church. For people who believe that 'small is beautiful' and that new is better than old, there is no merit in supporting what appear to them to be self-perpetuating institutions and structures, which continue to exist under the weight of tradition rather than the prompting of the Spirit.

Borrowing without recognition

Christopher Sugden points out perceptively that often the mission insights of Third World scholars are not credited as such in the West. He maintains (fairly in my opinion) that often Western theologians learn new insights in mission either from prolonged exposure to the Church overseas or through teaching and supervising Third World Christians studying in the West. They may (myself included), albeit unconsciously, not give due acknowledgement of their indebtedness. A particular case in point is the fieldwork carried out by Western scholars in the South. How can the ideas gleaned (say for a dissertation on the Church in India) serve the Church in that country?

> The question faces all Western missiologists and historians of mission: in our trade and practice are we genuinely empowering those whom we are engaging in partnership with by engaging with their ideas? . . . How can scholars in Indian and African churches be enabled to develop their own research? . . . For example, black Christians in South Africa have long wanted Christians from Latin America to come and engage with them missiologically, but the resources are never available. What are the ethics and rights of property over their information and the data they yield?[19]

Shared responsibility

I do not think there are easy solutions to these and other obstacles to authentic partnership. If long-established patterns of giving and receiving are going to change it will only be after much agonising. If, as we have suggested already, partnership is a matter of sharing together the full responsibility for mission in all situations, then the Church in the West in particular has a lot more learning to do. It still possesses an incipient paternalism, not to say racism, towards other Churches, often manifest in the surprise expressed at the vitality, spiritual maturity and intellectual strength of the Church elsewhere.

Shared responsibility means not only giving away control over financial resources, but receiving Christians from other nations whom the Churches there wish to send to be responsible with us for evangelism and discipling:

> Partnership in mission must mean partnership in the *whole* of mission. Churches in the South need to be involved with the North in the identification and articulation of mission issues as much as in addressing them. Indeed, part of the value of partnership is precisely that our partners may discern issues in our context which we cannot discern. If this is to be authentic, as well as comprehensive, it is important that mission partners are exposed to the whole of a pastoral and missionary situation and not restricted to bits of it.[20]

How hard it is for the Church in the West to receive. Our inclination is to be protective – they will be corrupted by materialism, not able to cope with secularism, unwilling to return to their own country – and dismissive of their cultural attitudes as being still 'pre-modern'. It is always apposite in this kind of context to quote Mahatma Gandhi's famous *bon mot*: when asked, on a visit to England in the 1930s, what he thought of European civilisation, replied, 'It would be a good idea!'

Power and powerlessness

Partnership is undoubtedly linked to questions of power. A truly mutual relationship cannot exist between two parties who possess unequal power. Power, principally, is the freedom and ability to make choices and act. It is invested in the things we possess: these may be wealth, status in the community, knowledge, educational qualifications, racial or ethnic identity, inherent gifts of leadership or the loyalty one can command. Powerlessness, by contrast, is generally the lack of these possessions: a lack of assets or the inability to use them effectively.

Contrary to much received opinion, power is not automatically corrupt. Lord Acton's famous saying is often misquoted,[21] but even in its original form it only expresses a half-truth: 'Power tends to corrupt and absolute power corrupts absolutely'. The fact that this aphorism resonates so easily with most of us is probably due to experience. We are all aware of too many examples of people unable to cope with the investiture of power, and too few who use it wisely and unassumingly. Power becomes corrupt when displayed with arrogance, disdain, presumption or a sense of superiority. In and of itself it is simply there. Most people have some power to make choices and act, even though this may be very unequally distributed through a society.

A biblical perspective

Power is a reality
Power is said to belong to a ruler (Eccles. 8:4; Dan. 8:24; Mark 10:42; Rom. 13:4), to a group of people (Josh. 17:17) or to an adviser (Prov. 24:5). It can be used for either good or evil. It does not have to be the latter: 'Do not withhold good from those to whom it is due, when it is in your power to do it' (Prov. 3:27).

The exercise of power is legitimate
Ultimately all power comes from God and is delegated to human beings (John 19:11; Eccles. 5:19; 2 Chron. 1:12). Power is given both to groups and individuals in a variety of circumstances – power to govern (with authority invested in a particular office), to denounce evil, in prayer, in wisdom and understanding (e.g. Ps. 8:5–8; 115:16). The New Testament speaks particularly of the power or authority of Jesus Christ in the coming of God's rule (Luke 4:14; 5:17; 11:20). The resurrection is the chief evidence of God's power at work (Rom. 1:4; Eph. 1:19–20).

Power is easily corrupted

The Bible speaks often of those who use power to oppress others: 'Again I saw all the oppressions that are practised under the sun. Look, the tears of the oppressed – with no one to comfort them! On the side of their oppressors there was power' (Eccles. 4:1; also Mic. 2:1–2; Eccles. 8:9; Jas. 5:1ff.). Power which is given by God to bring order and harmony to the world is distorted and used to dominate and manipulate others. That is why some have spoken of the 'disorder of order'.

Behind the corruption of power, the New Testament speaks of evil forces at work – 'principalities and powers'. Although their origin is in Christ (Col. 1:16), they exercise their power independently of, and therefore against, his purposes. The consequence of their activities may be seen in the political realm (1 Cor. 2:6,8; Acts 13:27), in intellectual life (Col. 2:8) and in religious observance (Col. 2:20ff.; Gal. 4:3).[22]

For this reason a Christian recognises that the misuse of power is not something that can be put right by purely human initiatives, using power wholly for righteous ends, for that would be to neglect the fact that power is exercised within a network of structures which are themselves perverted within a cycle of distortion.

Power is transformed by Christ

The Gospel represents a reversal of a common view of power: 'The word of the cross is folly to those who are perishing, but to us who are being saved it is the power of God' (1 Cor. 1:18; also Rom. 1:16). To receive as a gift the salvation which belongs to the new order of Jesus Christ, one has to give up trusting in those things that represent power in this age: wisdom, religious knowledge, status, prestige, wealth, high office (1 Cor. 1:26–8).

So power is redefined in the light of the crucifixion of Jesus Christ. In brief, it is the freedom to let go of all that hinders a life of sacrificial love (Mark 10:42–5; John 10:17–18; 3:1; Phil. 2:5ff.).[23]

The exercise of power

In its legitimate form, power is used to protect people from the arbitrary power of others. An act of empowerment establishes people's freedom and enables them to use it unselfishly and with integrity. When seen as an absolute right to possess, power inevitably leads to a struggle for power, as others seek to find an equal place in the sun.

If Christians wish to take seriously 'mission in the way of Christ', then their use of power must match his, 'who, though he was in the form of God, did not regard equality with God as something to be exploited, but emptied himself, taking the form of a slave' (Phil. 2:6). Power is seen in resistance to the temptation to use power to dominate. Power is not a kind of counterbalancing force which redresses inequalities, for in this way it will always lead to an inherently unstable situation – a kind of eternal struggle for rights denied or perceived to be denied. Rather, it is the transparent use of freedom to ensure, in so far as we are able, the freedoms of others.[24]

Power is a very subtle matter. Stephen Sykes recounts how the attempts within the Church to soften the suspicion surrounding all use of power – namely, associating it with the charisma of office and with the ministry of service – itself falls under suspicion:

> The first lends itself classically to analysis in terms of legitimation. One of the observable techniques of those who wish to exercise power over others is to clothe themselves with the mantle of divine approval . . . Were the theologians who endlessly celebrate servant-ministry less sociologically innocent they would know that the service conception of power is usually and especially favored by the powerful and those employed in defending and promoting their power.[25]

He is particularly critical of 'authoritarian liberals'. These are the people in the Church who attack hierarchy and bureaucracy, are antagonistic to elites and cabals and say they believe in increasing the participation in decision-making of those affected by the decisions. However, in Sykes's opinion, there is more than a whiff of hypocrisy in their stance:

> Power is exercised not just by the arguments of the articulate, but also by their control of the agenda . . . Authoritarian liberals are generally experts at concealing the fact that they are as ready as any totalitarian of the past to manipulate the

internal communications of the church to ensure that the mul-
titudes decide in favor of what they want confirmed . . . They
are expert in manipulation; they become spokespersons for
selected minorities whose campaigns entail the promulgation
of their own beliefs. In this way intellectual resistance to their
systems of belief can be represented as the persecution of a
minority and thus intolerable opinion.[26]

These harsh words appear to spring in part from personal experience of numerous meetings. They may be over-cynical, but there
is enough truth in them to show just how delicate and devious the
use of power can be. Sykes himself agrees that 'power is a term
indicative of resources available to human beings, the main types
of which are economic, military, legal and ideological'. He goes on
to say that its two most important features belong to a person's
intrinsic qualities and to the attributes appropriate to their public
position.[27]

From this discussion, we conclude that the controlled exercise
of power is intrinsic to sharing in partnership. This should be faced
openly and its implications confronted. The worst form of power
is not so much that of naked aggression or the flaunting of
authority but the disguised and manipulative schemings whose
aim is control of opinion and decision-making. I suppose the slogan
would have to be, 'In all things, transparency'.

The place of voluntary ('parachurch') agencies

One particular aspect of partnership is the position occupied by
agencies within the Church which are not directly linked to the
Churches' formal structures. Many of these are ecumenical or inter-
denominational in constitution. Most of them are recognised by
the Churches, but some may be operating rather as a law to themselves. All of them see themselves in some way as an arm of the
Church.

The Lausanne Covenant (1974) was positive about them: 'We
thank God for agencies which labour in Bible translation, theological education, the mass media, Christian literature, evangelism,
missions, church renewal and other specialist fields'. Their only

theological rationale is in the service they can give to the Churches, fulfilling those tasks which the Churches see as necessary but which they do not have the resources on a local level to accomplish. Their main objective should be to facilitate co-operation between local churches and across denominational boundaries. They may provide opportunities for fellowship, worship, teaching, evangelism and service, acting as catalysts and giving encouragement, but never trying to be substitutes for the Churches. They are in the words of the Pattaya Conference (1980), 'other Christian ministries'. In a complex and sophisticated world it is good to have specialist groups who can share their particular experience and expertise:

> I want to plead for the importance of voluntary movements in the Church for the fulfilment of the Church's mission. The partnership between the churches can be greatly assisted by people who are called to fulfil particular tasks. The whole Church is missionary, but people are called to fulfil particular tasks in that missionary Church.[28]

The existence of these voluntary organisations and their relationship to the established ecclesial structures has not always been benign. Michael Nazir Ali recognises, for example, that such organisations are sometimes formed because a group of Christians becomes impatient with what it regards as the failure of the Church to live up to its calling. Speaking of the Church Mission Society (CMS), he says: 'It saw itself as an independent organisation which could take initiatives in mission *without waiting for opinion to change in the Church's hierarchy*'.[29] Undoubtedly, members of the Church have sometimes unnecessarily succumbed to the entrepreneurial spirit of the age, initiating projects, and founding institutions and organisations which have been detrimental to mission rather than furthering it. On the other hand, where the Church at large is clearly failing to fulfil its mission vocation responsibly and with dedication, initiatives by groups of Christians in obedience to the Gospel seem to be perfectly in order.

There are therefore a number of questions that voluntary agencies must be prepared to wrestle with constantly, if they genuinely desire to promote mission.

The question of loyalties
Those involved in other Christian ministries often tend to remain
on the fringe of the local church, both critical of what they might
see as its traditionalism and fear of experimentation, and too
immersed in their own work to be able to support the local mission.
Of course, there are exceptions.

The question of openness to other Christians
Sometimes specialist groups are hesitant to share in discussion
with other Christians on those topics which they consider to belong
to their own field of expertise (e.g. medical ethics, education,
economics). They become possessive and dismissive of the ability
of others to have an informed opinion on matters into which they
may have done a lot of research. One of the consequences of such
an attitude is that Christians have had great difficulty in achieving
a genuinely multidisciplinary approach to important ethical and
social issues, and in being able to see them in a missiological
perspective.

The question of accountability
Voluntary agencies tend to be self-perpetuating, governed by a
board or council of individual people who do not necessarily act
as representatives of the Church or have a mandate from it, and
administered by people they appoint. Particularly in the case of
agencies which straddle denominations, there are few lines of
accountability to other structures. As long as they can persuade
the general Christian public to support their venture financially,
they can continue without having to answer for their decisions.
Again there are exceptions – particularly those that have an active
membership and representative councils.

The question of duplication
The entrepreneurial spirit looks for niches in the market. It can
almost become an end in itself. Rival organisations (for example,
in student work) are set up for no better reason than that somebody
else has different ideas, new techniques, a slightly different
theology or has identified another market. *The UK Christian Handbook*, for example, lists thousands of voluntary organisations in

almost every conceivable field of ministry. It is unlikely that all of
these are doing such a specialist job that a gap would be noticed
if they were to amalgamate with other similar organisations.

The question of long-term commitment

Some voluntary agencies exist as a kind of task-force. They see
their purpose in terms of engaging in highly concentrated evangelistic efforts which may last for weeks or even months, but not as
a permanent assignment in a locality. The rationale for this
approach lies either in their conviction that local Christians are not
effectively evangelising or that there are no local Christians. Quite
often, as we have mentioned before, they are able to recruit local
people (it has to be said, with some financial inducement) as temporary leaders to give the impression that the work is indigenous.

On the whole such agencies are inimical to genuine mission in
so far as they have not received a proper invitation from the local
churches, are not prepared to dedicate sufficient time to learning
local languages and culture and often come with strategies which
are hopelessly inappropriate to the local situation (everyone has
their horror story about such agencies working in Eastern Europe
and the former Soviet Union).[30] Quite often, as well, they have
not learnt the subtle sensitivities needed to deal with the secular
authorities. Their presence is therefore often an embarrassment to
local Christians who are left to pick up the pieces of an inade-
quately conceived evangelistic and church-planting strategy.

Co-operation in mission

The effects of non-co-operation

Failure of different Churches, agencies and individual Christians
to work together wherever they can has a detrimental effect on
mission. It causes a credibility gap between reality and the
message. Though the Gospel proclaims that faith in Christ brings
reconciliation, a healing of divisions and a release of love into
situations and relationships, people often see Christians adopting
policies which are based on suspicion, guilt by association and
conspiracy theories. It causes a tragic waste of resources in the
duplication of time, money and human abilities. 'Sheep stealing' –

the growth of some churches and mission agencies by attracting the disaffected from other bodies – is not checked. Such activities cause suspicion and resentment, making co-operation even less likely. Finally, it makes mutual correction more difficult: stereotypes from the past are not challenged and dealt with, and there is little fresh input to produce creative new ways of being involved in mission. Those who see no need to co-operate highlight their sense of self-sufficiency and their presumptuous belief that their ways are best. I think it is true that Christians do not really understand the meaning of communion and community until they feel deeply the pain of separation.[31]

Conditions for co-operation

The conditions for co-operation vary according to the objectives in view. In some cases – such as the Jubilee 2000 Coalition – a broad alliance of partners is possible. The aim is sharply focused and the strategies widely acceptable. In other examples of political activism, there need to be shared ideological positions reflecting similar views of the social implications of Christian faith.[32] In evangelism, there needs to be an agreement about the content of the message to be shared, the legitimate means for making it known and the identity of the recipients. Thus, for example, it would be difficult to co-operate in evangelism if some people held that it was inappropriate to share the message with people of (some) other religious traditions, or if some believed that salvation depended on joining a particular church, or if some were convinced that salvation was possible outside Jesus Christ.

Then there has to be a real concern for one another. Co-operation is much stronger when there is a commitment not just to a particular common task but to a deepening sense of responsibility for each other. Prior to the common engagement, those involved express a desire to grow together into a deeper fellowship of love and caring. If the co-operation is in an evangelistic programme, there needs to be prior agreement about the nurturing process of any who express faith and their integration into local fellowships – in order to avoid possible accusations and recriminations in the period following the joint enterprise.

Partnership in practice

There are already many examples of Christian communities, either within their own nation or across the world, linking with other Christian communities in shared ventures. The flow of mission partners has been one of the most obvious and a tangible expression of the universality of the Gospel. Of course, it has to be in all directions. One way of facilitating this is by globalising mission agencies so that they become truly intercontinental, operating with leadership from many nations, with local expressions and regular meetings for consultation. One organisation that has achieved this to some extent in recent years is The Navigators, a pioneering evangelistic operation that emphasises the study of the Bible as a means of witness. Many of the Roman Catholic orders have been working unobtrusively, but effectively, in this way for many years. Where these organisations have arisen in the West, it is crucial that leadership should not remain there but be distributed geographically according to gifts and abilities.

If agencies are truly international in their personnel, there is a better chance that resources will be distributed according to criteria agreed by people representing Churches in many nations. This may be a better model of partnership than the more common practice of national mission agencies, church districts or dioceses committing themselves to a companion relationship. In the latter case, the control of resources still remains with the body within one nation. In the international character of agencies, the principle of diversity in unity works itself out in a genuinely transnational practice.

Alongside these large-scale partnerships there is plenty of room for more localised expressions, where individual churches or small groups of churches engage in common tasks in two very different localities. One example of this is given by Robert Moffitt.[33] It concerned a co-operative enterprise between a Christian high school in Ohio and a village in the Dominican Republic, in which the former helped the latter achieve its vision of a development project that included a permanent source of clean water, provision of a staple diet and the means of work for the people. The value of this particular partnership lay in the fact that the initiative came from the village and the project was designed and owned by the people.

The dilemma of this kind of exchange is how to make it genuinely mutual, so that the traffic is not all one way – from the North to the South. Unless those who are involved are profoundly changed in their understanding of the Gospel and mission by their experience of another Christian community, the exercise may not be much more than the alleviation of an uneasy conscience. It would be better still if the community in the South could share in person, with communities in the North, their gifts and understanding of mission in the way of Christ.

Exercises

1. Draw up a list of what you consider to be the necessary aspects of genuine partnership.

2. Say how you would communicate to your church the criticisms of partnership you have heard during a recent trip overseas.

3. Consider one example of mission exchange known to you and comment on its strengths and weaknesses.

11

The Church in Mission

The enigma of the Church

Throughout this study we have assumed that, in one way or another, the Church is at the heart of God's mission. It is the Church that evangelises, finds appropriate cultural channels to express the faith of Jesus Christ, participates in the struggle for justice and the care of the environment, engages in dialogue with people of other faiths and builds peace. However, as we noted in chapter 2, the centrality of the Church continues to be disputed.

Under fire

There are a number of reasons why people engaged in or writing about mission are hesitant to give the Church too central a role. The first has to do with the Church's own self-consciousness. In seeking to explain itself both to itself and to those outside, it has often chosen inappropriate models – models which intrinsically contradict the idea of mission. One such is 'the ark of salvation'. This portrays the Church as a safe haven into which people may escape from the perplexities and dangers of a hostile and difficult world. It may be that individuals entrust their spiritual life to the Church, trustingly accepting the means of salvation which the Church claims to offer. Or it may be that finding intellectual problems (for example, in the realm of science and faith) or moral issues too difficult to cope with, they compliantly submit to the Church's official teaching. In this way they are rescued from the threat of being submerged by the beliefs and practices of a culture they do not understand or care much about.

The model of the ark tends to reflect an authoritarian institution. It is important that there are no leaks, no mutiny on board and few people trying to steer it. The leader (captain) is familiar with all the details of the vessel, who literally 'knows the ropes', who is a true professional seafarer. He (almost certainly) will seek to make the passengers as comfortable as possible, especially when going through particularly choppy seas. One of the many problems with the 'ark' model of the Church (which may exist in many different traditions – Catholic, Orthodox, evangelical or charismatic) is that its pastoral practice may be divorced from an understanding of its own historical context. This allows it to believe that any substantial change is already a surrender to forces hostile to its core self-understanding.[1]

Another reason to have serious misgivings about the role of the Church is its fear of contamination in public affairs. This may be seen in the Church's reluctance, due to a fear of being co-opted into someone else's agenda, to join forces with other agencies in condemning state oppression and political corruption or in campaigning for civil liberties, just wages or protection of the environment.

There is also the danger of triumphalism, in which the Church makes grandiose claims for itself as God's agent in order to increase its membership. The concern is that the Church will monopolise or domesticate God by giving the impression that it has some prior claim to or copyright on spiritual life or the divine order. Some see this as particularly serious in the context of the Church's relationship with other faith communities, in that their beliefs and practices tend to be assessed by the Church's understanding of the divine reality.

A final objection to the centrality of the Church springs from its failure on so many occasions to live up to its own principles, or even to values accepted as normal in open democratic societies. Thus, for example, it has a poor record in its treatment of women, and even when it claims to have rediscovered in the New Testament the essential equality of women and men in all aspects of ministry (why has this only happened following the rise of feminist movements?), it either acknowledges this with great reluctance or exempts certain offices from equal treatment.[2] Thus, it is argued, if God's mission is largely tied to the Church then God's freedom is seriously compromised.

These and other arguments are well known.[3] There will always be some – either those who have been nurtured in the Church from the beginning of their lives or those who have spent part of their later lives there – who find the contradictions and the constrictions too much to tolerate; if they remain believers at all, they will reinterpret God's purposes in the world in a non-ecclesial way. For others, nevertheless, although the Church is a chastened and weak vessel, it is quite indispensable to the fulfilment of God's mission in the world. It can, of course, never presume on God's favour. Its call to mission and its renewal in faithfulness are inseparable:

> There has been a great deal of reflection these last decades on the possibility and reality of change in the church ... There has been a sense of the need to assert the indefectibility of this church, which is the Lord's, and which receives from him ... nourishment, origin and life ... It has been considered urgent to emphasize the fact that this very life, this very nourishment require that the church, at once holy and in need of purification, ... be constantly renewed, reshaped in every age in conformity with the demands of its being and mission.[4]

Perplexed, but not driven to despair

The Church exists in mission because the restoration of a damaged humanity to wholeness can only happen in community. Because God's offer of salvation is universal (1 Tim. 2:3), the community which experiences the true meaning of life has to be universal as well. There is no other body which has the potential for demonstrating, across every conceivable divide, the healing of the wounds caused by hate, deception, selfishness and brutality.

The difference between the Old and New Testaments in God's way of bringing about salvation is between two different kinds of community – not that salvation is corporate in one and individual in the other. The discussion about whether Jesus intended to found the Church is hypothetical for two reasons. In the first place, the answer has to be quite clearly 'No' *if* the territorial Church of Christendom is envisaged. The question about this Church (and all subsequent expressions) is whether it is in recognisable continuity with Jesus' mission or represents such a deviation that it has become a body with incompatible aims to his. In the second place, the answer has to be quite clearly 'Yes' *if* it is believed that Jesus was the Messiah.

Although Jesus in his public ministry clashed with prevailing views about the task of the Messiah, there was no dispute about the centrality of a renewed community.[5] The differences (and they were major) were over the composition and purpose of the community. Apart from the use of 'church' (*ekklesia*) by Jesus on two occasions (Matt. 16:18; 18:17), which are disputed texts, there are at least three other strong indications that he saw the formation of a community as part of his strategy.

1. His use of imagery

Jesus uses a wide variety of figures to refer to his disciples as a group. They are drawn from the Old Testament, where they were used of God's people: for example, 'flock' (Luke 12:32; Mark 14:27); 'wedding guests' (Mark 2:19); 'God's building' (Matt. 5:14; Luke 16:8); 'family' (Mark 10:29ff.): 'There is no doubt that Jesus speaks repeatedly with the greatest variety of imagery about the gathering of the people of God that he is bringing about'.[6]

2. His calling of the Twelve

The symbolism of a core group of twelve to represent the first nucleus of the community of a renewed covenant would hardly be lost on any Jew of the first century:

> The very existence of the twelve speaks, of course, of the reconstitution of Israel; Israel had not had twelve visible tribes since the Assyrian invasion in 734 BC, and for Jesus to give twelve followers a place of prominence, let alone to make comments about them sitting on thrones judging the twelve tribes, indicates pretty clearly that he was thinking in terms of the eschatological restoration of Israel.[7]

Likewise, the call of a further 70 (Luke 10:1ff.) was designed to show that the new community was to be extended to all the nations,[8] fulfilling Israel's calling to be 'a light to the nations, that my salvation may reach to the ends of the earth' (Isa. 49:6).

3. His proclamation of the kingdom
Inherent in the notion of the kingdom of God is a renewed people fit for the Lord. This is to be the kind of community that God intended:

> The story Jesus was telling, the story of the kingdom, was Israel's story. He intended those who responded to him to see themselves as the true, restored Israel . . . If we rule out this whole sphere of Jesus' teaching as unhistorical, on the grounds that Jesus did 'not intend to found a church', we are quite simply failing to think historically.[9]

Although there is much confusion in the disciples' minds about Jesus' project (as the gospels record), it is historically credible that there should have been a rump group of about 120 (Acts 1:15) gathered in Jerusalem between the feasts of Passover and Pentecost in the year that Jesus died. This group, still muddled about their calling (Acts 1:6–7), gradually began to understand that the 'Israel' to whom Jesus would restore the kingdom was no longer geographically or ethnically defined, but precisely a community that would embrace people of every language who believed that Jesus was God's agent of final salvation (Acts 2:11; 2:36; 3:20–1; 10:45–8; 11:20–1). It is safe to conclude, therefore, that central to mission in the way of Christ is the life and witness of a renewed community.

Prepared for mission

The community of disciples that Jesus drew around himself and sent out to be witnesses to God's mighty acts of liberation had distinctive marks. These characteristics were (and are) a prerequisite for the faithful fulfilment of that community's mission calling. Let us note some of the most important.

Indiscriminate love
One of the most distinctive qualities of the Jesus community is its openness to all people. In Jesus' time this was a deliberate response to what one might call the 'remnant theology' of other groups (the ritual purity and legal correctness of the Pharisees and the monastic separateness of the Essenes). Their requirements for membership

were strict and excluding.[10] Jesus turns to those barred by the
'remnant' groups and expects his disciples to do likewise (Luke
14:13, 21; 10:37).

Unconditional trust in God

The relationship between Jesus' disciples and God is to be one of
intimacy. The nearest human analogy is that of children in the
closest possible relationship of confidence, reliance and safety with
their parents (Luke 11:11–12). The disciples can be assured of their
share in the salvation of the kingdom, quite apart from any merit
(Matt. 18:10, 14; Luke 12:32). They can rely on God for their
security; nothing is too insignificant for him (Matt. 6:8, 32ff.; Luke
12:30). They can have the courage to submit to uncertainty,
knowing that God's will for their lives is always the highest good.
When suffering comes (the result of faithfulness to the kingdom
project), they will understand the reasons (cf. John 9:2ff.; Luke
13:1–5; Mark 12:27). [11]

Distinctive behaviour

Jewish moral behaviour was based on *torah* (the written law) and
halakah (the oral interpretation, designed to ensure that the law
would not be abused and Israel discredited). In the Sermon on the
Mount Jesus taught the members of the new community the norms
of the new expression of God's rule.[12] He emphasised those qualities of life that were absolutely fundamental to the children of the
living God. Jesus did not abolish the law, nor even necessarily
criticise the attention to detail in the regulations set down for
keeping the sabbath, ritual purity and sacrifice. Rather, he challenged all his hearers to a fresh vision of God who requires
forgiveness, reconciliation, the utmost respect for the easily exploit-
able (women in particular), complete integrity, non-retaliation and
generosity (especially to enemies) (Matt. 5:21–48). Behaviour was
not a matter of codes of conduct, which inevitably leads to a
minimalist ethic, but a matter of 'like father, like son and daughter':
'You will be children of the Most High . . . be merciful, just as your
Father is merciful' (Luke 6:35–6).

    There is plenty of evidence in the rest of the New Testament to
suggest that the early Church took seriously the call to a distinctive

lifestyle.[13] The letter to the Ephesians is one case in point. The Christians were exhorted to live 'according to the likeness of God in true righteousness and holiness' (Eph. 4:24), which is the 'way you learned Christ... taught in him, as truth is in Jesus' (Eph. 4:20–1). The three fundamental principles that were to guide their life together were *absolute honesty tempered by love* (Eph. 4:15; 4:25–6), *provision for the needy* (Eph. 4:28), and *forgiveness* (Eph. 4:32; 5:2). Then they would be 'imitators of God, as beloved children' (Eph. 5:1). There are a number of echoes here of Jesus' teaching.

Discipline

However, if one might characterise the messianic community as being anti-sectarian (open membership) and anti-legalistic (not built on conventions and rules inherited from the past), is there not a danger of an unbridled antinomianism taking over? How does the Church work through in practice its witness to the fact that 'the kingdom is not a new legalism or a universal religious or political code, but rather a new order of grace fueled by the energy of love... not a kingdom without law and judgement, but... without legalism and vindictiveness'?[14] Are there any grounds for the Church disciplining (meaning regulating, reprimanding and punishing) those who fail to live 'according to the likeness of God'?

This is a matter which has concerned, among others, Stanley Hauerwas. He believes that 'the church seems caught in an irresolvable tension... Any attempt... For the church to be a disciplined and disciplining community seems antithetical to being a community of care'. The problem stems in part from the expectations of a culture that puts a high premium on accepting all, whatever mess their values or lifestyle may have got them into, with a wholly non-judgemental attitude: 'Care requires understanding the particularities of the individual's situation so that the very idea of disciplining someone in a personal crisis is unthinkable.'

Behind this concept of pastoral counselling is the further widespread belief that 'Christianity is... a belief system necessary for people to give meaning to their lives... salvation is for the individual'. The Church, at least in the West, has bought heavily into the prevailing expectation of the culture that the Church's task is to enable human beings to function better in a tolerant, liberal society, whose highest moral criterion seems to be that of not causing harm to others: 'We have underwritten a voluntaristic conception of the Christian faith, which presupposes that one can become a Christian without training'.

In contrast to this enfeebled view of Christianity, Hauerwas argues that the Church is a community in which one learns the discipline of discipleship at the hands of those who are qualified to pass on the skills of the craft: 'The teacher's authority must be accepted on the basis of a community of craft, which embodies the intellectual and moral habits we must acquire and cultivate if we are to become effective and creative participants in the craft'.[15]

The Church in mission has to be prepared to exert an internal discipline which demonstrates to the outside world that following in the way of Christ has well-defined boundaries which, if transgressed, make a mockery of the claims that a living relationship to Jesus Christ brings about a transformed existence in the world. Leaders have to be sensitive to the distinction in practice between legalism and righteousness.

Resources

Fortunately, the community has at its disposal immense assets to enable it to live up to its high calling. There is the story of Jesus which must be constantly retold as the fulfilment of God's promises to 'restore all things' (Acts 3:21; Eph. 1:10). There is the message of the apostolic community which both recites 'God's deeds of power' (Acts 2:11) and outlines the practical details of a redeemed life. In spite of much controversy over what is relevant and appropriate, there is the life of congregational worship centring on praise and thanksgiving. Here the Church recognises the author of its existence and life, and reminds itself 'that it lives by the amazing grace of a boundless kindness'.[16]

There is prayer by which one lives *in* God (in constant awareness of his personal presence) and *with* God (in his activity in the world). There is the encouragement given by testimonies of how sin and evil have been overcome in specific cases and how miracles of healing have happened. These are all signs of the reality of God's power at work in concrete situations 'to make all things new'. It

gives to Christians an 'audacious confidence that enables them to
go right on doing what others say is impossible or futile'.[17]

To divorce mission from life in community is to deprive oneself
of just those resources which make mission in the way of Christ
possible. However much the Church seems to fail to live up to
expectations, within this community alone the Jesus story is still
told, the grace and forgiveness of God are proclaimed, the 'subversive memory' of the crucified Messiah is still celebrated week
by week, there is encouragement and strength offered in the exercise of gifts. Those who have abandoned the Church have cut
themselves off from the gift of life. There is no adequate substitute.

Engaged in the world

Sacred and secular

In some societies the Church has a hard battle to rid itself of the
insidious distinction drawn between 'holy' and 'non-holy' things.
The sacred is often understood as referring to a special realm of
life associated with the spiritual, religion or God, or to special
events or places. Sacred things are to be reverenced and handled
with care. The secular, on the other hand, relates to worldly,
ordinary things not associated with religion or life beyond the
material. The West, defined by a set of common attitudes to life
built on a world-view with particular historical antecedents, is said
to be 'secular', meaning that its belief in God is no longer formative
and its religious commitment is marginal.[18]

Even if the two supposed spheres are not seen as being in
opposition to each other, it is a cultural commonplace to think of
them as separate. The first has to do with special moments of life,
when God (or equivalent divine presence) is felt to be close. The
second is ordinary, everyday, routine life. In order to enjoy the first
to the maximum it is necessary to get away from the second – by
going to church, participating in retreats, going to beautiful places,
listening to outstanding music or doing something exhilarating or
unusual.

From a Christian perspective the distinction is false. The secular,
understood as the legitimate tasks of ordinary life – family, work,
scientific investigation, gardening, hobbies, leisure, friendships,

political tasks, service in the community – is sacred. The sacred is
not another reality distinct from this, but the truly real life shorn
of all illusions. Encounter with God is possible in any place (John
4:21–4), all foods are clean for eating (Mark 7:19; Acts 10:15), the
sabbath is created for human beings (Mark 2:27), places of pilgrimage were unknown to the Church for some 300 years after its
birth, the scrupulous observance of special days and seasons signi-
fies a loss of freedom in Christ (Gal. 4:8–11; Col. 2:16–17, 20–3).

The modern distinction between the two probably originated
in the dichotomy erected between nature and grace in medieval
theology: nature was a medium sufficient for attaining a certain
knowledge of God, but had to be topped up by supernatural grace.
Gradually nature and supernature were seen as detached spheres,
only conjoined at special times and through special channels (the
sacraments). Later, under the influence of rationalism, discon-
nection became isolation and eventually autonomy. The natural no
longer needed supernature; because human reason was capable of
self-correction, nature was perfectable from within.

The dichotomy is fatal to a coherent view of mission, for it allows
a particular culture to believe that the message of Jesus Christ is
applicable only to some esoteric segments of life – what people do
in private. Lesslie Newbigin's sometimes misunderstood call for
the Church in the West to engage in the mission task of proclaiming the Gospel as 'Public Truth' should not cause the scandal
that it does among certain Christians.[19] It is but another way of
saying that no part of life (the so-called public or the so-called
private) is outside God's rule in judgement and grace. Such a
point of view seems perfectly obvious to anyone scanning quickly
through almost any passage in the Old or New Testaments. Perhaps
it is the word Truth (with a capital T) that causes offence – but a
moment's reflection should show that all Christians lay hold of the
idea of truth, even if only for the particular campaigns they are
interested in or for language they habitually use. In real life, simultaneously to deny that anything is true or good or that anything
is false or evil is preposterous, and in any case it does not happen.

Mission to political life

It has been said, half-mockingly though with some truth, that the only thing we learn from history is that we fail to learn anything much. Those who do not learn from past mistakes are condemned to repeat history. The Church has been as guilty as any other body, not least in its political involvement – a highly ambiguous area, if there ever was one.

The reality of politics is complex, with many hazards to trap the inexperienced. The Church finds itself in a wide variety of different situations: political life may be stable or rapidly changing; democratic principles may, or may not, be observed; the Christian faith may be the prevailing religion, either for historical reasons or because of the sheer number of Christians in the nation, or it may be a minority tradition; the Church may have some influence in the political arena or almost none; it may be tolerated, restricted or actively persecuted.

If the Church believes itself called to engage in political life generally or only in particular issues, it has to understand the distinctive nature of its own political context. This includes its own past involvement, key historical events and movements, cultural factors (like ethnicity) and ideological stances. Assuming, as we must, that one crucial aspect of mission in the way of Christ is the service of others through political means, we may speak of a triple role for the Church.[20]

1. The prophetic task

From a biblical perspective, the thing that those in politics most need to know is who God is and how he acts. As Paul declared to the Roman governor Felix and his Jewish wife Drusilla, God is about 'justice, self-control and the coming judgement' (Acts 24:25). Authorities in the state have been instituted to uphold the rule of law based on a clear distinction between good and evil (Rom. 13:3–4). They are to serve an ethical norm which finds its source in God's character. 'Submission' (Rom. 13:1) includes holding them to their high responsibility; in doing this we show that we take political authority seriously. They need to be reminded that they have no absolute role or status; they are not the arbiter of the

destiny of the people or of individuals.[21] They need to know
the consequences of breaking God's laws, the purposes of economic
life and the implications of God's justice in human affairs. The
Church can fulfil an important mission in monitoring all tendencies
by government to assume too much power or to credit itself with
messianic pretensions.

Sometimes, to the extent of great suffering and martyrdom, the
Church has been a strong prophetic voice against arrogant political
claims and brutal political repression. The one caution that has to
be sounded is that the Church, in carrying out a prophetic role,
seeks no political power or privileges for itself. In taking a prophetic stance it must not serve its own ends, only those of the
message entrusted to it.

2.   The servant task

The Church is called to intercessory prayer for civic leaders at all
levels, not merely on formal occasions but in the individual and
corporate prayer life of its members. Prayer witnesses to the conviction that life in society can only be harmonious when God
acts favourably towards a nation. But prayer also witnesses to a
separation between the Church and the state in which the political
leader is free from religious dictation, for the act of praying demonstrates a hesitation about being in the right – 'Not what I want,
but what you want' (Mark 14:36). As prayer is active, it implies
offering oneself for service in the community. Where it is possible
for Christians to be actively engaged, the idea of vocation – of
putting one's gifts, experience and training at the disposal of civil
society without expecting a large financial return – is indispensable
to mission.

3.   The evangelistic task

It might seem strange to include evangelism as part of the Church's
mission in political life. It would, however, be a mistake to interpret
the Church's place in politics as being solely direct, hands-on
action. There are some who have narrowed mission almost entirely
to mean the struggle for justice, interpreted as engagement at
all levels to bring about political structures which enable equal
opportunities for all and which, as a matter of priority, meet the

real needs of the disadvantaged. This, however, is to miss the very centre of the Christian faith. Evangelism is a visible witness to society concerning the core of all its basic problems: 'It is what comes out of a person that defiles. For it is from within, from the human heart, that evil intentions come . . .' (Mark 7:20–1) – and the fundamental solution is God's grace and forgiveness, reconciliation and a new beginning. Evangelism also points to the reality of a transforming power beyond daily political life.[22]

Of course, evangelism has a political dimension. At the same time, politics is carried out by people who need to hear for themselves the good news of Jesus Christ. If it is true that Christians should not privatise their faith, withdrawing it from any public expression, it is also true that no wedge can be driven between the public and private life of those involved in politics. It is a damaging piece of fiction to pretend that the public persona is divorced from what the private persona believes and does. It is an interesting commentary on the ethical confusion of modern cultures that a politician's personal financial affairs are considered of great public significance but infidelity in marriage is said to be of no public concern. The Church should witness against this false dualism.

The local church and mission

A considerable part of the renewal of the Church will happen when Christian thinking is properly integrated with Christian action and prayer at the local level. Although the term 'local church' can be used of the Church at a regional level, such as a diocese or district, I have in mind the local community of Christians gathered together for weekly worship, prayer and other activities. They are not an isolated body but belong to the Church organised at wider levels. Nevertheless, Christians gathered together in a unit within a definable geographical urban or rural boundary form the nucleus of the Church.

The nature of the going church
Assuming that going and being in the heart of the world is the essence of mission, the Church should see itself as a people on the move. At one and the same time Christians are to travel *into* the

heart of the world, being at the points of suffering and need, and *towards* God's new creation. The Church is a 'fellowship of the resurrection', an event of the past which anticipates the transformation of all decay and corruption into new life (Acts 2:24, 31). The Church is like a pin attracted to the magnet of the coming restoration of God's rule over the whole of life. It is a community 'with a view to' in both senses: 'looking towards' and 'having a goal'.

It has been said that the Church should live in the present as if the future was already a reality. Such a vision probably requires of most local churches a fundamental conversion from a view that the Church is *what it does* to a view that it is about *what God does*. It is natural, and the line of least resistance, to think of the Church in terms of its activities and to think of renewal as the updating or renovation of these activities. It is more common today for local churches to formulate a mission statement. How common is it, though, for this statement to make a fundamental difference to the way a church organises itself? How often does it reconsider its life in the light of its vision? How often does it re-examine the statement?

Structures to enable mission

If the church in mission is the community of Christians, either individually or together, engaged in activities that spring from mission in the way of Christ (John 17:15–18), the local church, to be church, must so order its life that this is facilitated. It simply has no rationale beyond that. This may mean that some churches need to reduce drastically their activities; others may need to reorder them.

By way of provoking discussion, I would suggest that (ideally) the local community of Christians should come together twice each week: once on Sunday (or, maybe, another convenient day) for corporate worship and training; during the week for sharing in smaller groups. I would further suggest that 'house fellowship groups' (they have a variety of different names) are the key to the local church in mission, whether in rural Norfolk or rural China, in urban Birmingham (UK or USA) or urban Johannesburg. Their role is to encourage and enable Christians to witness to the truth of the Gospel in everyday activities in the world. These groups focus on the *stories* of their members, on *prayer* for specific needs and on *Bible study* to seek the mind of Christ in particular situations and choices.

According to their gifts, callings and time available, Christians are involved in their local community in a variety of ways. Through prayer, study, discussion, sharing and acting, these groups are workshops of the kingdom which prepare Christians to relate the good news of Jesus Christ to every kind of situation. They can also act as 'intermediate churches' in the sense of being the first place where complete outsiders come to a Christian fellowship. The overwhelming task of the local church's leadership is to equip these groups to function well, particularly by enabling mature reflection to take place on emerging issues.

This emphasis on action in the local community may give the impression that the numerical growth of the church as a goal of mission is being neglected. We will discuss the issue of church growth below, suffice it to say here that the model I am suggesting in no way minimises the task of proclaiming Christ 'in all seasons' (2 Tim. 4:2). Rather, it proposes a new context for doing so by proclaiming and demonstrating in practice that Christ is for all seasons.

The true Church's struggle is very often not so much with an indifferent or hostile world as with its own heritage. Mission necessitates a faith-commitment from which 'religion' has been eliminated. By 'religion' I mean the stylised performance of set obligations which come from human traditions rather than from the heart of the Gospel.[23]

Church growth

In many parts of the world the Church is growing faster than the population. The numerical growth of the Church has become not only an object of social and cultural analysis, to explore the reasons why the number of church members has exploded in some places but not in others, but also the subject of mission theory.[24]

Reasons for growth

The reasons for growth cannot be reduced to easy formulas. Ultimately it is a mystery. Nevertheless, in all areas of church growth certain common features can be noticed.[25]

Expectations

There is a belief that numerical growth is God's will for his Church. This is a growth not so much by addition as by multiplication. Planting new churches is therefore seen as the fundamental task of mission. This belief is fed by prayer and stimulates prayer. Churches set goals for themselves, and it is not long before a newly established local congregation is founding another one in a nearby area. Growth is partly the result of a precise set of goals being carried out with dedication and competence.

Commitment to evangelism

In some churches, the main condition for pastoral ministry is having founded a new church. Whole congregations are mobilised for evangelism, going where people are. Everyone is expected to win others for Christ. New converts, in particular, are expected to witness immediately to their new faith. In some cases, it almost becomes the proof of one's salvation.

Healing ministry

Much of the growth is accompanied by an extensive ministry of healing through the laying on of hands and prayer. There is an expectation that God will act directly. This healing ministry, often in the context of evangelistic campaigns, is particularly appealing in areas where there is little access to conventional medicine. The effects of the healing of social evils – like drunkenness, violence in the family, and serious drug-addiction – are powerful testimonies to the life-transforming power of the message preached.

Social dislocation

The shanty towns of the major cities of Third World nations are the places where growth is most notable. These are communities made up of myriads of people, often of different ethnic backgrounds, who have come from remote rural areas looking for work.

The new churches act as substitute families, giving a feeling of belonging and a strong sense of worth in what has otherwise been a degrading life. New members are treated as genuine 'brothers' and 'sisters'. In these church communities the poor find an identity and a willingness to share (including jobs).[26]

Failure of the 'old gods'

The new churches have shown themselves better able to orientate their members to rapid social and personal change than the traditional beliefs. The latter are associated with the failure of the world they leave behind. The Christian message is linked with the hope of a new life.

Homogeneous units

As stated earlier, Church Growth (with capital letters) has been erected into a theory of mission, associated with the name of Donald McGavran, once a missionary in India. This school of thought is centred around two basic convictions: that church planting is the Church's first and foremost mission priority; that to become Christians, people should not have to cross unnecessary barriers.[27] This leads to two major assumptions.

1. The homogeneous unit principle

It is a matter of observation that people are more ready to respond to Christ if they are allowed to remain in their separate ethnic and cultural groupings. For the sake of the growth of the Church it would be wrong to concentrate too much on bringing together separated communities, if this means that such people, as a result, would not hear the Gospel.

2. People groups

The unfinished task of world evangelism should be concentrated on small, well-defined, culturally integrated groups of people: for example, Urdu-speaking Muslim farmers of the Punjab; Cantonese-speaking Chinese refugees from South-east Asia living in France; Tamil-speaking Indian workers on Malaysian rubber plantations. Each of these sub-groups, of which there are thousands in the world, should be identified and a culturally relevant church planted among them.

Defence of the principle

Miriam Adeney in her book, *God's Foreign Policy*,[28] gives five reasons for supporting the idea of ethnically kindred churches:

- God is glorified by cultural diversity, which can only find full expression in churches made up of people of a uniform culture;
- Every person has the right to worship in his or her own language;
- If mixed congregations are insisted on, the cultural tradition of the majority will prevail; the cultural minority will feel alienated;
- They are more effective in evangelism within their own ethnic community;
- They are the best way of supporting Christians who are temporary residents overseas.

Criticism of the principle

Eddie Gibbs in his book on church growth[29] says that sometimes the common traits of homogeneity which bind people together are evil (as in several instances of the *Volkkirche*). The Church is bad news if the ethnic identity of some is justified as a reason for not working for the overthrow of racial, cultural and class barriers: 'A church which identifies itself exclusively with one group may live a self-centred, impoverished life ... which may result in the exclusion of the majority of the surrounding population.'[30]

René Padilla, after an extensive survey of the New Testament material relevant to the debate, comes to the following conclusions: [31]

- The Jews and Gentiles heard the Gospel together;
- Breaking down the barriers separating people was regarded by the early Church as part of the good news of Jesus Christ, not merely the later result of believing the Gospel;
- The early Church not only grew, but grew across cultural barriers;
- Authentic unity is always unity in diversity, not uniformity;

- Adjustments to belief and practice were never made to avoid the charge that Christian believers acted as traitors in abandoning their own culture to join another one.

> The apostles . . . regarded Christian community across cultural barriers not as an optional blessing to be enjoyed whenever circumstances were favorable to it or as an addendum that could be omitted if it were deemed necessary to do so, in order to make the gospel more palatable, but rather as essential to Christian commitment.[32]

In the light of the overwhelming evidence from the New Testament that ethnically separate churches would have been perceived as a denial of the Gospel, it is incumbent on those who would defend ethnically centred evangelism (and the grounds for *beginning* there are strong) to say how it would result in multi-ethnic, multicultural churches. They also need to demonstrate in practice, for the evidence seems to be contrary, that these ethnically, culturally or linguistically conscious churches do not aid unacceptable ethnic or cultural chauvinism or perpetuate barriers already in existence in society.[33]

Christian presence

Some Christians believe strongly that in certain circumstances the Church's mission is fulfilled by Christians being present among non-believers, witnessing to their faith by the quality of their life in sacrificial service and by their recognition of God's 'footsteps' already planted in other faith traditions and people's histories. Such a view of mission is hesitant about verbal proclamation, at least as a first strategy. Where the Church is a small minority within a religiously motivated host society, making little headway in its desire to spread the Gospel and plant new churches, direct verbal communication through personal witness, evangelistic rally, literature distribution, radio or television programmes may not be appropriate.

There are a number of aspects to this view of mission:

- It follows the pattern of the incarnation (birth and growth

within a culture before mission), in which the Christian has to
spend much time in sharing his or her life alongside people;
friendship, understanding and trust are unreservedly prerequi-
sites for sharing the story of Jesus Christ with anyone;

- Rather than taking the initiative in making a first move, it is
  designed to provoke curiosity and questions; the impression
  of aggressive behaviour can be avoided, or at least minimised;

- It is concerned to correct the distorted image of mission that
  Christians are only interested in people as potential converts;

- It demonstrates reliance on God; response to the Gospel is not
  dependent on the technique of the evangelist, but the work of
  the Holy Spirit;

- It emphasises the truth that Christ is already ahead of the
  missionary at work in the lives and culture of people; it is
  deemed arrogant, if not idolatrous, to presume that the
  missionary somehow 'carries' Christ with him or her.[34]

In one sense, 'Christian presence' as sensitive listening to and
identification with others is indispensable as a preparation for
sharing the Gospel. However, in the minds of some, the approach
hides both a lack of conviction about the imperative of evangelism
to call people to repent, believe the Gospel and be identified as
followers of Jesus Christ, and an uncertainty about the content of
the message.[35]

Of course, it is dangerous to speak or act as if we took Christ
with us, as if we could possess the Lord of the universe. There is,
certainly, a tendency in some quarters to be overconfident about
the exact nature of the message, and a proneness to reduce it to
easy formulas which can then be repeated whatever the situation.
That is a travesty of apostolic mission. Such an approach is in
danger of treating the recipient of the message as an object to be
manipulated for the sake of getting a predetermined result.

Nevertheless, 'presence' is not sufficient on its own as a means
of mission. Human beings left to themselves would imagine that
salvation must depend on the kind of life they lead, living up to
the best standards of the ethical code they have adopted. Even
faith can be turned into a merit. God's offer of salvation in Jesus
Christ is *sui generis*; it will not be discovered on one's own:

> Everyone who calls on the name of the Lord shall be saved.
> But how are they to call on one in whom they have not
> believed? And how are they to believe in one of whom they
> have never heard? And how are they to hear without someone
> to proclaim him? And how are they to proclaim him unless
> they are sent? (Rom. 10:14–15).

Paul's logic is impeccable. It is borne out in experience. Witness is
more than awakening some truth already lying dormant in a
person's subconscious. People need to hear the apostolic word
about Christ and be urged to believe and be saved. If this was true
of the Jewish people in the first century (Rom. 1:16; 3:30; 10:1ff.),
why should it not be true of people of all beliefs today?[36]

So, then, receptive and perceptive identification with the lives
and aspirations of others is an essential aspect of Christian witness,
but so is telling the good news. Only reliance on the presence of
the Holy Spirit can enable anyone to be bold – a characteristic
of the early Church (Acts 4:29; 9:27; 13:46; 14:3; 28:31; Eph. 6:19;
Phil. 1:14) – without being arrogant and aggressive.

Exercises

1. Suggest appropriate symbols for the Church in mission.

2. Give your response to the commonly expressed belief that the
    Church and politics do not mix.

3. Draw up an outline for a training weekend on church growth
    for your local church.

Postscript:
Whither Mission?

It is tempting but hazardous to try to peer into the future and determine the way in which mission issues might develop. On the one hand, there is a natural curiosity about the possible shape of things to come. On the other hand, there is an awareness that attempts to predict trends on the basis of today's reality are notoriously fragile. Human beings are full of surprises. The history they create is full of countless unknown variables. That is why confident forecasts about the future usually turn out to miss the mark by a long way.

Nevertheless, to remain interested only in the present is both unadventurous and demotivating. Although certain kinds of interest in the future may be wholly speculative, or even manipulative (such as the ways in which commercial interests try to control future markets), there are others (such as care for the environment) which spring from a real concern not to repeat the mistakes of the past and present.

The Church in mission is forward-looking. Though it is dependent on the history and traditions that have been created behind it, like the various campsites established during an assault on a high mountain peak, the goal is to reach the summit; onwards and upwards. To have a view of distant landscapes, even if shrouded in mist, is thus to be aware in part of the terrain that has to be crossed.

I will attempt to cover three areas related to the missionary pilgrimage into the future: the context of the journey, the maps that may be used and the state of the travellers.

The context of a new millennium

Assuming that the ominous warnings that the year 2000 will be ushered in with cataclysmic events prove to be unfounded, we need to ask what kind of world is likely to stretch on into the twenty-first century. In no particular order, there are a number of signposts. Needless to say, they cannot be exhaustive.

There will continue to be a resurgence of local cultural identities across the globe. Ethnic groups who believe themselves to be disadvantaged historically, culturally, socially, politically, economically or religiously will strive for recognition, an end to discrimination and a certain degree of independence. The struggle to affirm difference, which will include other minority groups than those with a common ethnic origin, will be contested on national, cultural, economic and ethical grounds.

Hence there will continue to be an unresolved tension between the call for tolerance and self-determination and the desire for coherence and integration. Many communities will live in the midst of the competing forces of fragmentation and uniformity. There will continue to be a number of tough localised or regionalised conflicts (such as those which are ongoing in the Balkans and the Horn of Africa) which are the result of these tensions.

An increasing plurality of identities will affect religious institutions and religious consciousness. In some parts of the world, contrary to the expectations of a generation ago, there is a revival of religious experience. It is homespun, esoteric, deeply pragmatic, intrinsically syncretistic. The search for spiritualities that offer some measure of self-fulfilment will probably increase and will certainly be the object of commercialisation.

This trend is probably a more overt manifestation of the latent popular religiosity which, despite all attempts to debunk religion, has survived fairly strongly in the West, as elsewhere. Whether or not this trend is much comfort to organised, traditional religious traditions, which have seen a substantial decline in membership, is hotly debated. The debate will certainly go on.

The globalisation of the economic forces of late capitalism will continue to shape the destiny of every nation and all peoples. The struggle between the ideology of freedom in the market and the countervailing forces calling for substantial modifications in the interests of those excluded from a truly human life will go on.[1] It may become more intense, if not vicious. It remains to be seen whether the present world economic order can survive the resentment and contradictions which it creates.

There could be a change of attitudes, caused either by ethical convictions or by pragmatic considerations, which would direct economic goals more towards meeting the needs of the most deprived. There could be some meltdown of the system due to mutually contradictory forces getting out of control. It is more likely, at least in the short term, that the present way of operating will go on largely unmodified, with regional crises (East Asia, South America) being more or less contained on a fairly *ad hoc* basis.

If the present scenario is largely unchanged, increasing numbers of people will be condemned to subhuman existences, the environment will continue to be ravished and despoiliated and the megacities will become even more 'mega', and more ungovernable. Increasing destitution will be paralleled by increasing crime: tourists and other foreigners will feel less and less safe abroad; conscription into Mafia-type gangs will become easier; young children will continue to be exploited as cheap labour, sex-objects, front-line fighters or a combination of any of the three.

Scientific experimentation, allied to commercial technological objectives, will drive on, producing spectacular results. The most significant will probably be achieved in the area of genetics. There will be a fierce debate about the positive benefits and the potential perils of gene classification and modification, both in humans and in plant life. It is a moot point whether governments will be prepared to set any limits (such as forbidding human cloning) to changes that could be carried out.

Those societies where advanced scientific research is undertaken tend to lack a consensual ethic based on intrinsic notions of right and wrong. In the long run, consequential considerations are likely to overrule an inherited natural distaste for certain scientific procedures. At the same time, the creative ingenuity of the human species will be harnessed for wholly admirable ends in the alleviation of suffering, the promotion of successful agricultural innovations that will benefit millions, the fight against crime and other causes.

Where participatory democracy is still absent, there will be increasing pressure to institute political structures properly accountable to the people. In a number of instances this will be fraught with difficulty and strongly resisted by ruling elites. However, these elites are likely to come under increasing pressure through the global access to information and the resulting progressive difficulties in suppressing dissidence and propagating misinformation. Newly inaugurated democratic structures will often be weak and vulnerable to corruption, a lack of civic understanding and the play of factions. They may well depend on the ability of different strands in society, which wish to see them flourish, to organise themselves solidly in their defence.

Maps for missionary engagement

Given that at least some of the trends outlined above are likely to form the context in which Christians will seek to be faithful to mission in the way of Jesus Christ, can we predict which maps (missiological principles) they will use to guide them in their thinking and action?

Jongeneel and van Engelen (following Amstutz, Mitterhofer and Kramm) have suggested that there are three main mission theologies underlying most mission thinking today:[2]

1. There is the theology of the *missio Dei* which sees mission as God's initiative;

2. There is a missiology which focuses on the role and activity of the Church;

3. There is an emphasis on mission as redemptive history.

These categorisations may be helpful in offering broad-brush interpretations among Christians of distinct approaches to mission thinking. The problem with them, however, is in the detail. Our two authors show how the *missio Dei* concept has been interpreted both 'from above', using the Scriptures as a textbook for understanding God's purposes in and for the world, and 'from below', using the context as the factor that determines how God is involved. This bifurcation may simply reflect the basic division between 'conservatives' and 'liberals' which Nancey Murphy, among others, sees as a typical product of modernity.[3]

The same possibility occurs with the place of the Church in mission. The Church can be seen as the goal of mission – in ecclesio-centric interpretations – or as the agent of mission – in interpretations which focus on the reign of God as the end of history. The same is true when we think about mission as redemptive history: it could mean the redemption or salvation of those who respond to God's call to be a special people within history, or it could mean all peoples who do not explicitly reject God's gracious offer of forgiveness and new life, however that is mediated.[4]

Within the mapping task, I suspect that there will be at least four trends which will continue on into the future. One group of people will tend to see mission in terms of gathered communities of people seeking to live faithfully the life and teaching received from Jesus Christ. Though convinced that witness to the Gospel must, by its very nature, take place within the structures of society, they will be sceptical about the power of human wisdom, techno-logical mastery of nature, interreligious pressure or even Christian presence to effect significant changes in the world. Modelling the reign of God in self-conscious communities of faith and obedience will be their design for mission. Though committed in principle to the growth of Christian communities as cells of the kingdom in diverse societies, their emphasis will be on the quality of disciple-ship before the quantity of converts made. Underlying their thinking will be the notion of *election for responsibility.*

A second group of people will sit loose to the importance of the institutional Church. Their interest will be in interpreting the signs of God's presence in the movements of human history and being at the 'cutting edge' in order to further those proposals and actions which seem to reflect goodness and compassion. They will tend to seek alliances with non-Christians and accommodate theological language about God's kingdom to language acceptable to other religions or to secular people. Underlying their thinking will be a strong emphasis on the *doctrine of creation* and on *natural theology.* They will see the kingdom being realised in terms of human flourishing, which, wherever it happens, will be a manifestation of God's salvation.

A third group will see mission in the classic terms of planting churches and thus increasing the numerical witness of Christian believers in society. For them, finding the most appropriate forms of communication will be the chief task of mission. Much thought and experiment will go into finding innovative ways of adapting the Gospel to different cultural situations. Not only language, but also patterns of church life (liturgy, leadership, ceremonies) and values will be adapted in order to remove, as far as possible, unnecessary barriers to faith in Jesus Christ. The priority of mission for them will be pioneer evangelisation, reaching out to communities where the good news of Jesus has either not been heard or has not been properly communicated. Underlying their thinking will be a stress on the *personal calling* to believe and on *belonging to the body of Christ*.

Finally, some will continue to strive hard to integrate the best aspects of all these different emphases. Their missiology will stress the need to work with others on common social and political agendas, even where motivations may be quite distinct. At the same time, they will be cautious in interpreting this work as in itself redemptive. Indeed, they will wish to witness to salvation in Jesus Christ at appropriate times in their co-operative work with people of other faiths and none.

They believe that the mandate 'to go into all the world' has no exclusion zones. Although they will be aware of the need for great sensitivity in introducing the message of Jesus Christ in some circumstances, they will constantly seek for the right openings to make him known. They will interpret the essence of religious freedom to be freedom to convert. They will wish to ensure that new groups of Christians have all the necessary resources to live healthily and grow. Underlying their thinking will be Paul's affirmation to the Church in Rome: 'From Jerusalem and as far round as Illyricum I have *fully proclaimed the good news* of Christ' (Rom. 15:19). By proclamation is meant the testimony of word and life.

The people of God in transit

We return in a sense to where we began. Mission is travelling. It is being on a journey. It is a restless moving towards the time when God will be all in all in creation and salvation (1 Cor. 15:28). Christians are in transit. They have never landed at their final destination in this life. There is no vacation from the Gospel calling. The only thing that 'cannot be shaken' is the kingdom of God (Heb. 12:28).

Hence, the Church is because mission is: *missio sit ergo ecclesia sit*. And because the Church collectively is missionary by definition, every member individually is also a missionary by definition. And because mission is global, the missionaries will also be global in their outlook: 'Missionaries are at home everywhere, but not quite at home anywhere. They are persons who can move easily from one place to another, from one culture to another, and not become confused, or lost, or incapable of action.'[5]

It would be wishful thinking, unfortunately, to believe that the real Church will match its high calling. The experience of 2000 years suggests that much of the institution will remain immobile. It will not be in transit because it has not even begun the journey. The maintenance of institutions – whether buildings, structures, forms of training, societies or liturgical practices – will take priority over mission. Although this has been recognised in countless documents and forums, the predisposition to conserve energy will dictate the pace of change. Radical breaks with the forms inherited from the past are psychologically too costly for all but a handful to take the risks involved.[6]

Nevertheless, mission will go on. Sometimes it will happen by way of groups that break away from the mainstream Churches. Sometimes they are justified, as when institutions have become so sterile that they are incapable of pursuing new initiatives or when they act in a way which brings the Gospel into disrepute. Sometimes they are not, as when separation is caused by personality clashes or power-struggles. Quite often these groups in turn lose their vision, and the cycle is repeated.

Throughout the history of Christianity renewal has come at the margins of mainstream Church life. People have organised themselves into voluntary societies to do a piece of work which the Church as a whole is manifestly failing to perform. These societies or unions may exist within a particular Church or they may operate across church boundaries. In one sense they are para-Church, but in another they *are* the Church fulfilling a role left wide open, like a football substitute who comes on to the field to plug a gap in the field of play. If one accepts that the religious orders of the Catholic Church function to some extent in this way, and if one also takes notice of the thousands of non-official or semi-official agencies within the Protestant Churches, it is fair to say that a high percentage of mission activity occurs by this means.

This is almost truer of the 'Third Church' (in the Third World) than it is of the erstwhile Church of the West. Mission 'from everywhere to everywhere' is up and running in the Churches of Africa, Asia and Latin America. If one were able to know every missionary activity (in the broad sense assumed in this book) taking place across the world, it would be quite impossible to find a master plan or overall strategy, except perhaps in the intention of the Holy Spirit, so numerous and diverse are the actions and enterprises. One might fairly say that the age of the expansion of the Church is barely beginning.

I would hazard two guesses for the future of mission. First, particular contexts will always have a profound influence on how the Church shapes its response to the Gospel. Missionary hermeneutics (the interaction between a well-grounded faith and a shifting kaleidoscope of events) will always be a pivotal discipline to guide the Church's thinking and action. This is as it should be; as is often said today, the message of Jesus comes embodied, and bodies exist only in specific bits of time and space.

Secondly, the contours of mission will remain as described in the main section of this book. Thinking will alter and the means of mission will change to remain appropriate to new situations. There may be different ways of cutting the cake or skinning the cat – alternative combinations of the various aspects of mission can be put together. Nevertheless, announcing the good news in culturally authentic ways, struggling to right the wrongs caused by economic malfunctioning, environmental degradation and conflict, engaging with people of different beliefs, establishing new communities of disciples and seeking the unity of Christians and human communities will remain the core missionary activities of a Church still attuned in the third millennium to the voice of its leader saying, 'Come! Follow me!'

Notes

1 What is Theology? And Theology of Mission?

1. Harold Brown (quoting Trillhaas), 'On Method and Means in Theology' in John Woodbridge and Thomas McComiskey, *Doing Theology in Today's World* (Grand Rapids, Zondervan, 1991), p. 149.
2. cf. Paul Helm, *Faith and Understanding* (Edinburgh, Edinburgh University Press, 1997), pp. 3–76.
3. David Wells (quoting Brian Hebblethwaite and Maurice Wiles), 'The Theologian's Craft' in Woodbridge and McComiskey, *Doing Theology*, p. 182.
4. ibid. p. 184.
5. cf. J. Andrew Kirk, *The Mission of Theology and Theology as Mission* (Valley Forge, Trinity Press International, and Leominster, Gracewing, 1997), pp. 14–18.
6. James Nickoloff (ed.), *Gustavo Gutiérrez: Essential Writings* (Maryknoll, Orbis Books, 1996), p. 33.
7. ibid. p. 24; cf. also, Maria Pilar Aquino, *Our Cry for Life: Feminist Theology from Latin America* (Maryknoll, Orbis Books, 1993).
8. David Ford (ed.), *The Modern Theologians: An Introduction to Christian Theology in the Twentieth Century*, 2nd edn (Oxford, Blackwell, 1997), pp. 726–7. A very useful, multidisciplinary and international discussion of 'ways of doing theology' can be found in the journal *Gospel in Context* (vol. 1, no. 1, January 1978); cf. also, John Parratt, *A Guide to Doing Theology* (London, SPCK, 1996).
9. Schubert Ogden, 'Doing Theology Today' in Woodbridge and McComiskey, *Doing Theology in Today's World*, p. 422.
10. John Yoder, 'Thinking Theologically from a Free-Church Perspective' in Woodbridge and McComiskey, *Doing Theology in Today's World*, pp. 255–6.
11. A more elaborate discussion of this fine balance between form and freedom in theological exploration will be attempted later in the book, particularly in chapter 5, on the Gospel and culture.
12. Ogden, 'Doing Theology Today', p. 423 (the italics are mine).

13. Robert Schreiter, *Constructing Local Theologies* (London, SCM Press, 1985), p. 18.
14. An excellent example, at the time of writing, is the use of the biblical jubilee theme in the campaign for the total remission of the debt incurred by the poorest nations.
15. cf. Ford (ed.), *The Modern Theologians*, p. 724.
16. It will probably take some time for the theological curriculum to catch up with the realisation that theology is no longer defined by its development within one cultural context. There are already numerous experiments going on: within the Selly Oak Colleges, for example, an entirely new degree in Mission Theology has been developed, based on the pedagogical formula, 'see, judge, act'. For a variety of cultural perspectives on theological education, cf. Siga Arles, *Theological Education for the Mission of the Church in India: 1947–1987* (Frankfurt, Peter Lang, 1991); Daniel Schipani, *Religious Education Encounters Liberation Theology* (Birmingham, Religious Education Press, 1988); Joon Surh Park and Naozumi Eto (eds.), *Theology and Theological Education in Asia: Today and Tomorrow* (Seoul, NEAATS, 1992); Jack Seymour and Donald Miller, *Theological Approaches to Christian Education* (Nashville, Abingdon Press, 1990); Susan Thistlethwaite and George Cairns (eds.), *Beyond Theological Tourism: Mentoring as a Grassroots Approach to Theological Education* (Maryknoll, Orbis Books, 1994).
17. cf. Jon Sobrino and Ignacio Ellacuria, *Systematic Theology: Perspectives from Liberation Theology* (Maryknoll, Orbis Books, 1996), pp. 9ff.
18. cf. Donald Musser and Joseph Price (eds.), *A New Handbook of Christian Theology* (Nashville, Abingdon Press, and Cambridge, Lutterworth Press, 1992), pp. 490–1.
19. The three sources identified here might be called theology's external work-tools. There are also internal tools, which, though more difficult to assess, play an important and distinctive role: these are spirituality (which includes prophecies, dreams and prayer in the living presence of God) and conscience (a finely tuned moral sensitivity, based on the character of God and informed by contemporary ethical enquiry).
20. Among the most influential studies in the last 30 years have been Jürgen Moltmann, *A Theology of Hope* (London, SCM Press, 1967); Johann Baptist Metz, *Faith in History and Society: Toward a Practical Fundamental Theology* (London, Burns and Oates, 1980); Gustavo Gutiérrez, *A Theology of Liberation: History, Politics and Salvation* (London, SCM Press, 1974); Bernard Lonergan, *Method in Theology* (London, Darton, Longman and Todd, 1972); George Lindbeck, *The Nature of Doctrine: Religion and Theology in a Post-Liberal Age* (London,

SPCK, 1984); Rosemary Radford Ruether, *Sexism and God-Talk: Towards a Feminist Theology* (London, SCM Press, 1983).

21. cf. Lamin Sanneh, *Translating the Message: The Missionary Impact on Culture* (Maryknoll, Orbis Books, 1992); Anthony Thiselton, *New Horizons in Hermeneutics: The Theory and Practice of Transforming Biblical Reading* (London, HarperCollins, 1992); Nicholas Wolterstorff, *Divine Discourse: Philosophical Reflections on the Claim that God Speaks* (Cambridge, Cambridge University Press, 1995).

22. *Sensus literalis* is a technical term. It does not necessarily mean the 'literal sense', i.e. the primary or exact sense of a word or phrase. Rather, it conveys the attempt to find the obvious or normal sense, having paid due attention to the historical and literary context and to the way in which the use of language varies according to the type (or genre) of literature being used – for example, historical account, scientific description, legal definition, metaphor, symbol, allegory, poetry and so on. Failure to appreciate the text's reference and the richness and variety of language has resulted in some very bizarre interpretations of the Bible.

23. David Bosch, *Transforming Mission: Paradigm Shifts in Theology of Mission* (Maryknoll, Orbis Books, 1991, pp. 490–3; cf. also, J. Verkuyl, *Contemporary Missiology: An Introduction* (Grand Rapids, Eerdmans, 1978), pp. 6–17; Jan Jongeneel, *Philosophy, Science and Theology of Mission in the Nineteenth and Twentieth Centuries*, Part II (Frankfurt, Peter Lang, 1997), pp. 9ff.

24. Bosch, *Transforming Mission*, p. 492.

25. cf. F. J. Verstraelen, A. Camps, L. A. Hoedemaker and M. R. Spindler, *Missiology, an Ecumenical Introduction: Texts and Contexts of Global Christianity* (Grand Rapids, Eerdmans, 1995), pp. 1–7, 438–57. One of the groups participating in the course, 'Core Themes in Mission', at the Selly Oak Colleges' School of Mission in the spring term 1998 produced the following definition:

> Theology of mission is concerned with the basic presuppositions and underlying principles which determine, from the standpoint of Christian faith, the *motives*, *message*, *strategy* and *goals* of the Christian world mission.

26. Chapters 4 to 10 indicate the areas which I consider to be the most essential.

2 God's Mission and the Church's Response

1. R. K. Orchard (ed.), *Witness in Six Continents: Records of the CWME . . . Mexico City 1963* (London, Edinburgh House Press, 1964);

cf. also, *Minutes of the Second Meeting of the CWME* (Geneva, WCC, 1963), pp. 53, 125–7.

2. As we shall explore later in this chapter, some do not believe that the Church should be regarded as the primary agent of mission.

3. The convention of using capital letters in these kinds of phrases gives the misleading impression that there is a substantial Something behind the description. However, the whole point of using these formulas is to signify a fundamental uncertainty about the adequacy of language to describe a supreme being. Hence the process is essentially one of negation; cf. Kenneth Hamilton, *The System and the Gospel: A Critique of Paul Tillich* (London, SCM Press, 1963); Alistair Macleod, *Tillich: An Essay on the Role of Ontology in his Philosophical Theology* (London, George Allen and Unwin, 1973), pp. 61–7; Paul Badham, *A John Hick Reader* (London, Macmillan, 1990), pp. 12–13, 172–3; John Hick, *An Interpretation of Religion: Human Responses to the Transcendent* (London, Macmillan, 1989).

4. Is it significant that Nietzsche also used the metaphor of the sea (having already announced the death of God in *The Gay Science*): 'Once you said "God" when you gazed upon distant seas; but now I have taught you to say "superman"' (*Thus Spake Zarathustra*); cf. R. J. Holingdale, *A Nietzsche Reader* (Harmondsworth, Penguin Books, 1977), pp. 202–3; Nietzsche, *Thus Spake Zarathustra: A Book for Everyone and No One* (Harmondsworth, Penguin Books, 1961), p. 109.

5. Johannes Verkuyl, 'The Biblical Notion of Kingdom: Test of Validity for Theology of Religion', in Charles Van Engen, Dean Gilliland and Paul Pierson (eds.), *The Good News of the Kingdom: Mission Theology for the Third Millenium* (Maryknoll, Orbis Books, 1993), p. 72.

6. Emilio Castro, in Van Engen, Gilliland and Pierson (eds.), *The Good News of the Kingdom*, p. 133.

7. Wilbert Shenk, 'The Mission Dynamic' in Willem Saayman and Klippies Kritzinger (eds.), *Mission in Bold Humility: David Bosch's Work Considered* (Maryknoll, Orbis Books, 1996), p. 84.

8. John Hick, *God and the Universe of Faiths* (London, Macmillan, 1973).

9. cf. Marjorie Hewitt Suchoki, 'In Search of Justice: Religious Pluralism from a Feminist Perspective' in John Hick and Paul Knitter (eds.), *The Myth of Christian Uniqueness: Toward a Pluralist Theology of Religions* (Maryknoll, Orbis Books, 1987), p. 149:

> Universalizing one religion such that it is taken as the norm whereby all other religions are judged and valued leads to oppression, and hence falls short of the norm that liberationists consider ultimate – the normative justice that creates well-being in the world community.

10. According to James Scherer, during the early 1960s, under the influence of 'secular theologies', some missiologists came up with a deliberately non-trinitarian concept of mission: 'A theory about the transformation of the world and of history . . . by means of a divinely guided immanent historical process, somewhat analogous to deistic views of the Enlightenment' ('Church, Kingdom and *Missio Dei*: Lutheran and Orthodox Correctives to Recent Ecumenical Mission Theology', in Van Engen, Gilliland and Pierson [eds.], *The Good News of the Kingdom*, p. 86). According to Roger Bassham ('Mission Theology: 1948–1975' in *Occasional Bulletin of Missionary Research* [vol. 4, no. 2, 1980], p. 156), the most significant point of convergence between the three streams of the WCC, evangelicalism and Roman Catholicism 'has been the recognition of the trinitarian basis of the missionary enterprise'. I don't think this judgement needs revising 20 years later.

11. To mention but a few: Michael Nazir Ali, *From Everywhere to Everywhere: A World View of Christian Mission* (London, Collins, 1990), p. 9; Vinoth Ramachandra, *The Recovery of Mission* (Carlisle, Paternoster Press, 1996), pp. 237ff.; George Lemopoulos (ed.), *Your Will Be Done: Orthodoxy in Mission* (Geneva, WCC Publications, 1989), p. 80.

12. Michael Kinnamon (ed.), *Signs of the Spirit: Official Report, World Council of Churches Seventh Assembly* (Geneva, WCC Publications, 1992), para. 18.

13. According to the classical Greek legend, Narcissus was condemned by the goddess Nemesis to contemplate his own beauty, so that he fell ever deeper in love with himself.

14. The point is taken that when love is interpreted in a wholly disinterested direction, this can lead to exploitation – most particularly of women by men on the ideological ground that self-sacrifice most naturally befits their nature (cf. Musser and Price [eds.], *A New Handbook of Christian Theology*, p. 300). However, love is required from men in equal measure – perhaps more, for husbands are given the express command to love their wives (Eph. 5:28) – and the one who loves cannot, by definition, exploit.

15. Lesslie Newbigin, *The Open Secret: An Introduction to the Theology of Mission*, revised edn (London, SPCK, 1995), p. 49; cf. also, Richard Bauckham, *The Bible in Politics: How to Read the Bible Politically* (London, SPCK, 1989), pp. 148–9; Richard Bauckham, *The Theology of the Book of Revelation* (Cambridge, Cambridge University Press, 1993), p. 75.

16. Emilio Castro, 'Liberation, Development and Evangelism: Must We Choose in Mission?', *Occasional Bulletin for Missionary Research* (July 1978), p. 87.

17. The belief held by some people to whom missionaries came that

the Gospel brought with it an abundance of material benefits – cf. Friedrich Steinbauer, *Melanesian Cargo Cults: New Salvation Movements in the South Pacific* (London, George Prior, 1979); Carl Loegliger and Garry Trompf, *New Religious Movements in Melanesia* (Suva, University of the South Pacific, 1985).

18. cf. Newbigin, *The Open Secret*, pp. 77–8.

19. cf. Shenk, 'The Mission Dynamic', pp. 84–5; also, Howard Snyder, *Kingdom Lifestyle: Calling the Church to Live under God's Reign* (Basingstoke, Marshall Pickering, 1986).

20. cf. Scherer, 'Church, Kingdom and *Missio Dei*', pp. 82–3.

21. cf. Charles Taber, *The World is Too Much with Us: 'Culture' in Modern Protestant Missions* (Macon, Mercer University Press, 1991), pp. 60–1, 79–80.

22. Bassham, 'Mission Theology: 1948–1975', p. 53.

23. cf. A. T. Van Leeuwen, *Christianity in World History: The Meeting of Faiths East and West* (New York, Scribners, 1964) and J. C. Hoekendijk, *The Church Inside Out* (London, SCM Press, 1967).

24. For another interpretation of the false distinction between 'sacred' and 'secular', see chapter 11 of this book.

25. J. C. Hoekendijk, *Kirche und Volk in der deutscher Missionswissenschaft* (Munich, Kaiser Verlag, 1967).

26. Ismael Amaya, 'A Latin American Critique of Western Theology', *Evangelical Review of Mission* (vol. 7, 1, 1983), p. 20.

27. Stanley Hauerwas provocatively argues the thesis, abandoned in differing degrees, by most self-respecting modern theologians, that 'there is no salvation outside the Church':

> The church did not have an incidental part in God's story but was necessary for the salvation wrought in Christ. The church was not and is not a people gathered together in order to remember an impressive but dead founder. Rather the church is those gathered from the nations to testify to the resurrected Lord. Without the church the world literally has no hope of salvation since the church is necessary for the world to know it is part of a story that it cannot know without the church.
> (*After Christendom? How the Church is to Behave if Freedom, Justice and a Christian Nation are Bad Ideas* [Nashville, Abingdon Press, 1991], p. 36.)

cf. also the further discussion of the Church at the heart of mission in chapter 11 of this book.

28. cf. Lesslie Newbigin, *Sign of the Kingdom* (Grand Rapids, Eerdmans, 1980), p. 19.

29. As one might expect, the Orthodox Churches lay particular emphasis on worship as a powerful means of enabling witness to

the kingdom of God: 'It is the function of the liturgy to transform us as individuals into "living stones" of the church and as a community into an authentic image of the kingdom' (Ion Bria [ed.], *Go Forth in Peace: Orthodox Perspectives on Mission* [Geneva, WCC, 1986], p. 17.)
30. Emilio Castro, *Freedom in Mission: The Perspective of the Kingdom of God* (Geneva, WCC Publications, 1985), p. 62.
31. Shenk, 'The Mission Dynamic', p. 90.

3 Mission in the Way of Jesus Christ

1. cf. Frederick R. Wilson, *The San Antonio Report: Your Will be Done, Mission in Christ's Way* (Geneva, WCC Publications, 1990), pp. 5–6. The phrase also occurs in the document, *Mission and Evangelism: An Ecumenical Affirmation* (Geneva, WCC, 1983), Section 4.
2. Jürgen Moltmann, *The Way of Jesus Christ: Christology in Messianic Dimensions* (London, SCM Press, 1990).
3. ibid. pp. xiii–xiv.
4. cf. Tom Wright, *Jesus and the Victory of God* (London, SPCK, 1996), p. 59.
5. cf. Donald Senior and Carroll Stuhlmueller, *The Biblical Foundations for Mission* (London, SCM Press, 1983), pp. 144–6.
6. cf. Tom Wright, *The New Testament and the People of God* (London, SPCK, 1992), p. 445.
7. One might say that Jesus never played safe. The cultural expectations of how God would rule were so strong in first-century Palestine that Jesus took great risks of being misunderstood. His public ministry was largely a fulfilment of his own interpretation of God's reign and his struggle to make sure that this was communicated as effectively as possible to those who had 'ears to hear' (Mark 4:23).
8. At least, Matthew, Simon the Cananean and Judas Iscariot (Mark 3:18).
9. cf. J. Andrew Kirk, *A New World Coming* (Basingstoke, Marshalls, 1983), pp. 100–2.
10. 'Keeping the distinctive codes was *the* means of marking Israel out from her pagan neighbours' (Wright, *Jesus and the Victory of God*, p. 383).
11. Too radical apparently for the earliest Christian community (Acts 10:15; 15:5, 20).
12. cf. Gerd Theissen, *The Gospels in Context: Social and Political History in the Synoptic Tradition* (Minneapolis, Fortress Press, 1991), pp. 72–5; Helmut Koester, *Introduction to the New Testament; History, Culture and Religion in the Hellenistic Age* (Philadelphia, Fortress Press, 1982),

pp. 62–3; Sean Freyne, 'Bandits in Galilee: A Contribution to the Study of Social Conditions in First-Century Palestine', in Jacob Neusner *et al.*, *The Social World of Formative Christianity and Judaism* (Philadelphia, Fortress Press, 1988), pp. 62–4; Richard Horsley, *Sociology and the Jesus Movement* (New York, Continuum, 1994), pp. 71–80, 88–90.

13. Disease or physical disability was counted as a sign of God's displeasure due to sin.

14. Moltmann, *The Way of Jesus Christ*, p. 115. cf also Jon Sobrino, *Christology at the Crossroads: A Latin American Approach* (London, SCM Press, 1978), pp. 353–74; Jon Sobrino, 'The Epiphany of the God of Life in Jesus of Nazareth' in Pablo Richard *et al.*, *The Idols of Death and the God of Life* (Maryknoll, Orbis Books, 1983), pp. 66–102; Jorge Pixley and Clodovis Boff, *The Bible, the Church and the Poor* (Tunbridge Wells, Burns and Oates, 1989), pp. 56–65, 68–71.

15. Walter Wink, *Healing a Nation's Wounds: Reconciliation on the Road to Democracy* (Uppsala, Life and Peace Institute, 1997), p. 5.

16. Carlos Bravo, 'Jesus of Nazareth, Christ the Liberator' in Sobrino and Ellacuria, *Systematic Theology*, pp. 111–12.

17. Wright, *Jesus and the Victory of God*, pp. 403–5.

18. The sharp difference of views between Europeans and peoples of other cultures about the ownership of land became evident during the colonial period. To the European question, 'Whose land is that?', the answer often would be, 'Nobody's', meaning 'Everybody's'.

19. Bravo, 'Jesus of Nazareth, Christ the Liberator', p. 119; cf. also, J. Andrew Kirk, *God's Word for a Complex World: Discovering How the Bible Speaks Today* (Basingstoke, Marshall Pickering, 1987), pp. 130–4, for an exposition of the drama of Jesus' trial and execution and the unexpected, but highly significant, twist in the tail (tale).

20. Bravo, 'Jesus of Nazareth, Christ the Liberator', p. 119.

21. Perhaps the best picture of what this might mean within a human community is given in Isaiah's vision of a new heaven and a new earth (Isa. 65:17–25, also Mic. 4:1–4). For more on the meaning of *shalom*, see chapters 4 and 8.

4 Announcing Good News

1. I believe the two nouns can be used interchangeably: attempts to distinguish their respective meanings have not proved particularly helpful.

2. cf. Bosch, *Transforming Mission*, p. 409.

3. The phrase is said to have originated with A. T. Pierson, editor of the *Missionary Review of the World* until his death in 1911. It came to

prominence in the missionary commitment of the Student Volunteer Movement in North America and may go back to the evangelist D. L. Moody – cf. T. Yates, *Christian Mission in the Twentieth Century* (Cambridge, Cambridge University Press, 1994), pp. 12–13.

4. Bosch, *Transforming Mission*, p. 412, quoting the Evanston Assembly of the World Council of Churches.

5. cf., for example, The Grand Rapids Report, *Evangelism and Social Responsibility: An Evangelical Commitment* (Exeter, Paternoster Press, 1982).

6. John Stott, *Christian Mission in the Modern World* (London, Falcon Books, 1975), p. 30.

7. cf. Gustavo Gutiérrez, *Las Casas: in Search of the Poor of Jesus Christ* (Maryknoll, Orbis Books, 1993); Mario Rodriguez Leon, 'Invasion and Evangelization in the Sixteenth Century' in Enrique Dussel (ed.), *The Church in Latin America; 1492–1992* (Tunbridge Wells, Burns and Oates, 1992), pp. 43–54; Leonardo Boff and Virgil Elizondo, *The Voice of the Victims* (London, SCM Press, 1991); Leonardo Boff, *New Evangelization: Good News to the Poor* (Maryknoll, Orbis Books, 1991), pp. 95–103; L. Rivera, *A Violent Evangelism: the Political and Religious Conquest of the Americas* (Louisville, Westminster/John Knox Press, 1992).

8. cf. Hauerwas, *After Christendom?*; T. O. Beidelman, *Colonial Evangelism: A Socio-Historical Study of an East African Mission at the Grassroots* (Bloomington, Indiana University Press, 1982).

9. Donald McGavran, 'Will Uppsala Betray the Two Billion?' in Arthur Glasser and Donald McGavran (eds.), *The Conciliar-Evangelical Debate* (Waco, Word Books, 1972), p. 234.

10. Harvey Hoekstra, *The World Council of Churches and the Demise of Evangelism* (Wheaton, Tyndale House, 1979).

11. William Hocking, *Rethinking Missions: A Layman's Inquiry after One Hundred Years* (New York, 1933).

12. cf. Frederick, *The San Antonio Report*, pp. 100–14, 115–28, 129–38.

13. Eugene Smith, 'Renewal in Mission' in Glasser and McGavran (eds.), *The Conciliar-Evangelical Debate*, p. 261.

14. The literature on evangelism is vast. For a variety of views see William Abraham, *The Logic of Evangelism* (Grand Rapids, Eerdmans, 1989); Michael Green, *Evangelism in the Early Church* (London, Hodder and Stoughton, 1970); Michael Green, *Evangelism through the Local Church* (London, Hodder and Stoughton, 1990); Raymond Fung, *Evangelistically Yours: Ecumenical Letters on Contemporary Evangelism* (Geneva, WCC, 1992); Orlando Costas, *Liberating News: A Theology of Contextual Evangelism* (Grand Rapids, Eerdmans, 1989); Philip King, *Good News for a Suffering World: What Does the Christian Faith Really Have to Offer?* (Crowborough, Monarch Publications,

1996); David Wells, *God the Evangelist: How the Holy Spirit Works to Bring Men and Women to Faith* (Grand Rapids, Eerdmans, 1987); Colin Horseman, *Good News for a Postmodern World* (Cambridge, Grove Books, 1996); Harry Sawyer, *Creative Evangelism: Toward a New Christian Encounter with Africa* (London, Lutterworth Press, 1968); John Drane, *Evangelism for a New Age* (London, Marshall Pickering, 1994).

15. Bosch, *Transforming Mission*, pp. 412–13.

16. In addition the words 'preach' and 'proclaim' have been favoured in many church circles. However, their link with the formal sermon in a service of worship makes them less serviceable.

17. Daniel Niles, *That They May Have Life* (New York, Harper and Brothers, 1951) quoted in Norman Thomas (ed.), *Classic Texts in Mission and World Christianity* (Maryknoll, New York, 1995), p. 158. The quotation usually ends here; however, it is worth seeing how it continues:

> The Christians do not offer out of their bounty. They have no bounty. They are simply guests at their Master's table and, as evangelists, they call others too . . . The Christian stands alongside the non-Christian and points to the Gospel, the holy action of God.

18. Bria (ed.), *Go Forth in Peace*, p. 30.

19. Lemopoulos (ed.), *Your Will Be Done*, p. 11.

20. ibid. p. 412.

21. The order is new in comparison with the present order of things, said to be 'passing away' (1 Cor. 2:6). It is also a restoration (Acts 3:21) of God's original intentions.

22. In the English language, the deep personal significance of the good news has been beautifully captured by Charles Wesley in numerous hymns, of which these words from one of them give a flavour:

> Tis myst'ry all! th' Immortal dies: who can explore his strange design?
> In vain the first-born seraph tries to sound the depths of love divine!
> Tis mercy all! Let earth adore, let angel minds enquire no more . . .
> Long my imprisoned spirit lay fast bound in sin and nature's night;
> Thine eye diffused a quick'ning ray, I woke the dungeon flamed with light;
> My chains fell off, my heart was free; I rose, went forth, and followed thee.
> No condemnation now I dread; Jesus, and all in him, is mine!

Alive in him, my living Head, and clothed in righteousness divine,
Bold I approach the eternal throne, and claim the crown through Christ my own.

23. cf. Philip Clayton, *God and Contemporary Science* (Edinburgh, Edinburgh University Press, 1998), pp. 42–4.
24. René Padilla, *Mission Between the Times: Essays on the Kingdom* (Grand Rapids, Eerdmans, 1985), p. 75.
25. For further reflections on the nature and exercise of power, see chapter 10 of this book.
26. Mary Carroll Smith, 'Response' to Orlando Costas, 'A Radical Evangelical Contribution from Latin America' in Gerald Anderson and Thomas Stransky (eds.), *Christ's Lordship and Religious Pluralism* (Maryknoll, Orbis Books, 1981), pp. 156–8.
27. cf., for example, Zygmunt Bauman, *Postmodern Ethics* (Oxford, Blackwell, 1993), pp. 21–8.
28. Orlando Costas, in Anderson and Stransky (eds.), *Christ's Lordship and Religious Pluralism*, pp. 163–7.
29. This is also a valid criticism of the postmodern advocacy of a complete value-relativism or absolute tolerance – cf. Baumann, *Postmodern Ethics*, pp. 238–9.
30. By those who see it in terms of the martyrdom of a prophet, who interpret it as an example of sacrificial love or see it in terms of a victory over evil – cf. Alistair McGrath, *Historical Theology: An Introduction to the History of Christian Thought* (Oxford, Blackwell, 1998), pp. 283–97.
31. Jürgen Moltmann, *The Trinity and the Kingdom of God* (London, SCM Press, 1981), pp. 80–1.
32. For further reflection on the substance of the good news, cf. Padilla, *Mission Between the Times*, pp. 73–82; J. Andrew Kirk, *The Meaning of Freedom: A Study of Secular, Muslim and Christian Views* (Carlisle, Paternoster Press, 1998), pp. 206–12.
33. Zvomunondita Kurewa, 'Conversion in the African Context', *International Review of Mission* (68, 1979), p. 161. Further on the meaning and significance of conversion, cf. Andrew Wingate, *The Church and Conversion* (Delhi, ISPCK, 1997); Joseph Mattam and Sebastian Kim (eds.), *Mission and Conversion; A Reappraisal* (Bandra, Mumbai, St Paul's, 1996); Jim Wallis, *The Call to Conversion* (San Francisco, Harper and Row, 1981); Richard Longenecker, *The Road from Damascus: The Impact of Paul's Conversion on his Life, Thought and Ministry* (Grand Rapids, Eerdmans, 1997); Cyril Okorocha, *The Meaning of Religious Conversion in Africa: the Case of the Igbo of Nigeria* (Aldershot, Avebury, 1987).
34. David Bosch, 'Toward Evangelism in Context' in Vinay Samuel

and Chris Sugden, *The Church in Response to Human Need* (Oxford, Regnum Books, 1987), p. 188.

35. Bria, *Go Forth in Peace*, p. 31.

36. cf. Raymond Fung and Georges Leucopalos, *Not a Solitary Way: Evangelism Stories from Around the World* (Geneva, WCC, 1992).

37. Carl Braaten, *The Apostolic Imperative* (Minneapolis, Augsburg Press, 1985), p. 77.

38. From the Evangelical Methodist Church in Bolivia, 'A Bolivian Manifesto on Evangelism in Latin America Today' in Thomas (ed.), *Classic Texts in Mission*, p.164.

39. The motto of the duty free shop in Amsterdam's Schipol airport is: 'See, buy, fly'.

40. A Mission Affirmation (Selly Oak, School of Mission and World Christianity, 1992).

41. cf. John Finney, *Finding Faith Today: How Does it Happen?* (Swindon, Bible Society, 1992).

42. Commission I, 'Carrying the Gospel to All the Non-Christian World' in John Mott, *Addresses and Papers of John R. Mott*, vol. V, The International Missionary Council (New York, Association Press, 1947), p. 28.

5 The Gospel in the Midst of Cultures

1. cf. Alan Neely, *Christian Mission: A Case Study Approach* (Maryknoll, Orbis Books, 1995), p. 3; Roger Bowen, *So I Send You: A Study Guide to Mission* (London, SPCK, 1996), pp. 76–94.

2. cf. James Dunn, *The Parting of the Ways between Christianity and Judaism and their Significance for the Character of Christianity* (London, SCM Press, 1991), pp. 107–13.

3. For an extensive commentary on the significance of Genesis 10 for the plurality of culture, cf. George Hunsberger, *Bearing the Witness of the Spirit: Lesslie Newbigin's Theology of Cultural Plurality* (Grand Rapids, Eerdmans, 1998), pp. 244–55.

4. For the relation between racism and cultural factors, cf. Charles Kraft, *Anthropology for Christian Witness* (Maryknoll, Orbis Books, 1996), pp. 109–14; Charles Taber, *The World is Too Much with Us: Culture in Modern Protestant Missions* (Macon, Mercer University Press, 1991), pp. 38–41.

5. In English a similar (racist) use is made of the word 'philistine' to mean those indifferent to the arts.

6. It has been suggested that people cope with difference by either homogenising, demonising, romanticising or pluralising those who seem strange to them – cf. Robert Schreiter, 'Teaching Theology

from an Intercultural Perspective' in *Theological Education* (26, 1), p. 19.

7. Chris Sugden, 'God and the Nations' in Patrick Benson (ed.), *The Church and the Nations* (EFAC Bulletin, 47, 1996), p. 4.

8. An exception is the 'Christians of St Thomas' in India who claim direct descent from the first churches established along the Malabar coast by the apostle Thomas, according to tradition – cf. Nazir Ali, *From Everywhere to Everywhere*, pp. 25, 33–4.

9. Michael Poon Nai-Chiu, 'Christianity and the Destiny of China' in Benson (ed.), *The Church and the Nations*, p. 24.

10. Donald Jacobs, 'Contextualisation in Mission' in James Phillips and Robert Coote (eds.), *Toward the Twenty-First Century in Christian Mission* (Grand Rapids, Eerdmans, 1993), p. 237. John Pobee, puts it like this:

> That the practice of *tabula rasa* was characteristic of missions hardly needs arguing here. That practice said in not so many words that non-Christian culture could never be a *preparatorio evangelica* and, therefore, had to be destroyed before Christianity could be built up.
> ('A Passover of Language' in Saayman and Kritzinger [eds.], *Mission in Bold Humility*, p. 55.)

11. cf. Lamin Sanneh, 'Partnership, Mission and Cross-Cultural Sensitivity'; William Burrows, 'Catholics and Radical Inculturation', both in Saayman and Kritzinger (eds.), *Mission in Bold Humility*.

12. cf. Lamin Sanneh, *Translating the Message: the Missionary Impact on Culture* (Maryknoll, Orbis Books, 1992).

13. Lamin Sanneh, *Religion and the Variety of Culture: a Study in Origin and Practice* (Valley Forge, Trinity Press International, 1996).

14. Charles Taber, *The World is Too Much with Us*, pp. 105–6, 142, 153. He also believes that structuralism may be a more fertile tool for understanding important elements of cultures, not least the deeply similar underlying structures.

15. cf. Keith Ferdinando, 'Sickness and Syncretism in the African Context' in Antony Billington, Tony Lane and Max Turner (eds.), *Mission and Meaning* (Carlisle, Paternoster Press, 1995), pp. 272–84; Taber, *The World is Too Much with Us*, pp. 147, 154; Jerald Gort, Hendrik Voom, Rein Fernhout and Anton Wessels (eds.), *Dialogue and Syncretism: An Interdisciplinary Approach* (Grand Rapids, Eerdmans, 1989); Charles Stewart and Rosalind Shaw, *Syncretism/Anti-Syncretism: The Politics of Religious Synthesis* (London, Routledge, 1994); W.A. Visser't Hooft, *No Other Name: The Choice between Syncretism and Christian Universalism* (London, SCM Press, 1963).

16. Lesslie Newbigin deals with this question in *The Open Secret: An*

      Introduction to the Theology of Mission (London, SPCK, 1995), pp.
135ff., 144, 148; also, Taber, *The World is Too Much with Us*, p.168.

17. 'Generation X' represents the group of young people born to the
'baby boomers' around the early 1970s – cf. Douglas Coupland,
Generation X: Tales for an Accelerated Culture (London, Abacus, 1992);
Nick Mercer, 'Postmodernity and Rationality: the Final Credits or
Just a Commercial Break?' in Lane and Turner (eds.), *Mission and
Meaning*, pp. 322–8.

18. Neely, *Christian Mission*, p. 4.

19. Kraft, *Anthropology for Christian Witness*, p. 38.

20. Newbigin, *The Open Secret*, p. 142.

21. Taber, *The World is Too Much with Us*, p. 3.

22. Marguerite Kraft, *Worldview and the Communication of the Gospel: A
Nigerian Case Study* (Pasadena, William Carey Library, 1978); Guil-
lermo Cook (ed.), *Crosscurrents in Indigenous Spirituality: Interface of
Maya, Catholic and Protestant Worldviews* (Leiden, Brill, 1997).

23. Juan Luis Segundo has many pertinent observations to make about
beliefs and how they function, in *Faith and Ideologies* (London, Sheed
and Ward, 1984):

> To say society is to say faith: the universal, unfailing tendency to
> fill gaps in one's own experience with the borrowed experience
> of others. Faith is an absolutely universal dimension of being
> human (p. 7).

24. I have dealt at length with the many paradoxical elements within
contemporary views of freedom in my book, *The Meaning of Freedom*,
especially chapters 5, 6 and 7.

25. *The Concise Oxford Dictionary of Quotations* (Oxford, Oxford University Press, 1981), p. 135.

26. Paul Hiebert, *Anthropological Insights for Missionaries* (Grand Rapids,
Baker Book House, 1985), pp. 30–41. He also divides culture into
material, expressive and ritual parts: the creation of objects; art, and
rites, such as feasts, festivals and pilgrimages, pp. 171–83.

27. Taber, *The World is Too Much with Us*, pp. 163–4 (typology adapted).

28. However, the religious/secular divide is reckoned to be much more
problematical today than a generation ago, because more people
are inhabiting 'a world of spirituality' – cf. Bert Hoedemaker, *Secularization and Mission: A Theological Essay* (Harrisburg, Trinity Press
International, 1998), pp. 1–21.

29. cf. Neely, *Christian Mission*, p. 5.

30. ibid. pp. 32–50; Burrows, 'Catholics and Radical Inculturation' in
Saayman and Kritzinger (eds.), *Mission in Bold Humility*, pp. 12–13.
The process was in fact initiated by Alessandro Valignano's direction
to Mateo Ricci to enter fully into Chinese habits of mind and heart.

31. Quoted in Thomas (ed.), *Classic Texts in Mission and World Christianity*, pp. 172–3.

32. cf. David Paton, *The Ministry of the Spirit: Selected Writings by Roland Allen* (Grand Rapids, Eerdmans, 1962).

33. Newbigin, *The Open Secret*, p. 144.

34. Thomas Stransky, 'From Vatican II to *Redemptoris Missio*: a Development in the Theology of Mission' in Van Engen, Gilliland and Pierson (eds.), *The Good News of the Kingdom*, p. 142; also, Aylward Shorter, *Toward a Theology of Inculturation* (Maryknoll, Orbis Books, 1988).

35. cf. Burrows, 'Catholics and Radical Inculturation', p. 136.

36. Stransky, 'From Vatican II to *Redemptoris Missio*', p. 142.

37. Two relatively recent examples of the stretching of Roman Catholicism's limits have been the case of Archbishop Malinga of Zambia with regard to healing ministries in the African context, and Leonardo Boff's championing of the 'base ecclesial communities' as a 'reinvention of the Church': cf. Leonardo Boff, *Ecclesiogenesis: the Base Communities Reinvent the Church* (Maryknoll, Orbis Books, 1986). In neither case did the Vatican allow experimentation to go unchecked from the centre.

38. Tite Tienou, 'Forming Indigenous Theologies' in *Toward the Twenty-First Century in Christian Mission*, pp. 248–9.

39. One of the first studies that contributed to the rise of liberation theologies in the Third World was Richard Shaull, *Encounter with Revolution* (New York, Association Press, 1955).

40. Shoki Coe ('In Search of Renewal in Theological Education' in *Theological Education* [9, 1973], pp. 233–43), mentioned the particular influences of secularism, technology and the struggle for human justice. At the dawn of the twenty-first century, one would have to include the massive impact of the globalisation of capital and the means of communication: the first excludes large populations in many countries from active participation in the economy; the second, controlled from the West, tends to the flattening out and trivialisation of culture through 'pop' expressions.

41. Quoted in Thomas (ed.), *Classic Texts in Mission and World Christianity*, p. 175.

42. Richard Niebuhr, *Christ and Culture* (New York, Harper, 1951).

43. cf. Hiebert, *Anthropological Insights*, pp. 53–8.

44. cf. Arnold Snyder, 'The Relevance of Anabaptist Non-Violence for Nicaragua Today', and Jose Miguez Bonino, 'On Discipleship, Justice and Power', both in Daniel Schipani (ed.), *Freedom and Discipleship: Liberation Theology in Anabaptist Perspective* (Maryknoll, Orbis Books, 1989), pp. 112–27, 133–8.

45. Las Newman, 'The Church as a Source of Identity' in Benson (ed.), *The Church and the Nations*, pp. 32–3.
46. ibid. p. 33.
47. Emilio Castro, 'Themes in Theology of Mission Arising Out of San Antonio and Canberra' in Van Engen, Gilliland and Pierson (eds.), *The Good News of the Kingdom*, pp. 129–30.
48. John Paul II, Encyclical on Missionary Activity: Redemptoris Missio, op. cit., par. 53.

6 Justice for the Poor

1. Gustavo Gutiérrez, *The Truth Shall Make You Free: Confrontations* (Maryknoll, Orbis Books, 1990), pp. 8–9.
2. J. Remenyi, *Where Credit is Due* (London, Intermediate Technology Publications, 1991), p. 3.
3. Gutiérrez, *The Truth Shall Make You Free*, pp. 9–10; cf. also, Richard *et al.*, *The Idols of Death*.
4. cf. Richard Harries, *Is There a Gospel for the Rich?* (London, Mowbray, 1992), p. 8. Mother Teresa, on a visit to Britain, once said: 'Here in Britain you have a different kind of poverty. A poverty of loneliness and being unwanted, a poverty of spirit; and that is the worst disease in the world today'.
5. cf. Tony Beck, *The Experience of Poverty: Fighting for Respect and Resources in Village India* (London, Intermediate Technology Publications, 1944); Idriss Jazairy, Mohiuddin Alamgir and Theresa Panuccio, *The State of Rural Poverty: An Inquiry into its Causes and Consequences* (London, Intermediate Technology Publications, 1992); Tim Allen and Alan Thomas, *Poverty and Development in the 1990s* (Oxford, Oxford University Press, 1992).
6. Zygmunt Bauman, *Work, Consumerism and the New Poor* (Buckingham, Open University Press, 1998).
7. A phrase used first by Raymond Fung, 'Good News to the Poor – a Case for a Missionary Movement' in *Your Kingdom Come: Report on the World Conference on Mission and Evangelism* (Geneva, WCC, 1980), p. 84.
8. cf. Rhys Jenkins, *Transnational Corporations and Uneven Development: The Internationalization of Capital and the Third World* (London, Methuen, 1987); Paul Hirst and Grahame Thompson, *Globalization in Question* (Cambridge, Polity Press, 1996), chapter 4; John Gray, *False Dawn: The Delusions of Global Capitalism* (London, Granta Books, 1998), chapters 1–4.
9. cf. John Mihevc, *The Market Tells Them So: The World Bank and Economic Fundamentalism in Africa* (London, Zed Books, 1992); George Gelber (ed.), *Poverty and Power: Latin America after 500 Years* (London,

CAFOD, 1992), chapter 2; Graham Bird, *IMF Lending to Developing Countries: Issues and Evidence* (London, Routledge, 1995); Mariarosa Dalla Costa and Giovanna Dalla Costa (eds.), *Paying the Price: Women and the Politics of International Economic Strategy* (London, Zed Books, 1995), chapter 2.

10. H. Schlossberg *et al., Freedom, Justice and Hope: Toward a Strategy for the Poor and Oppressed* (Westchester, Crossway Books, 1988), pp. 89–90.

11. Ali Mazrui, *Cultural Forces in World Politics* (London, James Currey, 1990), p. 202.

12. Brian Griffiths sets out this position with clarity – cf. *The Creation of Wealth* (London, Hodder and Stoughton, 1984), pp. 30–1.

13. cf. Francis Fukuyama, *Trust: The Social Virtues and the Creation of Prosperity* (London, Penguin Books, 1996).

14. This action is backed by the Jubilee 2000 Coalition, a group of largely non-governmental organisations, trades unions and religious groups, who see this as not only economically necessary and right, but a fitting way of celebrating the dawn of a new millennium – cf. *Third World First: Freedom from Debt* (Oxford, Third World First, 1989).

15. I have already laid out some of the teaching given in the Bible concerning justice in my book, *God's Word for a Complex World: Discovering how the Bible Speaks Today* (Basingstoke, Marshall Pickering, 1987), pp. 86ff., 119ff. I will not repeat this material in the present book. See also the discussion on 'The Bible and Economics' between Stephen Mott, Milton Wan and Udo Middleman, and on 'Hermeneutical Issues' between Samuel Escobar, Nicholas Wolterstorff and Herbert Schlossberg, in *Transformation* (vol. 4, nos. 3–4, 1987); Michael Elliott, *Freedom, Justice and Christian Counter-Culture* (London, SCM Press, 1990), chapter 3.

16. Morris Ginsberg, *On Justice in Society* (Harmondsworth, Penguin Books, 1965).

17. A form of the so-called Golden Rule: 'In everything do to others as you would have them do to you' (Matt. 7:12).

18. For a recent discussion of social justice from different viewpoints, cf. James Sterba *et al., Morality and Social Justice: Point/Counterpoint* (Lamham, Rowman and Littlefield, 1995).

19. cf. Robert Wall, 'Social Justice and Human Liberation' in Samuel and Sugden, *The Church in Response to Human Need*, pp. 112ff.

20. The discussion is partly historical – was the jubilee ever practised in Israel? – and partly exegetical – is it most natural to interpret the Lucan text in this way? The material is too extensive to consider here. A useful summary of some of the main points is made by Robert Willoughby, 'The Concept of Jubilee and Luke 4:18–30' in Billington, Lane and Turner (eds.), *Mission and Meaning*, pp. 41–55;

cf. also John Nolland, *Luke 1–9:20*, World Biblical Commentary Volume 35A (Dallas, Word Books, 1989), pp. 196–8; Willard Swartley, *Israel's Scripture Tradition and the Synoptic Gospels: Story Shaping Story* (Peabody, Hendrickson Publishers, 1994), pp. 76–80, 87; Richard Horsley, *Jesus and the Spiral of Violence: Popular Jewish Resistance in Roman Palestine* (Minneapolis, Fortress Press, 1993), pp. 251–3; Johannes Nissen, *Poverty and Mission: New Testament Perspectives* (Leiden, IIMO, 1984), p. 75.

21. Newbigin, *The Open Secret*, p. 110.

22. cf. Duncan Forrester, *Christian Justice and Public Policy* (Cambridge, Cambridge University Press, 1997); Jon Sobrino, *The Principle of Mercy: Taking the Crucified People from the Cross* (Maryknoll, Orbis Books, 1994).

23. cf. Pedrito Maynard-Reid, *Poverty and Wealth in James* (Maryknoll, Orbis Books, 1987), pp. 81–98.

24. 'The worker is paid an equivalent for only a part of the working day, and the value produced in the other, unpaid part, is the surplus value' (Tom Bottomore [ed.], *A Dictionary of Marxist Thought* [Oxford, Blackwell, 1991], p. 532).

25. One may speculate about possible futures: whether, for example, capitalism could implode due to the contradictions inherent in its operation, as Marx predicted:

> The contradictions inherent in the movement of capitalist society impress themselves upon the practical bourgeois most strikingly in the changes of the periodic cycle through which modern industry runs, and whose crowning point is the universal crisis. That crisis is once again approaching, although as yet in its preliminary stage.
>
> (*Capital*, vol. I, text in David McLellan, *The Thought of Karl Marx* [London, Macmillan Press, 1995, 3rd edn] pp. 147–8.)

I think speculation is not very profitable. Up to now, capitalism has shown itself to be remarkably durable. One of the reasons that it is able to ride out the periodic storms is its indifference to the suffering which results (e.g. in the 1998 east Asian economic crisis). It will remain as long as (a) it can direct the political processes of governments, (b) it can persuade enough of the people who matter that, in the long run, it can bring about a maximisation of wellbeing, and (c) it can show that there is no viable alternative.

26. To refer to nations outside the league of the wealthy as 'Third World' has long been out of fashion. Much more common is to use the designation 'Two-Thirds World' or, more simply, 'the South'. I am persuaded by a conversation with a Filipino woman, Carmencita Karadag, that there is merit in returning to 'Third World'. Her

reasoning is that this label alone emphasises the ideological fact of dependence and powerlessness, while the others attempt an aseptic neutrality.

27. Further consideration of the meaning and practice of partnership will be given in chapter 10.

28. Wayne Bragg has given a masterful summary of the current discussion of development issues from a Christian perspective in 'From Development to Transformation' in Samuel and Sugden, *The Church in Response to Human Need*, pp. 20–51.

29. 'The Oxford Declaration on Christian Faith and Economics' (paragraph 48), *Transformation* (April/June 1990), pp. 1–8; cf. Susan Johnson and Ben Rohaly, *Microfinance and Poverty Reduction* (Oxford, Oxfam, 1997); Louise Dignard and Jose Havet, *Women in Micro- and Small-Scale Enterprise Development* (Boulder, Westview Press, 1995); Helen Todd (ed.), *Cloning Grameen Bank: Replicating a Poverty Reduction Model in India, Nepal and Vietnam* (London, Intermediate Technology Publications, 1996); Geoffrey Wood and Iffath Sharif, *Who Needs Credit? Poverty and Finance in Bangladesh* (London, Zed Books, 1997).

30. Gutiérrez, *The Truth Shall Make You Free*, p. 16. This statement takes into consideration the reality that in many places the poor have a deep sense of a personal God alongside them in their need. It also recognises the persistent problem of reconciling endemic poverty with a good and all-powerful God – cf. J. Andrew Kirk, *A New World Coming: A Fresh Look at the Gospel for Today* (Basingstoke, Marshalls, 1983), chapter 12.

31. Gustavo Gutiérrez, *We Drink from Our Own Wells: The Spiritual Journey of a People* (Maryknoll, Orbis Books, 1984), p. 1979.

32. Richard *et al.*, *The Idols of Death*, pp. 3–45.

33. It is a sad fact that Christians of all political persuasions, believing in God's presence in some political movement or ideological ideal, have fervently 'baptised' the latest political opinions in the name of Christ. As the epigram puts it: to be married to the world-view of this generation is to be divorced in the next. One of the strengths of liberation theology, in my opinion, has been its ability to revise its commitments to particular social currents and trends in the light of historical developments and further theological exploration, cf. Gustavo Gutiérrez, *Essential Writings* (Maryknoll, Orbis Books, 1996), pp. 42–9.

34. cf. Bosch, *Transforming Mission*, p. 437.

35. Ronaldo Muñoz, *The God of Christians* (Tunbridge Wells, Burns and Oates, 1991), pp. 31–2, 85–8; also, Gustavo Gutiérrez, *The Power of the Poor in History* (London, SCM Press, 1983), p. 13.

36. e.g. Calvin Beisner, *Prosperity and Poverty: The Compassionate Use of*

Resources in a World of Scarcity (Westchester, Crossway Books, 1988), p. 194.

37. Juan Luis Segundo, *The Humanist Christology of Paul* (Maryknoll, Orbis Books, 1986); also, the discussion in Curt Cadorette, 'Liberating Mission: a Latin American Perspective' in Saayman and Kritzinger (eds.), *Mission in Bold Humility*, pp. 66–72; Bosch, *Transforming Mission*, pp. 442–7; Newbigin, *The Open Secret*, pp. 110ff.

38. In this section we are drawing a direct line between the *material* poverty, which is the outcome of the present capitalist economic system, and the *spiritual* poverty of consumerism which sustains this system. Experience strongly suggests that the former cannot be resolved until the latter is recognised as a major contributing factor utterly destructive in different ways both to those who possess and those who do not.

39. cf. Bauman, *Work, Consumerism and the New Poor*, pp. 28–30, 58–9.

7 Encounter with Religions of the World

1. Bosch, *Transforming Mission*, p. 477.
2. cf. Carl Braaten, *No Other Gospel! Christianity Among the World's Religions* (Minneapolis, Fortress Press, 1992), p. 89:

    The question whether there is the promise of salvation in the name of Jesus, and in no other name, is fast becoming a life-and-death issue facing contemporary Christianity. In the churches this issue will become the test of fidelity to the gospel, a matter of *status confessionis* more urgent than any other.

3. cf. John Hick, *God has Many Names* (Basingstoke, Macmillan, 1980), pp. 43–58.
4. 'God' (with a capital 'G') is appropriate if one believes that the same God is invoked in all religions; 'god' (without a capital) is appropriate if one thinks that quite distinct manifestations of the divine are involved.
5. cf. J. Andrew Kirk, *Loosing the Chains: Religion as Opium and Liberation* (London, Hodder and Stoughton, 1992), chapter 2, 'Stealing Fire from the Gods'.
6. In the main discussions about Jesus Christ as the *locus* of salvation, these questions surprisingly are not often asked. One exception is J. A. DiNoia, 'Varieties of Religious Aims: Beyond Exclusivism, Inclusivism and Pluralism' in Bruce Marshall (ed.), *Theology and Dialogue: Essays in Conversation with George Lindbeck* (Notre Dame, University of Notre Dame Press, 1990), pp. 249–74.
7. 'Muslims believe the Qur'an is the final revelation of God and summarizes all former revelations. It is the criterion of all truth, for

it is in perfect harmony with all former revelations of God' (David Shenk, *Global Gods: Exploring the Role of Religions in Modern Societies* [Scottdale, Herald Press, 1995], p. 291).

8. Raimundo Panikkar, 'The Christian Challenge for the Third Millennium' in Paul Mojzes and Leonard Swidler (eds.), *Christian Mission and Interreligious Dialogue* (Lewiston, Edwin Mellen Press, 1990), p. 117.

9. Karl Barth, *Church Dogmatics: The Doctrine of the Word of God*, vol. I, 2 (Edinburgh, T. & T. Clark, 1978), pp. 299, 302, 326.

10. Paul Martinson, 'What's There to Worry About?' in Mojzes and Swidler (eds.), *Christian Mission and Interreligious Dialogue*, p. 210.

11. cf. Ninian Smart, *The Religious Experience of Mankind* (London, Collins, 1971).

12. For further discussion, cf. Kirk, *Loosing the Chains*, chapter 1, 'A Never Ending Story'; David Brown, *A Guide to Religions* (London, SPCK, 1975), pp. 8–13.

13. Central to all Melanesian religion is belief in ancestor-spirits who through their access to supernatural powers can bring good or ill to their living descendants. Gods, demons, land spirits (*masalai* in pidgin) and other forces of the unseen environment also intervene in human affairs . . . Prosperity and order in the small communities depends on effective control of spiritual power (sometimes called *mana*). (B. Colless and P. Donovan, 'Pacific Religions' in John Hinnells, *A Handbook of Living Religions* [London, Penguin Books, 1991], p. 420.)

14. cf. Stephen Sharot, *Messianism, Mysticism and Magic: A Sociological Analysis of Jewish Religious Movements* (Chapel Hill, University of North Carolina Press, 1982); Peter Clarke (ed.), *The Worlds Religions: Islam* (London, Routledge, 1990), pp. 2, 75, 132, 138ff., 188; Denis Maceoin and Ahmed Al-Shahi, *Islam in the Modern World* (Beckenham, Croom Hill, 1983), pp. 73–85; Bill Musk, *The Unseen Face of Islam: Sharing the Gospel with Ordinary Muslims* (Eastbourne, MARC, 1989); Jacques Van Nieuwenhove and Berma Klein Goldewijk (eds.), *Popular Religion, Liberation and Contextual Theology* (Kampen, Kok, 1991); Abraham Ayrookuzhiel, *The Sacred in Popular Hinduism* (Madras, Christian Literature Society, 1983).

15. Examples such as the Mormons, the Unification Church, Hare Krishna and Soka Gakkai readily spring to mind. There are literally thousands of others. As a manifestation of religion, it is baffling to know how to understand the phenomenon grouped around the very general heading of 'New Age'. Though related in a tenuous way to the world of the 'spirit' or 'meta-conscious', and certainly having some links to ancient religions of nature, New Age beliefs are unlike the historic or new religions, in that their adherents do

not generally form definable communities nor proscribe particular patterns of behaviour – cf. Paul Heelas, *The New Age Movement: The Celebration of the Self and Sacralization of Modernity* (Oxford, Blackwell, 1996); Ernest Lucas, *Science and the New Age Challenge* (Leicester, Apollos, 1996).

16. Kirk, *Loosing the Chains*, pp. 49–50; cf. also, J. Miguez Bonino, *Christians and Marxists: The Mutual Challenge to Revolution* (London, Hodder and Stoughton, 1975), pp 47–9.

17. 'Loving devotion and self-surrender to the deity, leading to inner transformation through grace' (John Hinnels [ed.], *The Penguin Dictionary of Religions* [Harmondsworth, Penguin Books, 1984], p. 63).

18. Seiichi Yagi, 'Plurality of the Treasure in Earthen Vessels' in Leonard Swidler and Paul Mojzes, *The Uniqueness of Jesus: A Dialogue with Paul F. Knitter* (Maryknoll, Orbis Books, 1997), pp. 140–1.

19. Stephen Neill, *Crises of Belief: The Christian Dialogue with Faith and No Faith* (London, Hodder and Stoughton, 1984), p. 121.

20. Pope John Paul II, *Encyclical on Missionary Activity: Redemptoris Missio* (printed in *Origins*, CNS documentary service, vol. 20, no. 34, January 31, 1991), par. 10.

21. John Hick, 'Five Misgivings' in Paul Mojzes and Leonard Swidler (eds.), *The Uniqueness of Jesus: A Dialogue with Paul F. Knitter* (Maryknoll, Orbis Books, 1997), p. 80.

22. Newbigin, *The Open Secret*, p. 177.

23. cf. Mark Heim, *Is Christ the Only Way? Christian Faith in a Pluralistic World* (Valley Forge, Judson Press, 1985), pp. 120–2.

24. cf. Yates, *Christian Mission in the Twentieth Century*, pp. 175–6; M. Ruokanen, *The Catholic Doctrine of the Non-Christian Religions According to the Second Vatican Council* (Leiden, IIMO, 1992).

25. cf. Jacob Kavunkal, 'Eschatology and Mission in Creative Tension: An Indian Perspective' in Saayman and Kritzinger (eds.), *Mission in Bold Humility*, pp. 75–8.

26. Hick, 'Five Misgivings', p. 80.

27. Samuel Rayan, 'Religions, Salvation and Mission' in Mojzes and Swidler (eds.), *Christian Mission and Interreligious Dialogue*, p. 129.

28. Gavin D'Costa offers a much more detailed account of the various options and gives his own assessment of the discussion in *Theology and Religious Pluralism: The Challenge of Other Religions* (Oxford, Blackwell, 1986). I have outlined my own approach to a theology of religion in *Loosing the Chains*. In this present book, I wish to try to lay bare the various issues and suggest what I believe are the fundamental ground-rules for a fruitful development of the debate.

29. Thus, for example, it is inadmissible to ascribe to the exclusivist the view that the non-Christian partner in dialogue is damned – cf. D'Costa, *Theology and Religious Pluralism*, p. 120. This is an emotive

word, which needs some refinement and setting in context. For a more nuanced view, see Clark Pinnock, 'Revelation' in Sinclair Ferguson and David Wright (eds.), *New Dictionary of Theology* (Leicester, Inter-Varsity Press, 1988), p. 586.

30. A common current example of this is the attempt to invalidate some people's opinions on the basis of geographical location. Thus some Asian theologians dismiss the views of any who have not lived in Asia, on the assumption that they either cannot understand or cannot sympathise with the convictions of adherents of other faiths. This is a mirror-image of the theological and cultural arrogance that has been so common in the West since the beginning of the modern expansion of Christianity.

31. Panikkar, 'The Christian Challenge for the Third Millennium', p. 118.

32. cf. Rayan, 'Religions, Salvation and Mission', p. 134.

33. cf. Kenneth Cracknell, *Towards a New Relationship: Christians and People of Other Faiths* (London, Epworth Press, 1986), pp. 107–8.

34. Paul Knitter, in Swidler and Mojzes (eds.), *The Uniqueness of Jesus*, p. 7.

35. 'Five Theses on the Uniqueness of Jesus,' in ibid. p. 11.

36. 'Can Our "One and Only" also Be a "One Among Many"? A Response to Responses', in ibid. p. 155.

37. 'What's So Special about Jesus?', in ibid. pp. 22–4.

38. 'Whose Uniqueness?' in ibid. p. 113.

39. 'Beguiled by a Word?' in ibid. p. 62.

40. 'A Simple Solution', in ibid. pp. 26–7.

41. 'Do Knitter's Theses Take Christ's Divinity Seriously?', in ibid. pp. 45–6.

42. 'An Evangelical Response to Knitter's Five Theses', in ibid. p. 117.

43. 'Five Misgivings', in ibid. p. 83.

44. As Hick does in *God Has Many Names*, pp. 59–79.

45. For an exposition of three representative attempts to approach Christology in this way – those of Stanley Samartha, Aloysius Pieris and Raimundo Panikkar – see Vinoth Ramachandra, *The Recovery of Mission: Beyond the Pluralist Paradigm* (Carlisle, Paternoster Press, 1996), pp. 3–142. Although Ramachandra does not agree with their views, he understands them well and is fair to them. He is particularly good at spelling out the fundamental issues involved in the debate between Christians about the significance of their confession of Christ.

46. The Orthodox Churches would dispute this statement, as they believe that the formulations of the creeds are, along with the New Testament, part of God's providential revelation.

47. A common device to avoid the implications of the Johannine lan-

guage is either to reinterpret it as mythological (i.e. conveying a non-literal and expressive kind of truth) or to assume that John's Gospel is the culmination of a long development from a moderate to an exalted Christology. In both cases, the conclusion has been reached first and the evidence then made to fit it.

48. Space only allows me to consider Colossians. The argument of Hebrews is that some Christians are in danger of falling away from their faith because they have not fully grasped the extraordinary nature and achievements of Jesus Christ. It begins with some of the most elevated of all statements about Christ, while also emphasising his true human nature.

49. Knitter, p. 148.

50. Ramachandra, p. 32.

51. John Sanders, 'Idolater Indeed!' in Swidler and Mojzes (eds.), *The Uniqueness of Jesus*, p. 122.

52. On the importance of truth in the encounter between different faiths, cf. Hendrik Vroom, *No Other Gods: Christian Belief in Dialogue with Buddhism, Hinduism and Islam* (Grand Rapids, Eerdmans, 1996), pp. 3–4, 130ff.

53. cf. A. C. Grayling (ed.), *Philosophy: A Guide through the Subject* (Oxford, Oxford University Press), pp. 470–7.

54. Peter Hicks, *Evangelicals and Truth: A Creative Proposal for a Postmodern Age* (Leicester, Apollos, 1998), p. 30.

55. ibid. p. 32. The author at this point is not presenting his own views, but those of others.

56. Some of the most important implications for mission of the contemporary epistemological debate have been explored in J. Andrew Kirk and Kevin Vanhoozer (eds.), *Staking a Claim: Christian Mission and the Western Crisis of Knowledge* (Maryknoll, Orbis Books, 1999).

8 Overcoming Violence and Building Peace

1. It does not figure, for example, in any of the elements of an emerging ecumenical missionary paradigm elaborated by Bosch in *Transforming Mission*. It is not mentioned either by Verkuyl, Nazir Ali, Yates or Senior and Stuhlmueller, and only briefly and minimally by Jongeneel.

2. For more on the causes of conflict in different regions of the world, cf. Peter Janke (ed.), *Ethnic and Religious Conflicts: Europe and Asia* (Aldershot, Dartmouth, 1994); Gerard Prunier, *The Rwanda Crisis (1959–1994): History of a Genocide* (London, Hurst and Co., 1995).

3. cf. John Driver, 'The Anabaptist Vision and Social Justice' in Samuel

Esobar and John Driver, *Christian Mission and Social Justice* (Scottdale, Herald Press, 1978), pp. 86–110.

4. cf. Willard Swartley, *Israel's Scripture Traditions and the Synoptic Gospels: Story Shaping Story* (Peabody, Hendrickson, 1994), pp. 135–7, 147–8.

5. 'To the majority of Christians, advocating a policy of total non-violence in the face of wickedness does seem to display, to say the least, a lack of realism about evil in the world' (Jerram Barrs, 'Justice and Peace Demand Necessary Force' in J. Andrew Kirk [ed.], *Handling Problems of Peace and War* [Basingstoke, Marshall Pickering, 1988], p. 10).

6. Paul Ramsey, *War and the Christian Conscience: How Shall Modern War be Conducted Justly?* (Durham, Duke University Press, 1961), pp. xv–xvii; Jean-Michel Hornus, *It is Not Lawful for Me to Fight: Early Christian Attitudes to War, Violence and the State* (Scottdale, Herald Press, 1980), pp. 158–99.

7. cf. John Helgeland *et al.*, *Christians and the Military: The Early Experience* (London, SCM Press, 1985); Peter Brock, *The Roots of War Resistance: Pacifism from the Early Church to Tolstoy* (Nyack, Fellowship of Reconciliation, 1981), pp. 9–13.

8. Augustine, *The City of God* (particularly Book XIX); cf. Ramsey, *War and the Christian Conscience*, pp. 15ff.

9. cf. Jeff McMahan, 'War and Peace' in Peter Singer, *A Companion to Ethics* (Oxford, Blackwell, 1993), pp. 386–7.

10. At the time of writing (August 1998), a number of countries are implementing the treaty on the total banning of land-mines as instruments of war.

11. cf. Oliver Barclay (ed.), *Pacifism and War* (Leicester, Inter-Varsity Press, 1984), pp. 17ff., 138ff., 165ff.; Paul Ramsey, *The Just War, Force and Political Responsibility* (Lanham, University Press of America, 1983).

12. Occasionally Christian groups have sought to exclude themselves entirely from any contact with society (e.g. the Amish). However, given that Christian discipleship is clearly meant to be carried out in the world, and not removed from it (Matt. 5:13–16; John 17:15; 1 Cor. 5:9–10), these examples are aberrations not norms.

13. By what criteria, for example, could the United Nations, strongly influenced by the USA, intervene in Iraq's invasion of Kuwait, but not in the case of China's annexation of Tibet or that of East Timor by Indonesia?

14. The following are some of the situations in which civil disobedience would be the right action: when a government requires its citizens to break God's laws, forbids the worship of God or the sharing of the message of the Gospel, enacts laws violating the dignity and

basic rights of its people, identifies itself with the state by sus-
pending the constitution or commits acts of gross injustice and
oppression.

15. cf. David Bosch, 'God's Reign and the Rulers of this World: Missiological Reflections on Church–State Relationships' in Van Engen,
Gilliland and Pierson (eds.), *The Good News of the Kingdom*, pp. 89–95.

16. For further reflection on the implications of the double citizenship,
cf. Kirk, *Handling Problems of Peace and War*, Part III: 'Christian
Responsibility within the Nation-State' (with contributions from
David Atkinson, John Gladwin, Donald Shell, Richard Bauckham,
Gordon McConville and Andrew Kirk).

17. Wink, *Healing a Nation's Wounds*, p. 54.

18. On this subject, cf. Olof Palme *et al.*, *Common Security: A Programme
for Disarmament* (London, Pan Books, 1982); Johann Galtung, *There
are Alternatives: Four Roads to Peace and Security* (Nottingham,
Spokesman, 1984); Paul Zagorski, *Democracy vs. National Security:
Civil-Military Relations in Latin America* (London, Lynne Rienner,
1992).

19. One of the most encouraging developments in international political
thinking is the move to privilege the integrity of peoples within a
state over the integrity of the state. This means that the doctrine of
non-interference in the internal affairs of a sovereign state can be
outweighed by the higher cause of the non-violation by the state of
the people's essential and intrinsic rights.

20. cf. Gerald Shenk, *God With Us? The Roles of Religion in the Former
Yugoslavia* (Uppsala, Life and Peace Institute, 1993).

21. Bo Wirmark (ed.), *Government–NGO Relations in Preventing Violence,
Transforming Conflict and Building Peace* (Stockholm, Peace Team
Forum, 1998), p. 8.

22. This is one of the major causes of racism. For more on racism, cf.
Philomena Essed, *Understanding Everyday Racism: An Interdisciplinary
Theory* (London, Sage Publications, 1991); Kenneth Leech, *Struggle
in Babylon: Racism in the Cities and Churches of Britain* (London,
Sheldon Press, 1988); Zolile Mbali, *The Churches and Racism: A Black
South African Perspective* (London, SCM Press, 1987); John Solomos,
Race and Racism in Contemporary Britain (Basingstoke, Macmillan,
1989); Dinesh D'Souza, *The End of Racism: Principles for a Multiracial
Society* (New York, The Free Press, 1995).

23. Mary Anne Warren, 'Abortion' in Singer, *A Companion to Ethics*, p.
313.

24. cf. Elaine Graham, *Making the Difference: Gender, Personhood and
Theology* (London, Mowbray, 1995); Ursula King (ed.), *Feminist
Theology from the Third World: A Reader* (London, SPCK, 1994); Paul
Tournier, *The Gift of Feeling* (London, SCM Press, 1981); Arthur

Britain, *Masculinity and Power* (Oxford, Blackwell, 1989); Morwena Griffiths, *Feminisms and the Self: The Web of Identity* (London, Routledge, 1995).

25. The classical discussion is to be found in H. Arendt, *On Violence* (Harmondsworth, Penguin Books, 1969); cf. also, Eric Moonman, *The Violent Society* (London, Frank Cass, 1987); Charles Villa-Vicencio (ed.), *Theology and Violence: The South African Debate* (Braamfontein, Skotaville, 1987); James Williams, *The Bible, Violence and the Sacred* (New York, HarperCollins, 1989); WCC, *Programme to Overcome Violence: An Introduction* (Geneva, WCC, 1994).

26. The example of the Community of San Egidio in Rome is instructive – cf. Claudio Mario Betti, 'Dealing with Conflicts: The Experience of the Community of S. Egidio' in Wirmark (ed.), *Government–NGO Relations in Preventing Violence*, pp. 102–9.

27. ibid. pp. 11–12.

28. A magnificent example of what can be achieved at the grass-roots in building confidence, developing skills and creating truly participatory forms of democracy as means of creating a culture of non-violence and resolving conflict, is the work of the 'Horn of Africa Programme' of the Life and Peace Institute: cf. Wolfgang Heinrich, *Building the Peace: Experiences of Collaborative Peacebuilding in Somalia 1993–1996* (Uppsala, Life and Peace Institute, 1997).

29. On mediation, cf. Michael Lund, *Preventing Violent Conflicts: A Strategy for Preventive Dipomacy* (Washington, US Institute of Peace, 1996); Various, *Steps Toward Reconciliation: Christian Faith and Human Enmity* (Budapest, Ecumenical Study Centre, 1996); Jack Porter and Ruth Taplin, *Conflict and Conflict Resolution* (Lanham, University Press of America, 1987); John Burton, *Deviance, Terrorism and War: The Process of Solving Unsolved Social and Political Problems* (Oxford, Martin Robertson, 1979).

30. cf. Peter Biddy (ed.), *Organised Abuse: The Current Debate* (Aldershot, Arena, 1996); Patrick Parkinson, *Child Sexual Abuse and the Churches* (London, Hodder and Stoughton, 1997).

31. cf. Carolyn Nordstrom, *Girls and Warzones: Troubling Questions* (Uppsala, Life and Peace Institute, 1997).

32. Wink, *Healing a Nation's Wounds*, p. 45.

9 Care of the Environment

1. 'Nature has been . . . degraded into a dumping ground for human refuse' (Moltmann, *The Way of Jesus Christ*, p. 305).

2. One of the main reasons for slashing and burning policies in the world's great forests (in Brazil, Malaysia, Indonesia and the Philippines) is to grow crops and produce beef (for export).

However, after only a short time the impoverished soil can no longer support the agricultural activities for which the trees were cleared in the first place – cf. Ian Barbour, *Ethics in an Age of Technology* (The Gifford Lectures, vol. 2) (London, SCM Press, 1992), p. 183.

3. *North–South: A Programme for Survival* (London, Pan Books, 1980).

4. cf. the discussion in Bryan Cartledge (ed.), *Population and the Environment* (Oxford, Oxford University Press, 1995); Philip Sarre and John Blundon (eds.), *An Overcrowded World? Population, Resources and the Environment* (Oxford, Oxford University Press, 1995).

5. The literature on environmental concerns is vast. The following are recommended as providing good summaries of the major questions: David Munro and Martin Holgate, *Caring for the Earth: A Strategy for Sustainable Living* (Grand, IUCN, UNEP, WWF, 1991); David Kemp, *Global Environmental Issues: A Climatological Approach* (London, Routledge, 1994); Paul Harrison, *The Third Revolution: Environment, Population and a Sustainable World* (London, Taurus, 1992); Steven Yearley, *Sociology, Environmentalism, Globalization: Reinventing the Globe* (London, Sage, 1996); Rosi Braidotti *et al.*, *Women, the Environment and Sustainable Development: Towards a Theoretical Synthesis* (London, Zed Books, 1994); Joan Davidson, Dorothy Myers and Manab Chakraborty, *No Time to Waste: Poverty and the Global Environment* (Oxford, Oxfam, 1992); Alan Durning, *How Much Is Enough? The Consumer Society and the Future of the Earth* (London, Earthscan, 1992).

6. Five headings are given on ecology and 60 on culture. Even allowing for the selective nature of the bibliographies, the disparity is rather large! cf. Jongeneel, *Philosophy, Science and Theology of Mission*, pp. 128–34. The following studies have been written from a Christian perspective; they represent only a selection from a large output: Sean McDonagh, *The Greening of the Church* (London, Geoffrey Chapman, 1990); Sean McDonagh, *Passion for the Earth: The Christian Vocation to Promote Justice, Peace and the Integrity of Creation* (London, Geoffrey Chapman, 1994); Tim Cooper, *Green Christianity: Caring for the Whole Creation* (London, Hodder and Stoughton, 1994); Michael Northcott, *The Environment and Christian Ethics* (Cambridge, Cambridge University Press, 1996); Lawrence Osborn, *Guardians of Creation: Nature in Theology and the Christian Life* (Leicester, Apollos, 1993); Ian Ball, Margaret Goodall, Clare Palmer and John Reader (eds.), *The Earth Beneath: A Critical Guide to Green Theology* (London, SPCK, 1992); Leonardo Boff, *Ecology and Liberation: A New Paradigm* (Maryknoll, Orbis Books, 1995); Leonardo Boff, *Cry of the Earth, Cry of the Poor* (Maryknoll, Orbis Books, 1997); Robert Gottfried, *Economics, Ecology and the Roots of Western Faith: Perspectives from the Garden* (Lanham,

Rowman and Littlefield, 1995); D. Hallmann (ed.), *Ecotheology: Voices from South and North* (Geneva, WCC, 1994).

7. The phrase was first used in the context of the Vancouver Assembly in 1983; cf. *Gathered for Life* (Geneva, WCC, 1983). In preparation for the Canberra Assembly in 1991 (whose theme was 'Come Holy Spirit: Renew the Whole Creation'), a major consultation on the subject was held in Seoul, Korea. Here, however, as in Canberra, major differences emerged among delegates concerning the missiological interpretation and imperatives regarding the environment – cf. Ulrich Duchrow and Gerhard Liedke, *Shalom: Biblical Perspectives on Creation, Justice and Peace* (Geneva, WCC, 1989); Preman Niles, *Resisting the Threats to Life: Covenanting for Justice, Peace and the Integrity of Creation* (Geneva, WCC, 1989); Gennadios Limouris, *Justice, Peace and the Integrity of Creation: Insights from Orthodoxy* (Geneva, WCC, 1990); Thomas Best and Wesley Granberg-Michaelson, *Koinonia and Justice, Peace and Creation: Costly Unity* (Geneva, WCC, 1993).

8. Frederick, *The San Antonio Report*, p. 54.

9. ibid. p. 58.

10. Moltmann, *The Way of Jesus Christ*, p. 308.

11. It would be unfair to give the impression that science has been driven largely by pragmatic concerns. Scientists have been inspired by an authentic desire to expand knowledge, by wonder at the beautiful intricacies of nature as a created given to be explored and by a compassionate longing to overcome disease, suffering and impotence.

12. cf. Andrew Linzey, *Christianity and the Rights of Animals* (London, SPCK, 1987), pp. 114–25.

13. 'Creation' in *A New Handbook of Christian Theology*, p. 112.

14. Connected to the views of Henry David Thoreau and his followers, cf. *Walden* (New York, W. W. Norton, 1951 [reprint of 1854 original]).

15. A technical way of distinguishing between the essential and non-essential moral value of different living things: 'Something is morally considerable if it enters into ethical evaluation in its own right, independently of its usefulness as a means to other ends' (Robert Elliott, 'Environmental Ethics' in Singer, *A Companion to Ethics*, p. 286).

16. ibid. p. 287.

17. On the distinction in essence between humans and animals, cf. Roger Scruton, *Modern Philosophy: An Introduction and Survey* (London, Mandarin, 1994), pp. 224, 232–3, 236, 299–301.

18. ibid. p. 351.

19. For further discussion, cf. J. Baird Callicott, 'Animal Liberation: A

Triangular Affair' in Robert Elliott (ed.), *Environmental Ethics* (Oxford, Oxford University Press, 1995), pp. 29–59; Robin Attfield, *Environmental Philosophy: Principles and Prospects* (Aldershot, Ashgate, 1994), pp. 93–102; Andrew Linzey, *Animal Theology* (London, SCM Press, 1994); John Cobb, *Matters of Life and Death* (Louisville, Westminster/John Knox Press, 1991), pp. 31–43; Andrew Linzey and Tom Reagan (eds.), *Animals and Christianity: A Book of Readings* (London, SPCK, 1989).

20. Moltmann, *The Way of Jesus Christ*, p. 308.

21. Peter Singer, *Animal Liberation*, 2nd edn (New York, Random House, 1990), p. 50; cf. also, Singer, *A Companion to Ethics*, p. 351.

22. Tom Regan, *The Case for Animal Rights* (Berkeley, University of California Press, 1983).

23. This term is used in the literature. Some environmental scientists think it is misleading and prefer a holistic approach to balancing habitats.

24. Bill Deval and George Sessions, *Deep Ecology* (Salt Lake City, Peregrine Smith Books, 1985), p. 17.

25. Barbour, *Ethics in an Age of Technology*, p. 63.

26. The belief that 'the material and the spiritual, the physical and the mental, are aspects of one being or substance' (Hinnells, *A Handbook of Living Religions*, p. 219).

27. L. S. Cousins, 'Buddhism' in Hinnells, *A Handbook of Living Religions*, pp. 304, 306.

28. Bernard Williams, 'Ethics' in Grayling (ed.), *Philosophy: A Guide Through the Subject*, p. 553.

29. Barbour, *Ethics in an Age of Technology*, p. 66. Decisions for the future have to be taken with all due care about the risks involved. However, if irreversible changes to biological processes are contemplated, a much greater degree of certainty about probable outcomes is needed. The degree of short-term expediency evident in political and economic decision-making does not inspire confidence.

30. Jongeneel, *Philosophy, Science and Theology of Mission*, p. 129. Scylla in Greek mythology was a monster with six heads, each mouth having a triple set of teeth. Charybdis was a whirlpool. The two were on the opposite shores of the Strait of Messina, a narrow channel running between Sicily and mainland Italy, so it was almost impossible for sailors to navigate between the two without destruction.

31. Church of England, *Alternative Service Book* (London and Cambridge, SPCK and Cambridge University Press, 1980), p. 129.

32. Roger Scruton, *Modern Philosophy: An Introduction and Survey* (London, Mandarin, 1996), p. 223.

33. ibid. pp. 224–5.

34. The theological status of pantheism in relation to an orthodox trinitarian view of God and creation is highly disputed. It may well depend on how it is defined. For defence of this perspective which distinguishes it clearly from all forms of pantheism, cf. Philip Clayton, *God and Contemporary Science* (Edinburgh, Edinburgh University Press, 1997), pp. 89–100.

35. For more on Christian understandings of freedom, cf. Kirk, *The Meaning of Freedom*, chapter 9.

36. Antony Giddens has noticed how the concept of nature is being 'recreated' by the Green Movement just as (as a result of) it is disappearing. It becomes personified (Nature) as the source of true values for humans, in contrast to the values espoused by the ethics of production and consumption which underlie Marxism and capitalism respectively. He quotes Ulrich Beck (*Ecological Politics in an Age of Risk*, p. 65):

> Nature is not nature, but rather a concept, norm, memory, utopia, counter-image. Today more than ever, now that it no longer exists, nature is being rediscovered, pampered . . . 'Nature' is a kind of anchor by whose means the ship of civilisation, sailing over the open seas, conjures up, cultivates, its contrary: dry land, the harbour, the approaching reef.

He then goes on to make the valid point that nature is not an originator of meaning nor is it self-explanatory; it always comes already interpreted – cf. *Beyond Left and Right: The Future of Radical Politics* (Cambridge, Polity Press, 1994), pp. 202–12.

37. 'Fortune' and 'Destiny' (Gad and Meni) were astral deities taken from the religions of Canaan and Egypt respectively. They were the male and female gods of fate.

38. Paulus Mar Gregorios suggests that the desire for affluence is stimulated by hidden persuasion and the collusion of the heart. However, instant gratification marks a serious loss for it implies the possession of cheap workmanship (which costs little) instead of skilled craftsmanship (which requires patient waiting); cf. 'New Testament Foundations for Understanding the Creation' in W. Granberg Michaelson, *Tending the Earth* (Grand Rapids, Eerdmans, 1987), p. 92.

39. Donella Meadows *et al.*, *The Limits to Growth* (New York, Universe, 1972).

40. Moltmann, *The Way of Jesus Christ*, p. 309.

41. cf. Paul Brand, 'A Handful of Mud: A Personal History of My Love for the Soil' in Michaelson, *Tending the Earth*, p. 146.

42. cf. Ulrich Duchrow, *Alternatives to Global Capitalism Drawn from Bib-*

lical History, Designed for Political Action (Utrecht, International Books, 1995), pp. 256–9.

10 Sharing in Partnership

1. The common habit in the West of couples cohabiting is symptomatic of a culture which highly favours 'keeping one's options open' – separation does not involve the legal complications of divorce. In this context the word 'partner' is being used in a weak sense of 'the person I happen to be sharing my life with at present'. In business ventures, a 'partnership' is a contractual relationship in which two or more persons agree to share both the right to profits and liability for losses. In the context of mission (as in the Christian view of marriage), it would be better to speak of a 'covenantal' relationship in which two or more Christian bodies undertake before God to support one another in their respective tasks.

2. cf. Bosch, *Transforming Mission*, p. 465.

3. cf. Nazir Ali, *Mission and Dialogue*, p. 51.

4. cf. Jongeneel, *Philosophy, Science and Theology of Mission*, p. 180.

5. The most obvious examples are the many Pentecostal churches in Latin America and the African Initiated churches in that continent; cf. Andrew Chesnut, *Born Again in Brazil: The Pentecostal Boom and the Pathogens of Poverty* (New Brunswick, Rutgers University Press, 1997); Daniel Miller (ed.), *Coming of Age: Protestantism in Contemporary Latin America* (Lanham, University Press of America, 1994), pp. 65–88, 89–116; Diane Austin-Broos, *Jamaica Genesis: Religion and the Politics of Moral Order* (Chicago, University of Chicago Press, 1997); Harvey Cox, *Fire from Heaven: The Rise of Pentecostal Spirituality and the Reshaping of Religion in the Twenty-First Century* (London, Cassell, 1996), chapter 9; David Martin, *Tongues of Fire: The Explosion of Protestantism in Latin America* (Oxford, Blackwell, 1990); Allan Anderson, *Tumelo: The Faith of African Pentecostals in South Africa* (Pretoria, University of South Africa, 1993); M-L Martin, *Kimbangu: An African Prophet and his Church* (Oxford, Blackwell, 1985); Adrian Hastings, *A History of African Christianity, 1950–1975* (Cambridge, Cambridge University Press, 1979), pp. 248–57; Edward Fashole-Luke, Richard Gray, Adrian Hastings and Godwin Tasie (eds.), *Christianity in Independent Africa* (London, Rex Collins, 1978), pp. 44–59, 96–110, 111–21; David Shenk (ed.), *Ministry in Partnership with African Independent Churches* (Elkhart, Mennonite Board of Missions, 1991); Allan Anderson, *African Reformation: The Rise and Development of African Instituted Churches in the Sub-Sahara* (forthcoming).

6. Nacpil, 'Mission but not Missionaries', *International Review of Mission* (vol. 60, 1971), pp. 356–62. John Gatu of Kenya was also prominent

in the debate – cf. Yates, *Christian Mission in the Twentieth Century*, p. 199; also, Pius Wakatama, *Independence for the Third World Church: An African's Perspective on Missionary Work* (Downers Grove, IVP, 1976).

7. At a later date (in the late 1970s), it was also observed that the national Churches (of all denominations) which were most supportive of radical social and political change (as in Nicaragua) were also those with the fewest missionaries in attendance.

8. Nacpil, 'Mission but not Missionaries', p. 360.

9. Examples were the United Society for the Propagation of the Gospel in the UK and the United Methodist Church and the Presbyterian Church of America in the USA.

10. A recent example known to me is of a couple (the husband from Israel, the wife from Chile) going to South America with a British mission society. Gradually the idea that cross-cultural mission is international, in both personnel and financial support, is beginning to be accepted.

11. Wilbert Shenk, *Write the Vision: The Church Renewed* (Valley Forge, Trinity Press International, 1995), pp. 51–2.

12. cf. John Fleming, *Structures for a Missionary Congregation: The Shape of the Christian Community in Asia Today* (Singapore, EACC, 1964); *The Church for Others* (Geneva, WCC, 1967); *Planning for Mission* (New York, 1966); Herbert Neve, *Sources for Change: Searching for Flexible Church Structures* (Geneva, WCC, 1968).

13. Hence the scandal caused by Jesus eating with 'tax collectors' and 'sinners' (Mark 2:16; Luke 15:2; 19:7), and Peter's breaking table fellowship with Gentile Christians (Gal. 2:11–14).

14. Nazir Ali, *Mission and Dialogue*, p. 50.

15. cf. Jerome Murphy O'Connor, *The Theology of the Second Letter to the Corinthians* (Cambridge, Cambridge University Press, 1991), chapter 6; Ralph Martin, *Word Biblical Commentary* vol. 40, *2 Corinthians* (Waco, Word Books, 1986), pp. 248–96; Stephen Kraftchick, 'Death in Us, Life in You: The Apostolic Medium' in David Hay (ed.), *Pauline Theology* vol. II, *1 and 2 Corinthians* (Minneapolis, Fortress Press, 1993), pp. 177–9.

16. 'In the context of God's saving purpose for humankind, Paul establishes a sense of mutuality and reciprocity between those who first received the Gospel and those who later on were evangelised by them' (Samuel Escobar, 'A Pauline Paradigm of Mission: A Latin American Reading' in Van Engen, Gilliland and Pierson [eds.], *The Good News of the Kingdom*, p. 63).

17. Frederick, *The San Antonio Report*, p.37.

18. Gutiérrez, *Essential Writings*, pp. 299ff. Here 'solidarity' means the

commitment of one's whole being to a person or group of people
in sympathy with their cause.

19. Christopher Sugden, 'Placing Critical Issues in Relief: A Response
to David Bosch' in Saayman and Kritzinger (eds.), *Mission in Bold
Humility*, p. 149.

20. cf. Nazir Ali, *From Everywhere to Everywhere*, p. 211.

21. Thus, Stephen Sykes says, 'The association of the terms (in English,
German and French) has to do ... with Lord Acton's dictum,
"Power corrupts, absolute power corrupts absolutely" ' ('Episcope
and Power in the Church' in Bruce Marshall [ed.], *Theology and
Dialogue: Essays in Conversation with George Lindbeck* [Notre Dame;
University of Notre Dame Press, 1990], p. 197). For the original, cf.
Life and Letters of Mandell Creighton, i. 372; also, William Pitt:
'Unlimited power is apt to corrupt the minds of those who possess
it' (Speech to the House of Lords, 9 January 1770).

22. The literature on the 'powers' in the New Testament is considerable.
Perhaps, the most extensive treatment in recent years has been given
by Walter Wink: *Naming the Powers: The Language of Power in the New
Testament* (Philadelphia, Fortress Press, 1984); *Unmasking the Powers:
The Invisible Forces that Determine Human Existence* (Philadelphia,
Fortress Press, 1986); *Engaging the Powers: Discernment and Resistance
in a World of Domination* (Philadelphia, Fortress Press, 1993); *The
Powers that Be* (London, Cassell, 1998).

23. cf. Bauckham, *The Bible in Politics*, pp. 147–9; Bauckham, *The Theology
of the Book of Revelation*, pp. 73–6; John Piper, *Love Your Enemies:
Jesus' Love Command in the Synoptic Gospels and the Early Christian
Paraenesis* (Cambridge, Cambridge University Press, 1979), pp.
76–88.

24. Frederick, *The San Antonio Report*, has a section on 'creative power'
(pp. 38–40). Although tending to the rhetorical (as ecumenical documents have a habit of doing), this is a useful description of how
power can be used positively in supporting and sustaining the
building of community for justice by telling the truth, sharing information, building trust, training and planning.

25. Sykes, 'Episcope and Power in the Church', pp. 198–9.

26. ibid. pp. 209–10.

27. ibid. p. 205.

28. Nazir Ali, *Mission and Dialogue*, p. 53.

29. Nazir Ali, *From Everywhere to Everywhere*, p. 49 (my italics).

30. cf. Peter Deyneka and Anita Deyneka, 'Evangelical Foreign Missionaries in Russia', in *IBMR* (*International Bulletin of Missionary Research*)
(vol. 22, 2, April 1998), pp. 56–62.

31. It is beyond the scope of this study to enter into the twists and
turns of the discussion of unity and the advances that have been

made. One helpful exploration of some of the theological questions has been made by Michael Root, 'Identity and Difference: The Ecumenical Problem' in Marshall (ed.), *Theology and Dialogue*, pp. 165–90; cf. also, Bosch, *Transforming Mission*, pp. 463ff.

32. In the United Kingdom, to give one example, there is considerable cross-party support for the central aims of the Movement for Christian Democracy (founded in 1990). It is 'an all-party, non-denominational, mass-membership organisation. It exists to promote Christian principles in politics through active campaigning in Parliament, and by encouraging service to our nation and communities.' Its six principles are: social justice, empowerment, wise stewardship, respect for life, active compassion and reconciliation.

33. Robert Moffitt, 'The Local Church and Development' in Samuel and Sugden, *The Church in Response to Human Need*, pp. 246–7.

11 The Church in Mission

1. cf. Alvaro Quiroz Magana, 'Ecclesiology in the Theology of Liberation' in Sobrino and Ellacuria, *Systematic Theology: Perspectives from Liberation Theology*, p. 182.

2. On the question of women in ministry, cf. Kathy Keay (ed.), *Men, Women and God* (Basingstoke, Marshall Pickering, 1987); Elaine Storkey, *What's Right with Feminism* (London, SPCK, 1985); Elsa Tamez (ed.), *Through Her Eyes: Women's Theology from Latin America* (Maryknoll, Orbis Books, 1989); Lisa Cahill, *Sex, Gender and Christian Ethics* (Cambridge, Cambridge University Press, 1996), chapter 5; Elisabeth Schüssler Fiorenza, *Discipline of Equals: A Critical Feminist Ecclesia-logy of Liberation* (London, SCM Press, 1993); Gretchen Gaebelein Hull, *Equal to Serve: Women and Men in the Church and Home* (London, Scripture Union, 1989); Susanne Heine, *Women and Early Christianity: Are the Feminist Scholars Right?* (London, SCM Press, 1987); Ben Witherington, *Women in the Earliest Churches* (Cambridge, Cambridge University Press, 1988).

3. I have recorded elsewhere a number of general instances in which the Church has badly betrayed its purpose – cf. *A New World Coming: A Fresh Look at the Gospel for Today* (Basingstoke, Marshalls, 1983), pp. 14–22; 86–9; 92–4; *Loosing the Chains*, pp. 115–18; 126–34.

4. Magana, 'Ecclesiology in the Theology of Liberation', p. 179.

5. cf. Gerd Theissen, *Social Reality and the Early Church: Theology, Ethics and the World of the New Testament* (Minneapolis, Fortress Press, 1992), chapter 2; Gerhard Lohfink, *Jesus and Community: The Social Dimension of Christian Faith* (London, SPCK, 1985), pp. 7–73.

6. Joachim Jeremias, *New Testament Theology*, vol. I (London, SCM Press, 1971), p. 170.

7. Wright, *Jesus and the Victory of God*, p. 300. Tom Wright also thinks that the inner group of three – Peter, James and John – may be modelled on David's three closest bodyguards (2 Sam. 23:8–23; 1 Chr. 11:10–25): 'The symbolism fits well with Jesus' persona, . . . anointed-but-not-yet-enthroned king of Israel'.

8. On the mission of the 70/72, cf. Robert Tannehill, *The Narrative Unity of Luke–Acts: A Literary Interpretation*, vol. 1, *The Gospel according to Luke* (Philadelphia, Fortress Press, 1986), pp. 232–7.

9. Wright, *Jesus and the Victory of God*, pp. 316–17.

10. cf. Jeremias, *New Testament Theology*, vol. I, pp. 175–6.

11. Although it might appear a thorough contradiction, Christian people who suffer for their faith are a sign that a new age is dawning . . . Paul informed the new Christians of Asia Minor that the kingdom of God could only be enjoyed in its completeness through suffering (Acts 14:22).
    (Kirk, *A New World Coming*, p. 130)

12. cf. John Stott, *Christian Counter-Culture: The Message of the Sermon on the Mount* (Leicester, IVP, 1978); Pinchas Lapide, *The Sermon on the Mount: Utopia or Program for Action* (Maryknoll, Orbis Books, 1986); George Strecker, *The Sermon on the Mount: An Exegetical Commentary* (Edinburgh, T. and T. Clark, 1988).

13. cf. Wolfgang Schrage, *The Ethics of the New Testament* (Edinburgh, T. and T. Clark, 1988); C. E. B. Cranfield, *On Romans and Other New Testament Essays* (Edinburgh, T. and T. Clark, 1998), chapter 4.

14. Howard Snyder, *Models of the Kingdom* (Nashville, Abingdon Press, 1991), p. 151.

15. Hauerwas, *After Christendom?*, pp. 93, 95, 96, 98, 105.

16. Lesslie Newbigin, *The Gospel in a Pluralist Society* (London, SPCK, 1989), p. 228.

17. Snyder, *Models of the Kingdom*, p. 154.

18. The extent and influence of 'folk' or 'implicit' religion in the West is debatable:

    > Folk religion is an *ad hoc* mixture of formal religion and local beliefs. It is a set of loosely related practices, often mutually contradictory, used not to present a coherent view of reality, but to produce immediate results and to offer strategies for living . . . It suggests ways in which one can ward off the bad and align oneself to the good.
    > (Mission Theological Advisory Group, *The Search for Faith and the Witness of the Church* [London, Church House Publishing, 1996], p. 48)

cf. also, Kirk, *Loosing the Chains*, chapter 1. The case of the phenomena loosely gathered together under the title 'New Age' is also intriguing. An excellent study of this manifestation of spiritual inclinations is given by Lars Johannson, 'Mystical Knowledge, New Age and Missiology' in Kirk and Vanhoozer (eds.), *To Stake a Claim*.

19. A weighty, comprehensive and sympathetic interpretation of New-bigin's mission engagement with contemporary culture is given in Hunsberger, *Bearing the Witness of the Spirit*.

20. There are many approaches to the Church's mission to political life: cf. Oliver O'Donovan, *The Desire of the Nations: Rediscovering the Roots of Political Theology* (Cambridge, Cambridge University Press, 1996); John de Gruchy, *Christianity and Democracy* (Cambridge, Cambridge University Press, 1995); Philip Wogaman, *Christian Perspectives on Politics* (London, SCM Press, 1988); Jack Nelson-Pallmeyer, *The Politics of Compassion* (Maryknoll, Orbis Books, 1986); Glenn Tinder, *The Political Meaning of Christianity: The Prophetic Stance* (New York, HarperCollins, 1991); Robert Aboagye-Mensah, *Mission and Democracy in Africa: The Role of the Church* (Accra, Asempa Publishers, 1994).

21. In the twentieth century people as diverse as Stalin, Hitler, the Japanese emperor, Lyndon Johnson (in Vietnam), Ian Smith, Ronald Reagan (in Nicaragua) and countless military dictators have assumed this position for themselves.

22. Although accused of restricting mission to political action (on the widest stage), liberation theologians at their best have emphasised that politics is a deeply spiritual matter: thus, for example, Gutiérrez, *On Job: God-Talk and the Suffering of the Innocent* (Maryknoll, Orbis Books, 1987); *We Drink from our Own Wells: The Spiritual Journey of a People* (Maryknoll, Orbis Books, 1984); Jon Sobrino, 'Spirituality and the Following of Jesus' in Sobrino and Ellacuria, *Systematic Theology*, pp. 233–56; Sobrino, *The Principle of Mercy*.

23. I have discussed in some detail elsewhere what I understand the 'religionless' nature of Christian faith to be and why it is important to grasp it in this light: cf. *Loosing the Chains*, chapters 6 and 7.

24. The literature on the 'Church Growth School of Missiology' is immense. It is not my intention to enter at length into the missiological debate surrounding certain affirmations about the nature and task of the Church, but to indicate briefly some lines of enquiry. Undoubtedly the discussion continues to be important and the views expressed enormously influential – cf. Donald McGavran, *Understanding Church Growth*, 3rd edn, revised and edited by Peter Wagner (Grand Rapids, Eerdmans, 1990); Eddie Gibbs, *I Believe in Church Growth* (London, Hodder and Stoughton, 1981); Orlando Costas, *Christ Outside the Gate: Mission Beyond Christendom*

(Maryknoll, Orbis Books, 1982), chapter 3; Wilbert Shenk (ed.), *Exploring Church Growth* (Grand Rapids, Eerdmans, 1983); Wayne Zunkel, *Church Growth under Fire* (Scottdale, Herald Press, 1987); Bowen, *So I Send You.*

25. In the case of the Church in Latin America, cf. Philip Berryman, *Religion in the Megacity: Catholic and Protestant Portraits from Latin America* (London, Latin American Bureau, 1996); also, Shenk (ed.), *Exploring Church Growth*, part 1.

26. Berryman, *Religion in the Megacity.*

27. It has not been easy in the recent history of mission to achieve a clear distinction between the principle of growing churches as part of the aim of mission and the theory of Church Growth as a particular interpretation of, and strategy for, growth. To have serious questions about some aspects of the latter does *not* imply a rejection of the former.

28. Miriam Adeney, *God's Foreign Policy* (Grand Rapids, Eerdmans, 1984), pp. 94ff.; cf. also, Bowen, *So I Send You.*

29. Eddie Gibbs, *I Believe in Church Growth.*

30. ibid. p. 128.

31. Padilla, *Mission Between the Times*, pp. 166–8.

32. ibid. pp. 167–8.

33. cf. Verkuyl, *Contemporary Missiology*, p. 192; Derek Tidball, 'Scandal of the Church' in Billington, Lane and Turner (eds.), *Mission and Meaning*, p. 365.

34. The best and most famous modern advocate of 'Christian presence' is Kenneth Cragg who, beginning with two remarkably influential books, *The Call of the Minaret*, 2nd edn (Maryknoll, Orbis Books, 1985) and *Sandals at the Mosque: Christian Presence amid Islam* (Oxford, Oxford University Press, 1959), advocated a long and painful 'retrieval' of Christ for the Muslim: undoing the alienation Muslims feel at the mention of Christ and restoring to them the Christ they have missed. Cragg himself offers a living example of the process he advocates – a highly sympathetic exploration into the interior of the Muslim's faith, discovering ways in which Islam cannot fulfil its own ideals because it lacks the knowledge of God revealed in Jesus Christ. For a brief summary of Cragg's views, cf. Yates, *Christian Mission*, pp. 150–5, 158. For a fuller interpretation, cf. Christopher Lamb, *The Call to Retrieval: Kenneth Cragg's Christian Vocation to Islam* (London, Grey Seal, 1997).

35. cf. Yates, *Christian Mission*, p. 159.

36. Unlike the contemporary pluralist, those who have advocated 'presence' as a valid aspect of mission have not usually dismissed the call to speak about Christ with a view to salvation. With all his

proper sensitivity towards Muslims, Cragg did not evade the
responsibility of witness:

> As long as Christ is Christ and the Church knows both itself
> and him, there will be a mission to Islam . . . We present Christ
> for the sole sufficient reason that he deserves to be presented . . .
> We cannot neglect that Christ claims discipleship and that his
> Gospel is something expecting a verdict.
> (*The Call of the Minaret*, p. 305.)

Postscript: Whither Mission?

1 cf. John Gray, *False Dawn: The Delusions of Global Capitalism* (London,
   Granta Publications, 1998).
2. Jan Jongeneel and Jan van Engelen, 'Contemporary Currents in
   Missiology' in Verstraelen, Camps, Hoedemaker and Spindler, *Missiology, an Ecumenical Introduction*, pp. 446ff.
3. cf. Nancey Murphy, *Beyond Liberalism and Fundamentalism: How
   Modern and Postmodern Philosophy set the Theological Agenda* (Valley
   Forge, Trinity Press International, 1996).
4. cf. Michael Amaladoss, 'The Challenges of Mission Today' in
   William Jenkinson and Helene O'Sullivan, *Trends in Mission: Toward
   the Third Millennium* (Maryknoll, Orbis Books, 1991), pp. 363–6.
5. Anthony Bellagamba, *Mission and Ministry in the Global Church*
   (Maryknoll, Orbis Books, 1992), p. 10.
6. In mitigation, some might argue that the Church is in for the long
   haul and cannot afford therefore to be identified with momentary
   movements that might turn out to be faddish and ephemeral. There
   is some truth in this assertion. It all depends on what reason and
   in what context it is being used.

Bibliography

Robert Aboagye-Mensah, *Mission and Democracy in Africa: The Role of the Church* (Accra: Asempa Publishers, 1994)

William Abraham, *The Logic of Evangelism* (Grand Rapids: Eerdmans, 1989)

Tim Allen and Alan Thomas, *Poverty and Development in the 1990s* (Oxford: OUP, 1992)

Allan Anderson, *Tumelo: The Faith of African Pentecostals in South Africa* (Pretoria: University of South Africa, 1993)

Allan Anderson, *African Reformation: The Rise and Development of African Instituted Churches in the Sub-Sahara* (forthcoming)

Gerald Anderson and Thomas Stransky (eds), *Christ's Lordship and Religious Pluralism* (Maryknoll: Orbis Books, 1981)

Maria Pilar Aquino, *Our Cry for Life: Feminist Theology from Latin America* (Maryknoll: Orbis Books, 1993)

Hannah Arendt, *On Violence* (Harmondsworth: Penguin Books, 1969)

Siga Arles, *Theological Education for the Mission of the Church in India: 1947–1987* (Frankfurt: Peter Lang, 1991)

Robin Attfield, *Environmental Philosophy: Principles and Prospects* (Aldershot: Ashgate, 1994)

Diane Austin-Broos, *Jamaica Genesis: Religion and the Politics of Moral Order* (Chicago: University of Chicago Press, 1997)

Abraham Ayrookuzhiel, *The Sacred in Popular Hinduism* (Madras: Christian Literature Society, 1983)

Paul Badham, *A John Hick Reader* (London: Macmillan, 1990)

Ian Ball, Margaret Goodhall, Clare Palmer and John Reader (eds), *The Earth Beneath: A Critical Guide to Green Theology* (London: SPCK, 1992)

Ian Barbour, *Ethics in an Age of Technology* (The Gifford Lectures, Vol. 2) (London: SCM Press, 1992)

Oliver Barclay (ed), *Pacifism and War* (Leicester: IVP, 1984)

Karl Barth, *Church Dogmatics: The Doctrine of the Word of God* (Vol.I, 2) (Edinburgh: T and T Clark, 1978)

Richard Bauckham, *The Bible in Politics: How to read the Bible Politically* (London: SPCK, 1989)

Richard Bauckham, *The Theology of the Book of Revelation* (Cambridge: CUP, 1993)

Zygmunt Bauman, *Postmodern Ethics* (Oxford: Blackwell, 1993)

Zygmunt Bauman, *Work, Consumerism and the New Poor* (Buckingham: Open University Press, 1998)

Tony Beck, *The Experience of Poverty: Fighting for Respect and Resources in Village India* (London: Intermediate Technology Publications, 1994)

T.O. Beidelman, *Colonial Evangelism: A Socio-Historical Study of an East African Mission at the Grassroots* (Bloomington: Indiana University Press, 1982)

Calvin Beisner, *Prosperity and Poverty: The Compassionate Use of Resources in a World of Scarcity* (Westchester: Crossway Books, 1988)

Patrick Benson (ed), *The Church and the Nations* (EFAC Bulletin, 47, 1996)

Philip Berryman, *Religion in the Megacity: Catholic and Protestant Portraits from Latin America* (London: Latin American Bureau, 1996)

Thomas Best and Wesley Granberg-Michaelson, *Koinonia and Justice, Peace and Creation: Costly Unity* (Geneva: WCC Publications, 1993)

Peter Biddy (ed), *Organised Abuse: The Current Debate* (Aldershot: Arena, 1996)

Anthony Billington, Tony Lane, Max Turner (eds), *Mission and Meaning* (Carlisle: Paternoster Press, 1995)

Graham Bird, *IMF Lending to Developing Countries: Issues and Evidence* (London: Routledge, 1995)

Leonardo Boff, *Ecclesiogenesis: The Base Communities Reinvent the Church* (Maryknoll: Orbis Books, 1986)

Leonardo Boff, *New Evangelization: Good News to the Poor* (Maryknoll: Orbis Books, 1991)

Leonardo Boff, *Ecology and Liberation: A New Paradigm* (Maryknoll: Orbis Books, 1995)

Leonardo Boff, *Cry of the Earth, Cry of the Poor* (Maryknoll: Orbis Books, 1997)

Leonardo Boff and Virgil Elizondo, *The Voice of the Victims* (London: SCM Press, 1991)

David Bosch, *Transforming Mission: Paradigm Shifts in the Theology of Mission* (Maryknoll: Orbis Books, 1991)

Tom Bottomore (ed), *A Dictionary of Marxist Thought* (Oxford: Blackwell, 1991)

Roger Bowen, *So I Send You: A Study Guide to Mission* (London: SPCK, 1996)

Carl Braaten, *The Apostolic Imperative* (Minneapolis: Augsburg Press, 1985)

Carl Braaten, *No Other Gospel! Christianity among the World's Religions* (Minneapolis: Fortress Press, 1992)

Rosi Braidotti (et al), *Women, the Environment and Sustainable Development: Towards a Theoretical Synthesis* (London: Zed Books, 1994)

Brandt Report, *North-South: A Programme for Survival* (London: Pan Books, 1980)

Ion Bria, *Go Forth in Peace: Orthodox Perspectives on Mission* (Geneva: WCC Publications, 1992)

Arthur Britain, *Masculinity and Power* (Oxford: Blackwell, 1989)

Peter Brock, *The Roots of War Resistance: Pacifism from the Early Church to Tolstoy* (Nyack: Fellowship of Reconciliation, 1981)

John Burton, *The Process of Solving Unsolved Social and Political Problems* (Oxford: Martin Robinson, 1979)

Lisa Cahill, *Sex, Gender and Christian Ethics* (Cambridge: CUP, 1996)

Bryan Cartledge (ed), *Population and the Environment* (Oxford: OUP, 1995)

Emilio Castro, *Freedom in Mission: The Perspective of the Kingdom of God* (Geneva: WCC Publications, 1985)

Andrew Chesnut, *Born Again in Brazil: The Pentecostal Boom and the Pathogens of Poverty* (New Brunswick: Rutgers University Press, 1997)

Peter Clarke (ed), *The World's Religions: Islam* (London: Routledge, 1990)

Philip Clayton, *God and Contemporary Science* (Edinburgh: Edinburgh University Press, 1998)

John Cobb, *Matters of Life and Death* (Louisville: Westminster/John Knox Press, 1991)

Guillermo Cook (ed), *Crosscurrents in Indigenous Spirituality: Interface of Maya, Catholic and Protestant Worldviews* (Leiden: Brill, 1997)

Tim Cooper, *Green Christianity: Caring for the Whole Creation* (London: Hodder and Stoughton, 1994)

Mariarosa Dalla Costa and Giovanna Dalla Costa (eds), *Paying the Price: Women and the Politics of International Economic Strategy* (London: Zed Books, 1995)

Orlando Costas, *Christ Outside the Gate: Mission Beyond Christendom* (Maryknoll: Orbis Books, 1982)

Orlando Costas, *Liberating News: A Theology of Contextual Evangelism* (Grand Rapids: Eerdmans, 1989)

Douglas Coupland, *Generation X: Tales for an Accelerated Culture* (London: Abacus, 1992)

Harvey Cox, *Fire from Heaven: The Rise of Pentecostal Spirituality and the Reshaping of Religion in the Twenty First Century* (London: Cassell, 1996)

Kenneth Cracknell, *Towards a New Relationship: Christians and People of Other Faiths* (London: Epworth Press, 1986)

Kenneth Cragg, *The Call of the Minaret* (Maryknoll: Orbis Books, 1985 – 2nd edition)

Kenneth Cragg, *Sandals at the Mosque: Christian Presence and Islam* (Oxford: OUP, 1959)

C.E.B. Cranfield, *On Romans and Other New Testament Essays* (Edinburgh: T and T Clark, 1998)

Joan Davidson, Dorothy Myers and Manab Chakraborty, *No Time to Waste: Poverty and the Global Environment* (Oxford: Oxfam, 1992)

Gavin D'Costa, *Theology and Religious Pluralism: The Challenge of Other Religions* (Oxford: Blackwell, 1986)

John de Gruchy, *Christianity and Democracy* (Cambridge: CUP, 1995)

Bill Deval and George Sessions, *Deep Ecology* (Salt Lake City: Peregrine Smith Books, 1985)

Louise Dignard and Jose Javet, *Women in Micro- and Small-Scale Enterprise Development* (Boulder: Westview Press, 1995)

John Drane, *Evangelism for a New Age* (London: Marshall Pickering, 1994)

Dinesh D'Souza, *The End of Racism: Principles for a Multiracial Society* (New York: The Free Press, 1995)

Ulrich Duchrow, *Alternatives to Global Capitalism Drawn from Biblical History, Designed for Political Action* (Utrecht: International Books, 1995)

Ulrich Duchrow and Gerhard Liedke, *Shalom: Biblical Perspectives on Creation, Justice and Peace* (Geneva: WCC Publications, 1989)

James Dunn, *The Parting of the Ways Between Christianity and Judaism and their Significance for the Character of Christianity* (London: SCM Press, 1991)

Alan Durning, *How Much is Enough? The Consumer Society and the Future of the Earth* (London: Earthscan, 1992)

Enrique Dussel (ed), *The Church in Latin America: 1492–1992* (Tunbridge Wells: Burns and Oates, 1992)

Michael Elliott, *Freedom, Justice and Christian Counter-Culture* (London: SCM Press, 1990)

Robert Elliott (ed), *Environmental Ethics* (Oxford: OUP, 1995)

Samuel Escobar and John Driver, *Christian Mission and Social Justice* (Scottdale: Herald Press, 1978)

Philomena Essed, *Understanding Everyday Racism: An Interdisciplinary Theory* (London: Sage Publications, 1991)

Edward Fashole-Luke, Richard Gray, Adrian Hastings and Godwin Tasie (eds), *Christianity in Independent Africa* (London: Rex Collins, 1978)

Sinclair Ferguson and David Wright (eds), *New Dictionary of Theology* (Leicester: Inter-Varsity Press, 1988)

John Finney, *Finding Faith Today: How Does it Happen?* (Swindon: Bible Society, 1992)

Elisabeth Schüssler Fiorenza, *Discipline of Equals: A Critical Feminist Ecclesia-logy of Liberation* (London: SCM Press, 1993)

John Fleming, *Structures for a Missionary Congregation: The Shape of the Christian Community in Asia Today* (Singapore: EACC, 1964)

David Ford, *The Modern Theologians: An Introduction to Christian Theology in the Twentieth Century* (Oxford: Blackwell, 1997)

Duncan Forrester, *Christian Justice and Public Policy* (Cambridge: CUP, 1997)

Frederick, *The San Antonio Report: Your Will Be Done, Mission in Christ's Way* (Geneva: WCC Publications, 1990)

Francis Fukuyama, *Trust: The Social Virtues and the Creation of Prosperity* (London: Penguin Books, 1996)

Raymond Fung, *Evangelistically Yours: Ecumenical Letters on Contemporary Evangelism* (Geneva: WCC Publications, 1992)

Raymond Fung and Georges Leucopolos, *Not a Solitary Way: Evangelism Stories from Around the World* (Geneva: WCC Publications, 1992)

Johann Galtung, *There are Alternatives: Four Roads to Peace and Security* (Nottingham: Spokesman, 1984)

George Gelber (ed), *Poverty and Power: Latin America after 500 Years* (London: CAFOD, 1992)

Eddie Gibbs, *I Believe in Church Growth* (London: Hodder and Stoughton, 1981)

Anthony Giddens, *Beyond Left and Right: The Future of Radical Politics* (Cambridge: Polity Press, 1994)

Maurice Ginsberg, *On Justice in Society* (Harmondsworth: Penguin Books, 1965)

Arthur Glasser and Donald McGavran (eds), *The Conciliar-Evangelical Debate* (Waco: Word Books, 1972)

Jerald Gort, Hendrik Voom, Rein Fernhout and Anton Wessels (eds), *Dialogue and Syncretism: An Interdisciplinary Approach* (Grand Rapids: Eerdmans, 1989)

Robert Gottfried, *Economics, Ecology and the Roots of Western Faith: Perspectives from the Garden* (Lanham: Rowman and Littlefield, 1995)

Elaine Graham, *Making the Difference: Gender, Personhood and Theology* (London: Mowbray, 1995)

John Gray, *False Dawn: The Delusions of Global Capitalism* (London: Granta Books, 1998)

A.C. Grayling (ed), *Philosophy: A Guide through the Subject* (Oxford: Oxford University Press)

Michael Green, *Evangelism in the Early Church* (London: Hodder and Stoughton, 1970)

Michael Green, *Evangelism through the Local Church* (London: Hodder and Stoughton, 1990)

Brian Griffiths, *The Creation of Wealth* (London: Hodder and Stoughton, 1984)

Morwena Griffiths, *Feminisms and the Self: The Web of Identity* (London: Routledge, 1995)

Gustavo Gutiérrez, *A Theology of Liberation: History, Politics and Salvation* (London: SCM Press, 1974)

Gustavo Gutiérrez, *The Power of the Poor in History* (London: SCM Press, 1983)

Gustavo Gutiérrez, *On Job: God-Talk and the Suffering of the Innocent* (Maryknoll: Orbis Books, 1987)

Gustavo Gutiérrez, *The Truth Shall Make You Free: Confrontations* (Maryknoll: Orbis Books, 1990)

Gustavo Gutiérrez, *We Drink from Our Own Wells: The Spiritual Journey of a People* (Maryknoll: Orbis Books, 1984)

Gustavo Gutiérrez, *Las Casas: in Search of the Poor of Jesus Christ* (Maryknoll: Orbis Books, 1993)

D. Hallman (ed), *Ecotheology: Voices from South and North* (Geneva: WCC, 1994)

Kenneth Hamilton, *The System and the Gospel: A Critique of Paul Tillich* (London: SCM Press, 1963)

Richard Harries, *Is There a Gospel for the Rich?* (London: Mowbray, 1992)

Paul Harrison, *The Third Revolution: Environment, Population and a Sustainable World* (London: Taurus, 1992)

Adrian Hastings, *A History of African Christianity, 1950–1975* (Cambridge: CUP, 1979)

Stanley Hauerwas, *After Christendom? How the Church is to Behave if Freedom, Justice and a Christian Nation are Bad Ideas* (Nashville: Abingdon Press, 1991)

David Hay (ed), *Pauline Theology (Vol II), 1 and 2 Corinthians* (Minneapolis: Fortress Press, 1993)

Paul Heelas, *The New Age Movement: The Celebration of Self and Sacralization of Modernity* (Oxford: Blackwell, 1996)

Mark Heim, *Is Christ the Only Way? Christian Faith in a Pluralistic World* (Valley Forge: Judson Press, 1985)

Susanne Heine, *Women and Early Christianity: Are the Feminist Scholars Right?* (London: SCM Press, 1987)

Wolfgang Heinrich, *Building the Peace: Experiences of Collaborative Peacebuilding in Somalia 1993–1996* (Uppsala: Life and Peace Institute, 1997)

John Helgeland (et al), *Christians and the Military: The Early Experience* (London: SCM Press, 1985)

Paul Helm, *Faith and Understanding* (Edinburgh: Edinburgh University Press, 1997)

John Hick, *God and the Universe of Faiths* (London: Macmillan, 1973)

John Hick, *God Has Many Names* (Basingstoke: Macmillan, 1980)

John Hick, *An Interpretation of Religion: Human Responses to the Transcendent* (London: Macmillan, 1989)

John Hick and Paul Knitter (eds), *The Myth of Christian Uniqueness: Toward a Pluralist Theology of Religions* (Maryknoll: Orbis Books, 1987)

Peter Hicks, *Evangelicals and Truth: A Creative Proposal for a Postmodern Age* (Leicester: Apollos, 1998)

John Hinnels (ed), *A Handbook of Living Religions* (London: Penguin Books, 1991)

John Hinnels (ed), *The Penguin Dictionary of Religions* (London: Penguin Books, 1997)

Paul Hirst and Grahame Thompson, *Globalization in Question* (Cambridge: Polity Press, 1996)

William Hocking, *Rethinking Missions: A Layman's Inquiry after One Hundred Years* (New York: 1933)

Bert Hoedemaker, *Secularization and Mission: A Theological Essay* (Harrisburg: Trinity Press International, 1998)

J.C. Hoekendijk, *The Church Inside Out* (London: SCM Press, 1967)

J.C. Hoekendijk, *Kirche und Volk in der deutscher Missionswissenschaft* (Munich: Kaiser Verlag, 1967)

Harvey Hoekstra, *The World Council of Churches and the Demise of Evangelism* (Wheaton: Tyndale House, 1979)

R.J. Holingdale, *A Nietzsche Reader* (Harmondsworth: Penguin Books, 1977)

Jean-Michel Hornus, *It is Not Lawful for Me to Fight: Early Christian Attitudes to War, Violence and the State* (Scottdale: Herald Press, 1980)

Colin Horseman, *Good News for a Postmodern World* (Cambridge: Grove Books, 1996)

Richard Horsley, *Jesus and the Spiral of Violence: Popular Jewish Resistance in Roman Palestine* (Minneapolis: Fortress Press, 1993)

Richard Horsley, *Sociology and the Jesus Movement* (New York: Continuum, 1994)

Gretchen Gaebelein Hull, *Equal to Serve: Women and Men in the Church and Home* (London: Scripture Union, 1989)

George Hunsberger, *Bearing the Witness of the Spirit: Lesslie Newbigin's Theology of Cultural Plurality* (Grand Rapids: Eerdmans, 1998)

Peter Janke (ed), *Ethnic and Religious Conflicts: Europe and Asia* (Aldershot: Dartmouth, 1994)

Idriss Jazairy, Mohiuddin Alamgir and Theresa Pannucio, *The State of Rural Poverty: An Inquiry into its Causes and Consequences* (London: Intermediate Technology Publications, 1992)

Rhys Jenkins, *Transnational Corporations and Uneven Development: The Internationalization of Capital and the Third World* (London: Methuen, 1987)

Joachim Jeremias, *New Testament Theology, Vol. I* (London: SCM Press, 1971)

John Paul II, *Encyclical on Missionary Activity: Redemptoris Missio*

Susan Johnson and Ben Rohaly, *Microfinance and Poverty Reduction* (Oxford: Oxfam, 1997)

Jan Jongeneel, *Philosophy, Science and Theology of Mission in the Nineteenth and Twentieth Centuries, Vols I and II* (Frankfurt: Peter Lang, 1995, 1997)

Kathy Keay (ed), *Men, Women and God* (Basingstoke: Marshall Pickering, 1987)

David Kemp, *Global Environment Issues: A Climatological Approach* (London: Routledge, 1994)

Philip King, *Good News for a Suffering World: What does the Christian Faith Really Have to Offer?* (Crowborough: Monarch Publications, 1996)

Ursula King (ed), *Feminist Theology from the Third World: A Reader* (London: SPCK, 1994)

Michael Kinnamon (ed), *Signs of the Spirit: Official Report, World Council of Churches Seventh Assembly* (Geneva: WCC Publications, 1992)

J. Andrew Kirk, *A New World Coming: A Fresh Look at the Gospel for Today* (Basingstoke: Marshalls, 1983)

J. Andrew Kirk, *God's Word for a Complex World: Discovering How the Bible Speaks Today* (Basingstoke: Marshall Pickering, 1987)

J. Andrew Kirk, *Loosing the Chains: Religion as Opium and Liberation* (London: Hodder and Stoughton, 1992)

J. Andrew Kirk, *The Mission of Theology and Theology as Mission* (Valley Forge: Trinity Press International, 1997)

J. Andrew Kirk, *The Meaning of Freedom: a Study of Secular, Muslim and Christian Views* (Carlisle: Paternoster Press, 1998)

J. Andrew Kirk (ed), *Handling Problems of Peace and War* (Basingstoke: Marshall Pickering, 1988)

J. Andrew Kirk and Kevin Vanhoozer (eds), *To Stake a Claim: Mission and the Western Crisis of Knowledge* (Maryknoll: Orbis Books, 1999)

Helmut Koester, *Introduction to the New Testament: History, Culture and Religion in the Hellenistic Age* (Philadelphia: Fortress Press, 1982)

Charles Kraft, *Anthropology for Christian Witness* (Maryknoll: Orbis Books, 1996)

Marguerite Kraft, *Worldview and the Communication of the Gospel: A Nigerian Case Study* (Pasadena: William Carey Library, 1978)

Christopher Lamb, *The Call to Retrieval: Kenneth Cragg's Christian Vocation to Islam* (London: Grey Seal, 1997)

Pinchas Lapide, *The Sermon on the Mount: Utopia or Program for Action* (Maryknoll: Orbis Books, 1986)

Lausanne Committee, The, *Evangelism and Social Responsibility: An Evangelical Commitment (The Grand Rapids Report)* (Exeter: Paternoster Press, 1982)

Kenneth Leech, *Struggle in Babylon: Racism in the Cities and Churches of Britain* (London: Sheldon Press, 1988)

George Lemopolous (ed), *Your Will Be Done: Orthodoxy in Mission* (Geneva: WCC Publications, 1989)

Gennadios Limouris, *Justice, Peace and the Integrity of Creation: Insights from Orthodoxy* (Geneva: WCC Publications, 1990)

George Lindbeck, *The Nature of Doctrine: Religion and Theology in a Post-Liberal Age* (London: SPCK, 1984)

Andrew Linzey, *Christianity and the Rights of Animals* (London: SPCK, 1987)

Andrew Linzey, *Animal Theology* (London: SCM Press, 1994)

Andrew Linzey and Tom Reagan (eds), *Animals and Christianity: A Book of Readings* (London: SPCK, 1989)

Carl Loegliger and Garry Trompf, *New Religious Movements in Melanesia* (Suva: University of the South Pacific, 1985)

Gerhard Lohfink, *Jesus and Community: The Social Dimension of Christian Faith* (London: SPCK, 1985)

Bernard Lonergan, *Method in Theology* (London: Darton, Longman and Todd, 1972)

Richard Longenecker, *The Road from Damascus: The Impact of Paul's Conversion on his Life, Thought and Ministry* (Grand Rapids: Eerdmans, 1997)

Ernest Lucas, *Science and the New Age Challenge* (Leicester: Apollos, 1996)

Michael Lund, *Preventing Violent Conflicts: A Strategy for Preventive Diplomacy* (Washington: US Institute of Peace, 1996)

Alistair MacLeod, *Tillich: An Essay on the Role of Ontology in his Philosophical Theology* (London: George, Allen and Unwin, 1973)

Denis Maceoin and Ahmed Al-Shahi, *Islam in the Modern World* (Beckenham: Croom Hill, 1983)

Bruce Marshall, *Theology and Dialogue: Essays in Conversation with George Lindbeck* (Notre Dame: University of Notre Dame Press, 1990)

David Martin, *Tongues of Fire: The Explosion of Protestantism in Latin America* (Oxford: Blackwell, 1990)

M-L Martin, *Kimbangu: An African Prophet and his Church* (Oxford: Blackwell, 1985)

Ralph Martin, *Word Biblical Commentary (Vol 40), 2 Corinthians* (Waco: Word Books, 1986)

Joseph Mattam and Sebastian Kim (eds), *Mission and Conversion: A Reappraisal* (Bandra, Mumbai: St Paul's, 1996)

Pedrito Maynard-Reid, *Poverty and Wealth in James* (Maryknoll: Orbis Books, 1987)

Ali Mazrui, *Cultural Forces in World Politics* (London: James Currey, 1990)

Zolile Mbale, *The Churches and Racism: A Black South African Perspective* (London: SCM Press, 1987)

Nancey Murphy, *Beyond Liberalism and Fundamentalism: How Modern and Postmodern Philosophy Set the Theological Agenda* (Valley Forge: Trinity Press International, 1996)

Sean McDonagh, *The Greening of the Church* (London: Geoffrey Chapman, 1990)

Sean McDonagh, *Passion for the Earth: The Christian Vocation to Promote Justice, Peace and the Integrity of Creation* (London: Geoffrey Chapman, 1994)

Donald McGavran, *Understanding Church Growth* (Third Edition revised and edited by Peter Wagner) (Grand Rapids: Eerdmans, 1990)

Alistair McGrath, *Historical Theology: An Introduction to the History of Christian Thought* (Oxford: Blackwell, 1998)

David McLellan, *The Thought of Karl Marx* (London: Macmillan, 1995–3rd edition)

Donella Meadows (et al), *The Limits to Growth* (New York: Universe, 1972)

Johann Baptist Metz, *Faith in History and Society: Toward a Practical Fundamental Theology* (London: Burns and Oates, 1980)

W Granberg Michaelson (ed), *Tending the Earth* (Grand Rapids: Eerdmans, 1987)

John Mihevc, *The Market Tells Them So: The World Bank and Economic Fundamentalism in Africa* (London: Zed Books, 1992)

Jose Miguez Bonino, *Christians and Marxists: The Mutual Challenge to Revolution* (London: Hodder and Stoughton, 1975)

Daniel Miller (ed), *Coming of Age: Protestantism in Contemporary Latin America* (Lanham: University Press of America, 1994)

Mission Theological Advisory Group, *The Search for Faith and the Witness of the Church* (London: Church House Publishing, 1996)

Jürgen Moltmann, *A Theology of Hope* (London: SCM Press, 1967)

Jürgen Moltmann, *The Way of Jesus Christ: Christology in Messianic Dimensions* (London: SCM Press, 1990)

Jürgen Moltmann, *The Trinity and the Kingdom of God* (London: SCM Press, 1981)

Paul Mojzes and Leonard Swidler (eds), *Christian Mission and Interreligious Dialogue* (Lewiston: Edwin Mellen Press, 1990)

Paul Mojzes and Leonard Swidler (eds), *The Uniqueness of Jesus: A Dialogue with Paul F. Knitter* (Maryknoll: Orbis Books, 1997)

Eric Moonman, *The Violent Society* (London: Frank Cass, 1987)

John Mott, *Addresses and Papers of John R. Mott: Volume V, The International Missionary Council* (New York: Association Press, 1947)

Ronaldo Munoz, *The God of Christians* (Tunbridge Wells: Burns and Oates, 1991)

David Munro and Martin Holgate, *Caring for the Earth: A Strategy for Sustainable Living* (Grand: IUCN, UNEP, WWF, 1991)

Bill Musk, *The Unseen Faces of Islam: Sharing the Gospel with Ordinary Muslims* (Eastbourne: MARC, 1989)

Donald Musser and Joseph Price (eds), *A New Handbook of Christian Theology* (Nashville: Abingdon Press and Cambridge: Lutterworth Press, 1992)

Michael Nazir Ali, *From Everywhere to Everywhere: A World View of Christian Mission* (London: Collins, 1990)

Michael Nazir Ali, *Mission and Dialogue* (London: SPCK, 1995)

Alan Neely, *Christian Mission: A Case Study Approach* (Maryknoll: Orbis Books, 1995)

Stephen Neill, *Crises of Belief: The Christian Dialogue with Faith and no Faith* (London: Hodder and Stoughton, 1984)

Jack Nelson-Pallmeyer, *The Politics of Compassion* (Maryknoll: Orbis Books, 1986)

Jacob Neusner (ed), *The Social World of Formative Christianity and Judaism* (Philadelphia: Fortress Press, 1988)

Herbert Neve, *Sources for Change: Searching for Flexible Church Structures* (Geneva: WCC Publications, 1968)

Lesslie Newbigin, *The Open Secret: An Introduction to the Theology of Mission* (London: SPCK, 1995)

Lesslie Newbigin, *Sign of the Kingdom* (Grand Rapids: Eerdmans, 1980)

Lesslie Newbigin, *The Gospel in a Pluralist Society* (London: SPCK, 1989)

James Nickoloff (ed.), *Gustavo Gutiérrez Essential Writings* (Maryknoll: Orbis Books, 1996)

Richard Niebuhr, *Christ and Culture* (New York: Harper, 1951)

Friedrich Nietzsche, *Thus Spake Zarathustra: A Book for Everyone and No One* (Harmondsworth: Penguin Books, 1961)

Daniel Niles, *That They May Have Life* (New York: Harper and Brothers, 1951)

Preman Niles, *Resisting the Threats to Life: Covenanting for Justice, Peace and the Integrity of Creation* (Geneva: WCC Publications, 1989)

Johannes Nissen, *Poverty and Mission: New Testament Perspectives* (Leiden: IIMO, 1984)

John Nolland, *Luke 1–9.20 (World Biblical Commentary Volume 35A)* (Dallas: Word Books, 1989)

Carolyn Nordstrom, *Girls and Warzones: Troubling Questions* (Uppsala: Life and Peace Institute, 1997)

Michael Northcott, *The Environment and Christian Ethics* (Cambridge: CUP, 1996)

Jerome Murphy O'Connor, *The Theology of the Second Letter to the Corinthians* (Cambridge: CUP, 1991)

Oliver O'Donovan, *The Desire of the Nations: Rediscovering the Roots of Political Theology* (Cambridge: CUP, 1996)

Cyril Okorocha, *The Meaning of Religious Conversion in Africa; The Case of the Igbo of Nigeria* (Aldershot: Avebury, 1987)

R.K. Orchard (ed), *Witness in Six Continents: Records of the CWME . . . Mexico City 1963* (London: Edinburgh House Press, 1964)

Lawrence Osborn, *Guardians of Creation: Nature in Theology and the Christian Life* (Leicester: Apollos, 1993)

René Padilla, *Mission Between the Times: Essays on the Kingdom* (Grand Rapids: Eerdmans, 1985)

Olof Palme (et al), *Common Security: A Programme for Disarmament* (London: Pan Books, 1982)

Joon Suth Park and Naozumi Etop (eds), *Theology and Theological Education in Asia: Today and Tomorrow* (Seoul: NEAATS, 1992)

Patrick Parkinson, *Child Sexual Abuse and the Churches* (London: Hodder and Stoughton, 1997)

John Parratt, *A Guide to Doing Theology* (London: SPCK, 1996)

David Paton, *The Ministry of the Spirit: Selected Writings by Roland Allen* (Grand Rapids: Eerdmans, 1962)

John Piper, *Love Your Enemies: Jesus' Love Command in the Synoptic Gospels and the early Christian Paraenesis* (Cambridge: CUP, 1979)

Jorge Pixley and Clodovis Boff, *The Bible, the Church and the Poor* (Tunbridge Wells: Burns and Oates, 1989)

Jack Porter and Ruth Taplin, *Conflict and Conflict Resolution* (Lanham: University of America Press, 1987)

Gerard Prunier, *The Rwanda Crisis (1959–1994): History of a Genocide* (London: Hurst and Co., 1995)

Vinoth Ramachandra, *The Recovery of Mission: Beyond the Pluralist Paradigm* (Carlisle: Paternoster Press, 1996)

Paul Ramsay, *War and the Christian Conscience: How Shall Modern War Be Conducted Justly?* (Durham: Duke University Press, 1961)

Paul Ramsay, *The Just War, Force and Political Responsibility* (Lanham: University Press of America, 1983)

Tom Regan, *The Case for Animal Rights* (Berkeley: University of California Press, 1983)

J. Remenyi, *Where Credit is Due* (London: Intermediate Technology Publications, 1991)

Rosemary Radford Reuther, *Sexism and God-Talk: Toward a Feminist Theology* (London: SCM Press, 1983)

Pablo Richard (et al), *The Idols of Death and the God of Life* (Maryknoll: Orbis Books, 1983)

L. Rivera, *A Violent Evangelism: The Political and Religious Conquest of the Americas* (Louisville: Westminster/John Knox Press, 1992)

M. Ruokanen, *The Catholic Doctrine of the Non-Christian Religions According to the Second Vatican Council* (Leiden: IIMO, 1992)

Willem Saayman and Klippies Kritzinger (eds), *Mission in Bold Humility: David Bosch's Work Considered* (Maryknoll: Orbis Books, 1996)

Vinay Samuel and Chris Sugden, *The Church in Response to Human Need* (Oxford: Regnum Books, 1987)

Lamin Sanneh, *Translating the Message: The Missionary Impact on Culture* (Maryknoll: Orbis Books, 1992)

Lamin Sanneh, *Religion and the Variety of Culture: A Study in Origin and Practice* (Valley Forge: Trinity Press International, 1996)

Philip Sarre and John Blundon (eds), *An Overcrowded World? Population, Resources and the Environment* (Oxford: OUP, 1995)

Harry Sawyerr, *Creative Evangelism: Towards a New Christian Encounter with Africa* (London: Lutterworth Press, 1968)

Daniel Schipani (ed), *Religious Education Encounters Liberation Theology* (Birmingham, Al.: Religious Education Press, 1988)

Daniel Schipani (ed), *Freedom and Discipleship: Liberation Theology in Anabaptist Perspective* (Maryknoll: Orbis Books, 1989)

H. Schlossberg (et al), *Freedom, Justice and Hope: Toward a Strategy for the Poor and Oppressed* (Westchester: Crossway Books, 1988)

Wolfgang Schrage, *The Ethics of the New Testament* (Edinburgh: T and T Clark, 1988)

Robert Schreiter, *Constructing Local Theologies* (London: SCM Press, 1985)

Roger Scruton, *Modern Philosophy: An Introduction and Survey* (London: Mandarin, 1994)

Juan Luis Segundo, *Faith and Ideologies* (London: Sheed and Ward, 1984)

Juan Luis Segundo, *The Humanist Christology of Paul* (Maryknoll: Orbis Books, 1986)

Donald Senior and Carroll Stuhlmueller, *The Biblical Foundations for Mission* (London: SCM Press, 1983)

Jack Seymour and Donald Miller, *Theological Approaches to Christian Education* (Nashville: Abingdon Press, 1990)

Stephen Sharot, *Messianism, Mysticism and Magic: A Sociological Analysis of Jewish Religious Movements* (Chapel Hill: University of North Carolina Press, 1982)

Richard Shaull, *Encounter with Revolution* (New York: Association Press, 1955)

David Shenk, *Global Gods: Exploring the Role of Religions in Modern Societies* (Scottdale: Herald Press, 1995)

David Shenk (ed), *Ministry in Partnership with African Independent Churches* (Elkhart: Mennonite Board of Missions, 1991)

Gerald Shenk, *God with Us? The Roles of Religion in the Former Yugoslavia* (Uppsala: Life and Peace Institute, 1993)

Wilbert Shenk, *Write the Vision: The Church Renewed* (Valley Forge: Trinity Press International, 1995)

Wilbert Shenk (ed), *Exploring Church Growth* (Grand Rapids: Eerdmans, 1983)

Aylward Shorter, *Toward a Theology of Inculturation* (Maryknoll: Orbis Books, 1988)

Peter Singer, *Animal Liberation* (New York: Random House, 1990 – 2nd edition)

Peter Singer, *A Companion to Ethics* (Oxford: Blackwell, 1993)

Ninian Smart, *The Religious Experience of Mankind* (London: Collins, 1971)

Howard Snyder, *Kingdom Lifestyle: Calling the Church to Live under God's Reign* (Basingstoke: Marshall Pickering, 1986)

Howard Snyder, *Models of the Kingdom* (Nashville: Abingdon Press, 1991)

Jon Sobrino, *Christology at the Crossroads: A Latin American Approach* (London: SCM Press, 1978)

Jon Sobrino, *The Principle of Mercy: Taking the Crucified People from the Cross* (Maryknoll: Orbis Books, 1994)

Jon Sobrino and Ignacio Ellacuria, *Systematic Theology: Perspectives from Liberation Theology* (Maryknoll: Orbis Books, 1996)

John Solomos, *Race and Racism in Contemporary Britain* (Basingstoke: Macmillan, 1989)

Friedrich Steinbauer, *Melanesian Cargo Cults: New Salvation Movements in the South Pacific* (London: George Prior, 1979)

James Sterber (et al), *Morality and Social Justice; Point/Counterpoint* (Lanham: Rowman and Littlefield, 1995)

Charles Stewart and Rosalind Shaw, *Syncretism/Anti-Syncretism; The Politics of Religious Synthesis* (London: Routledge, 1994)

Elaine Storkey, *What's Right with Feminism* (London: SPCK, 1985)

John Stott, *Christian Mission in the Modern World* (London: Falcon Books, 1975)

John Stott, *Christian Counter-culture: The Message of the Sermon on the Mount* (Leicester: IVP, 1978)

George Strecker, *The Sermon on the Mount: An Exegetical Commentary* (Edinburgh: T and T Clark, 1988)

Willard Swartley, *Israel's Scripture Tradition and the Synoptic Gospels: Story Shaping Story* (Peabody: Hendrickson Publishers, 1994)

Charles Taber, *The World is Too Much with Us: 'Culture' in Modern Protestant Missions* (Macon: Mercer University Press, 1991)

Elsa Tamez (ed), *Through Her Eyes: Women's Theology from Latin America* (Maryknoll: Orbis Books, 1989)

Robert Tannehill, *The Narrative Unity of Luke-Acts: A Literary Interpretation (Volume I, The Gospel according to Luke)* (Philadelphia: Fortress Press, 1986)

Gerd Theissen, *The Gospels in Context: Social and Political History in the Synoptic Tradition* (Minneapolis: Fortress Press, 1991)

Gerd Theissen, *Social Reality and the Early Church: Theology, Ethics and the World of the New Testament* (Minneapolis: Fortress Press, 1992)

Third World First, *Freedom from Debt* (Oxford: Third World First, 1989)

Anthony Thiselton, *New Horizons in Hermeneutics: The Theory and Practice of Transforming Biblical Reading* (London: HarperCollins, 1992)

Susan Thistlethwaite and George Cairns (eds), *Beyond Theological Tourism: Mentoring as a Grassroots Approach to Theological Education* (Maryknoll: Orbis Books, 1994)

Norman Thomas (ed), *Classic Texts in Mission and World Christianity* (Maryknoll: Orbis Books, 1995)

Henry David Thoreau, *Walden* (New York: WW Norton, 1951 (reprint of 1854 original))

Glenn Tinder, *The Political Meaning of Christianity: The Prophetic Stance* (New York: HarperCollins, 1991)

Helen Todd (ed), *Cloning Grameen Bank: Replicating a Poverty Reduction Model in India, Nepal and Vietnam* (London: Intermediate Technology Publications, 1996)

Paul Tournier, *The Gift of Feeling* (London: SCM Press, 1981)

Charles Van Engen, Dean Gilliland and Paul Pierson (eds), *The Good News of the Kingdom: Mission Theology for the Third Millenium* (Maryknoll: Orbis Books, 1993)

A.T. Van Leeuwen, *Christianity in World History: The Meeting of Faiths East and West* (New York: Scribners, 1964)

Jacques Van Nieuwenhove and Berma Klein Goldewijk (eds), *Popular Religion, Liberation and Contextual Theology* (Kampen: Kok, 1991)

Johannes Verkuyl, *Contemporary Missiology: An Introduction* (Grand Rapids: Eerdmans, 1978)

F.J. Verstraelen, A. Camps, L.A. Hoedemaker and M.R. Spindler, *Missiology, an Ecumenical Introduction: Texts and Contexts of Global Christianity* (Grand Rapids: Eerdmans, 1995)

Charles Villa-Vicencio (ed), *Theology and Violence: The South African Debate* (Braamfontein: Skotaville, 1987)

W.A. Visser't Hooft, *No Other Name: The Choice between Syncretism and Christian Universalism* (London: SCM Press, 1963)

Hendrik Vroom, *No Other Gods: Christian Belief in Dialogue with Buddhism, Hinduism and Islam* (Grand Rapids: Eerdmans, 1996)

Pius Wakatama, *Independence for the Third World Church; An African's Perspective on Missionary Work* (Downers Grove: IVP, 1976)

Jim Wallis, *The Call to Conversion* (San Francisco: Harper and Row, 1981)

David Wells, *God the Evangelist: How the Holy Spirit Works to Bring Men and Women to Faith* (Grand Rapids: Eerdmans, 1987)

James Williams, *The Bible, Violence and the Sacred* (New York: Harper-Collins, 1989)

Andrew Wingate, *The Church and Conversion* (Delhi: SPCK, 1997)

Walter Wink, *Naming the Powers: The Language of Power in the New Testament* (Philadelphia: Fortress Press, 1984)

Walter Wink, *Unmasking the Powers: The Invisible Forces that Determine Human Existence* (Philadelphia: Fortress Press, 1986)

Walter Wink, *Engaging the Powers: Discernment and Resistance in a World of Domination* (Philadelphia: Fortress Press, 1993)

Walter Wink, *Healing a Nation's Wounds: Reconciliation on the Road to Democracy* (Uppsala: Life and Peace Institute, 1997)

Walter Wink, *The Powers that Be* (London: Cassell, 1998)

Bo Wirmark (ed), *Government-NGO Relations in Preventing Violence, Transforming Conflict and Building Peace* (Stockholm: Peace Team Forum, 1998)

Ben Witherington, *Women in the Earliest Churches* (Cambridge: CUP, 1988)

Philip Wogaman, *Christian Perspectives on Politics* (London: SCM Press, 1988)

Nicholas Wolterstorff, *Divine Discourse: Philosophical Reflections on the Claim that God Speaks* (Cambridge: CUP, 1995)

Geoffrey Wood and Iffath Sharif, *Who Needs Credit? Poverty and Finance in Bangladesh* (London: Zed Books, 1997)

John Woodbridge and Thomas McComiskey, *Doing Theology in Today's World* (Grand Rapids: Zondervan, 1991)

World Council of Churches, *Planning for Mission* (New York: 1966)

World Council of Churches, *The Church for Others* (Geneva: WCC Publications, 1967)

World Council of Churches, *Your Kingdom Come: Report on the World Conference on Mission and Evangelism* (Geneva: WCC Publications, 1980)

World Council of Churches, *Gathered for Life: Report of the Vancouver Assembly* (Geneva: WCC Publications, 1983)

World Council of Churches, *Mission and Evangelism: An Ecumenical Affirmation* (Geneva: WCC Publications, 1983)

World Council of Churches, *Programme to Overcome Violence: An Introduction* (Geneva: WCC Publications, 1994)

Tom Wright, *Jesus and the Victory of God* (London: SPCK, 1996)

Tom Wright, *The New Testament and the People of God* (London: SPCK, 1992)

Tim Yates, *Christian Mission in the Twentieth Century* (Cambridge: CUP, 1994)

Steven Yearley, *Sociology, Environmentalism, Globalization: Reinventing the Globe* (London: Sage, 1996)

Paul Zagorski, *Democracy vs National Security: Civil-Military Relations in Latin America* (London: Lynne Rienner, 1992)

Wayne Zunkel, *Church Growth under Fire* (Scottdale: Herald Press, 1987)

Biblical References

Index

Printed in the United States
37208LVS00004B/97-204